WE ARE THE LEADERS WE'VE BEEN WAITING FOR

A Companion Facilitator Guide Also Available
Women and Leadership Development in College: A Facilitation Resource
Edited by Jennifer M. Pigza, Julie E. Owen and Associates

WE ARE THE LEADERS WE'VE BEEN WAITING FOR

Women and Leadership Development in College

Julie E. Owen

Foreword by Heather D. Shea and Kristen A. Renn

STERLING, VIRGINIA

Published by Stylus Publishing, LLC.
22883 Quicksilver Drive
Sterling, Virginia 20166-2019

Library of Congress Cataloging-in-Publication Data

Names: Owen, Julie E., author. | Stylus Publishing.
Title: We are the leaders we've been waiting for : women and leadership
    development in college / Julie E. Owen ; foreword by Heather D. Shea and
    Kristen A. Renn.
Other titles: We are the leaders we have been waiting for Description: First
    Edition. | Sterling, Virginia : Stylus, 2020. | Includes bibliographical
    references and index.
Identifiers: LCCN 2020024812 | ISBN 9781642670097 (Paperback : acid-
    free paper | ISBN 9781642670080 (Hardcover : acid-free paper) |
    ISBN 9781642670110 (eBook) | ISBN 9781642670103 (PDF)
Subjects: LCSH: Women--Education (Higher)--United States. | Leadership-
    -United States. Classification: LCC LC1756 .O94 2020 | DDC
    378.1/9822--dc23
LC record available at https://lccn.loc.gov/2020024812

13-digit ISBN: 978-1-64267-008-0 (cloth)
13-digit ISBN: 978-1-64267-009-7 (paperback)
13-digit ISBN: 978-1-64267-010-3 (library networkable e-edition)
13-digit ISBN: 978-1-64267-011-0 (consumer e-edition)

Printed in the United States of America

All first editions printed on acid-free paper
that meets the American National Standards Institute
Z39-48 Standard.

Bulk Purchases

Quantity discounts are available for use in workshops and
for staff development.

Call 1-800-232-0223

First Edition, 2020

I dedicate this book to my mother, Constance Aikens Owen, for showing me the world.

And to all who work toward creating a more just, equitable, nonviolent, and sustainable world, especially the alumnae from a decade of Integrative Studies Women and Leadership classes.

CONTENTS

Heather: I first met Julie Owen when I was a new professional at an ACPA: College Student Educators convention nearly two decades ago within a commission I had joined. Julie, a doctoral student working with Susan Komives at the University of Maryland, warmly welcomed me into the group. From there, our overlapping circles of friends kept us in touch and each time our paths crossed at convention—in her distinct style—Julie greeted me warmly, expressed her interest in my pathway, and encouraged me to keep my sights on new opportunities. Over the years since then, I have closely followed her work with the National Clearinghouse of Leadership Programs and the Multi-Institutional Study of Leadership, and on leadership models and student-facing resources. I have also looked to her as one of the leadership scholars who is specifically responding to the needs of women in leadership development. Julie has been a constant voice and leader in this work.

Sometime later in my career, while serving as a director of a campus-based women's center, I was confronted directly with the reality that much of the existing women's leadership texts and women's leadership development initiatives were ill-fitted for the feminist student organizations with whom I was working. I had witnessed an interesting phenomenon among the student leaders of these feminist groups: often, they were competitive, hierarchical, and independent versus collaborative, inclusive of all perspectives, and interdependent. And so, I went searching for leadership texts that could work for a women's leadership and mentoring course I was teaching.

I quickly grew weary of what I found within the "women's leadership" literature; I later dubbed them *feminine* models of leadership. These models that turned attention toward—and even encouraged—traditional gender roles as important aspects of how women enacted leadership (as if there was one singular style applicable to all women), or they sought to *remake* and "empower" women leaders to effectively deploy the hierarchical and competitive leadership styles in order to fit into a "man's" world. In addition to being extremely limiting in application, these models also propelled readers toward a gender binary (e.g., women lead one way, men lead another).

Within the leadership development resources geared toward college students, I found engaging models that refrained from emphasizing positional leadership and encouraged interdependence while also bringing in concepts of social justice, social change, and relational styles of leadership. However, these texts didn't directly or intentionally center women's experiences in leadership.

In desperation, I entered the search keywords "feminist + leadership" and found a third strand of leadership texts, which embraced feminist approaches (many of the authors Julie cites in this text) and was inspired to integrate readings into the course. However, I quickly gathered that these legal and academic texts were often dense and unappealing for college students. I continued my search, to no avail, for leadership texts embracing feminist approaches that would (a) appeal to college students and (b) specifically and intentionally examine women's experiences in feminist leadership.

Kris: I first came to know Julie through her scholarship. As someone studying student leaders and identity development (though I had not put those two concepts directly together) I attended a session at an ACPA convention in which she presented with Susan Komives on a new model of leadership identity development. Leadership *identity* development? I had to hear what they and their research colleagues were talking about. I was intrigued by the session and snagged the handout to ponder further. Within a few months I e-mailed Susan to find out how to cite the model, when it would be published, and where. I used this model to inspire my examination of leaders of identity-based student organizations and focused work on LGBTQ student leaders. Julie's involvement with Multi-Institutional Study of Leadership further contributed to the depth of my understanding of student leadership.

It was not surprising when I learned that Julie was writing the book you hold in your hands—and which I am certain you will find as enriching, challenging, and empowering as Heather and I have. Like Heather, I have been seeking a new way to think and teach about women's leadership, feminist leadership, and women leaders. Also like Heather and Julie, I do so in a way that both names women and women's experience while being gender expansive to interrupt binary conceptions of who is a woman (and thus by default, who is not).

Both: Several years ago, we were invited to write a closing "Call to Action" in the *Gender and Leadership* New Directions for Student Leadership monograph (Shea & Renn, 2017). In that chapter, we focused on the ways that gender is conceptualized and the many implications for leadership education and development. Upon finishing that chapter, we both lamented the few student-facing resources focusing on women's experiences in leadership to which we might refer folks for additional reading. Back then, nothing really quite fit our audiences who we imagined desiring an approachable yet challenging text. We were both thrilled to hear of Julie's book in the works and grateful to have this opportunity to preview it. In short, as coauthors of the foreword to Julie's book, we exclaim *We Are the Leaders We've Been Waiting For* is the student leadership textbook WE have been waiting for!

This book accomplishes many things simultaneously, which we believe makes it invaluable to students and leadership educators alike.

First, Julie's student-facing book is particularly accessible to college students because she features students' voices throughout the text. Gathered through an autoethnographic process, the narratives and counternarratives of students from many different perspectives and backgrounds add depth and richness to the foci of the chapters. Some narratives are powerful stories of resilience, others are difficult to read—dealing directly with discrimination and violence. All stories are, as Julie describes, an "authentic expression of the lived experiences of unique individual college women and gender nonconforming people" (p. 6, this volume). This glimpse into the lives of students helps readers make a direct application of the concepts of the text. We found the inclusion of these student voices to be uniquely feminist. In the second chapter, Julie provides a model for readers to author their own stories as an important step as leaders seek to understand the experiences that shaped their own perspectives on gender and personal leadership pathways.

Second, the book situates intersectional identities, critical consciousness, and student development theory lenses. We agree with Julie that the women's leadership canon, including much student leadership literature, has been written by and largely for white women leaders. Centering the experiences and concerns of women from a range of backgrounds and identities makes space for intersectional considerations; creates counterspaces within leadership literature; and provides possibility models for a world where leaders come in all genders, races, ethnicities, and other identities.

Third, as Julie notes in the text and Heather described previously, this book complicates the gendered notions of "women's leadership" by separating these two words . . . in what ways is the possessive "women's" limiting the readers' broader understanding of leadership? Is there such a thing as a universal "woman" whose leadership should be emulated? This text also delves more deeply into the concept of "feminine" versus "feminist" leadership approaches, which, given Heather's prior experience working with feminist student organizations, is sorely needed.

Fourth, we loved the concept that women who practice leadership particularly effectively shouldn't be put on pedestals as "SHE-roes." Leadership is present in everyday acts of engagement within a group to promote positive change. This accessible approach makes this book exceedingly useful with groups of students, whether they decide they want to identify as "leaders"—or "women" for that matter—or not.

We believe this book will be useful for students interested in women's experiences in leadership and the educators who work with them. It will be useful to leadership educators in all settings, and particularly those educators who seek to center women's experiences. Student affairs administrators across functional areas may find it useful in their work with students and for their own professional development and exploration. The content will resonate with faculty teaching leadership courses and advising student organizations. Activists on and off campus will find inspiration, challenge, and resonance.

We reiterate elements of our 2017 call to action, put forth again throughout this book. It is critical for student leaders and educators who care about them to subvert power structures, complicate difference, and enact social change. As is clear in this book, student leaders are not always from privileged groups, but we argue that by nature of their formal or informal leadership positions, they have privileges that not all other students have. It is imperative to act through this privilege to work toward social justice.

We are grateful to Julie for the opportunity to introduce readers to this important book, and grateful for the place this book will take in the leadership education literature. It is the book—indeed the student leadership movement—we have been waiting for.

Heather D. Shea, PhD
Kristen A. Renn, PhD
Michigan State University

ACKNOWLEDGMENTS

I offer words of gratitude to people who were instrumental in the process of thinking about and writing this book. To the brilliant student research team: Alliyah Fabijan, Arnèle Francis, Sharrell Hassell-Goodman, Cia Makrigiorgos, Katherine Quigley, Rukan Said, and Aoi Yamanaka. Also to Diana Fernandez, Kalia Harris, Shannon Naquin, Kelly Purtell, Shauna Rigaud, Emily Vaughan, and Michelle Wallerstedt. Thank you for sharing your stories, insights, and encouragement. You are the foundation and reason for this work.

To Jennifer Pigza and the many talented authors of modules for the *Woman and Leadership Development in College: A Facilitation Resource*, thank you for sharing your wisdom and commitment to critical pedagogy. Special thanks to Jennifer to being a companion, counselor, and champion on this long journey.

To critical readers and wise friends Adrian Bitton, Danyelle Reynolds, and Trisha Teig; and to student editors, especially Gilly Kelly and Alliyah Fabijan, I am forever grateful to each of you for the gifts of your time and talents—this book is better because of you. Thank you for helping me practice vulnerability and for your diligence in making this book more inclusive and readable.

To the faculty, staff, and students at the Leadership Learning Research Center at Florida State University for hosting me as a visiting scholar and for providing me space and inspiration for this work; especially Jenni Batchelder, Cameron Beatty, Brittany Brewster, Vivechkanand Chunoo, Brittany Devies, Jesse Ford, Kathy Guthrie, Julie LeBlanc, Marianne Lorensen, Laura Osteen, Maritza Torres, and Sally Watkins, among others.

To George Mason University, the College of Humanities and Social Science, and the School of Integrative Studies (SIS) Executive Director Kelly Dunne for granting a study leave and support for this kind of project. Thanks to Suzanne Scott Constantine, Kim Eby, Marsha Guenzler-Stevens, and Elizabeth Miller, who pioneered women and leadership classes on three campuses—your expertise is foundational. To the powerful women of SIS, especially dear friends and colleagues Cher Chen, Pamela Garner, Elizabeth Freeman, Misty Krell, Nance Lucas, Duhita Mahatmya, Wendi

Manuel-Scott, Shayna Maskell, Patty Mathison, Graziella McCarron, Julia Shadur, and Stephanie Zeher. To Fu (James) Zhao for unending support.

Importantly, to John von Knorring, David Brightman, and the team at Stylus for going on this journey with me. To Alexandra Hartnett, managing production editor, for her diligence, patience, and attention to detail that made this book readable.

To the American Association of University Women for their continued advocacy for gender equity in leadership as represented in their report on *Barriers and Bias: The Status of Women and Leadership* (2016). To Craig Slack and the National Clearinghouse for Leadership Programs for a lifetime of support.

To my predecessors in this work from whom I've learned so much. You'll see my admiration for them reflected in the numerous times I quote and borrow from their work. Gloria Anzaldúa, Helen Astin, Stephen Brookfield, Brené Brown, Judith Butler, Linda Carli, Kimberlé Crenshaw, Barbara Crosby, Alice Eagly, Roxane Gay, Gil Hickman, Patricia Hill Collins, bell hooks, Crystal Hoyt, Adrianna Kezar, Jean Lipman-Bluman, Audre Lorde, Susan Madsen, Sonia Ospina, Deborah Rhode, Janis Sanchez-Hucles, and Rosalind Wiseman. Special thanks to John Dugan, Paige Haber-Curran, Kerry Priest, Kris Renn, Rian Satterwhite, Heather Shea, and Daniel Tillapaugh, among others, for bringing criticality to leadership studies.

To my personal leadership SHE-roes in higher education, Susan R. Komives, Marylu McEwen, Susan Jones, Jan Arminio, Nance Lucas, and Gretchen Metzelaars. To lifelong friends and instigators, John Dugan, John Garland, Wendy Wagner, and Kristan Cilente Skendall.

To my family, Connie, Kenneth, Laura, and Bennett Owen, and posthumously, to Donald Owen.

WE ARE THE LEADERS
WE'VE BEEN WAITING FOR

Consider the following scenarios:

You are the only woman on a team working on a group project in class. The teacher suggests someone in your group takes notes. Your group members all turn to you and hand you a pen.

You make a worthwhile comment in a group meeting and seemingly everyone ignores your contribution. Five minutes later, a man makes a similar comment and everyone remarks on how clever and fantastic his idea is.

Your friends encourage you to run for an officer position in student government. You decline because you do not want people to think you are bossy.

You disagree with a colleague at work, and after you voice your objections someone asks if you are having your period.

Your teacher pulls you aside and tells you that the clothes you are wearing, while well within the school's dress code, are distracting to the boys in class.

You have always dreamed about being a drummer in a band. When band tryouts occur at school, the adviser suggests you take up the flute or clarinet.

You go to use the bathroom and someone questions whether you are in the right place.

You are walking down the street by yourself thinking about a book you are reading, when a man stops you and tells you that you should smile more because you have such a pretty face.

You try on 15 different outfits for a party you are invited to, then decide not to go because you aren't happy with how you look.

You care deeply about women's issues. Members of your family refer to you as a femi-Nazi.

Even though you are majoring in conservation science, a man decides to explain global warming to you.

If you have experienced one or more of these situations, then you do not need me to make the case for why the world needs another book about the challenges women face in schools, work, and leadership. If you have yet to experience these phenomena, then you might take a closer look at the dynamics going on around you. While overt sexism is still rampant in our culture, it is now also accompanied by much more subtle, even internalized, forms of stereotyping and discrimination such as what characterizes some of the previously mentioned examples. Some discrimination even appears benevolent—when people tell you that women are more compassionate, nurturing, or better listeners, it may sound like a compliment, but consider what is not being said. These backward compliments may actually be used to get you to take on unpaid emotional labor in groups or organizations. They also support binary or dualistic thinking about both gender and leadership. If women are by nature caring and collaborative, then the opposite must also be true—that men are naturally more assertive and decisive, and thus built for leadership. It is the task of this book to interrogate these assumptions. For example, you'll notice the title of this book includes the words "women *and* leadership," rather than "women's leadership." This is an intentional choice, as all women do not lead in the same way.

The scenarios that open this chapter reflect real-life experiences drawn from conversations with dozens of college-aged cisgender, transgender, and gender nonconforming individuals who were part of research teams and focus groups contributing to this book. You will hear more personal stories from these people throughout this text. These individuals were also essential to selecting the title for this book, *We Are the Leaders We've Been Waiting For.* You may be familiar with this phrase because Barack Obama used a similar phrase—"We are the ones we have been waiting for"—frequently on the presidential campaign trail in 2008. Or perhaps you know it from the music of the collective Sweet Honey in the Rock, who blend folk, roots, gospel, and world music (and if so, I applaud you on your excellent taste in music). Or you may know it from a collection of essays from feminist author Alice Walker, or from the work of human rights activist Grace Lee Boggs. I first became aware of the phrase from the poetry of June Jordan, who presented her "Poem for South African Women" to the United Nations on August 9, 1978, in commemoration of a 1956 event when 40,000 women and children protested against apartheid.

The implication in these words is that change will not come if we wait for someone else to make it. Creating more just and equitable systems requires our own deep engagement. This book title is an invitation for you to join with others and engage in a critical examination of the ways gender and leadership function in our world and to envision a more inclusive and generative approach to leadership.

Like many books designed for higher education, this volume's name includes a subtitle: *Women and Leadership Development in College.* The idea that leadership can and should be developed is an essential part of this book. If you think that leadership is strictly an innate quality —that you either have it at birth or you don't—then this volume may not be for you. I can refer you to dozens of other women and leadership books that would be more in line with the thinking that leadership is restricted to a chosen few people who go on to accomplish history-changing deeds. Indeed, much of the existing literature on women in leadership tends to focus on charismatic elite heroes—or *she*-roes if they also happen to be women. These books glorify strong competent women who overcame tough circumstances to lead and make a difference. This intrapersonal storytelling approach to leadership learning can be seductive. Who doesn't want to be inspired by the lives of Susan B. Anthony, Harriet Tubman, Eleanor Roosevelt, or Rosa Parks, or modern exemplars like Ruth Bader Ginsberg and Oprah Winfrey? However, if you are like many college students today, you may suffer from some level of anxiety about your own talents and abilities. As one student told me, "If leadership means I have to be totally put together and know exactly who I am and what I want out of life, then I will never be a leader." One of the side-effects of *she*-ro narratives is that, while they may inspire some, they may cause others to drop out. This is especially true if you do not identify with the identities or experiences of the person being held up as a model.

Fortunately, the evolving field of leadership studies recognizes that leadership is far more than the cultivation of a particular set of traits or innate behaviors. There is monumental evidence that leadership is not something you are gifted with at birth; rather, leadership can and must be learned. This book does not assume that leadership can only happen when you have got everything going for you. Rather, it will acknowledge that we all face challenges in becoming our best selves, and that occasionally even the best of intentions can result in flawed outcomes. Leadership learning involves the complex interplay among leadership capacity, motivation, identity, efficacy, and enactment (Dugan, 2017). It also involves aspects of human and interpersonal development such as values and identity development (Guthrie & Jenkins, 2018). It can refer to the process of expanding people's abilities to engage effectively in leadership roles and processes (Day, 2001). I include all these aspects under the heading of "leadership development." This book will look at how concepts of gender and concepts of leadership are socially constructed and developed over time. It is primarily intended for college students, but does not focus exclusively on the college experience. The text looks at how gender is socialized across the lifespan, including formative, collegiate, and workplace experiences. It includes short exercises in each chapter designed to support your own personalized leadership development, and narratives from college students about their own experiences navigating gender and leadership. It is not a "one-size-fits-all" endeavor.

Framing

I had originally included much of the information in this chapter as a preface to the book until my student collaborators informed me that almost no one reads prefaces and that by placing this material there I was essentially assuring it would be ignored. I want to offer a few pieces of framing information that are important for when you read the ensuing chapters, so have included them here as an essential component of chapter 1.

1. *This book does not assume that leadership means being at the top of an organization or profession.* Rather, I suggest that leadership refers to a process between and among people who seek to make a positive influence in the world. This approach will be explored much more thoroughly in the coming chapters. In fact, one of my reasons for writing this book is that I was so disheartened by existing women and leadership books that mainly take a corporate and positional approach to leadership. In my experience, while a small handful of college students are interested in climbing the corporate ladder in search of C-suite executive positions, most have vastly different career aspirations. They want to do policy work, work for not-for profit organizations, become social innovators and entrepreneurs, stay home and raise families, or, most frequently, a combination of several of these paths. It struck me that the textbooks on women and leadership that I was using for my classes did not speak to my students' aspirations or experiences and we need to look beyond executive leadership for examples of everyday leadership.

2. *This book situates intersectional identities, critical consciousness, and student development theory as important lenses throughout the text.* The vast majority of the women's leadership canon is written by white women, and I would venture to add, for white women. I am also a white, middle-class, cisgender, able-bodied, heterosexual woman living in the United States and these identities certainly shape the approach and information included, and not included, as part of this book. As a tenured professor at a large public research-extensive university, I also hold academic privilege. I work hard to be critically conscious of the way my privileged identities shape my own gender identity and expression, as well as my approach to leadership. I make many mistakes in my journey and I also actively seek and learn from those around me. One of my lifetime commitments is to work toward creating more just and equitable spaces for all people within leadership.

As someone acutely aware of the lack of representation among leadership authors, I hope to use my privileged status and positionality to invite more voices into the conversation. I am fortunate to work at a university that is one of the most structurally diverse in the world. The students at my institution hail from numerous countries; represent numerous ethnicities, cultures, and religions; and have a variety of experiences I am only beginning to comprehend. I have students who are in the United States on political asylum, who identify as undocumented, who are first-generation Americans and first-generation college students, who are paying for college themselves, and some who cannot return to their home countries because of recent travel restrictions. I continue to learn from and with them, and many students' voices are represented in this volume. When teaching, I often find that my required course readings are woefully inadequate in addressing anything close to my students' experiences. Even the most respected books in leadership and gender studies rarely address intersectionality and multiple identities. If these concepts are new to you, they will be explained more fully in ensuing chapters. This book will attempt to get at the complex and intrapersonal nature of leadership and will begin to address the intersection of leadership, multiple intersectional identities, and student development.

3. *This book is multi-vocal in that it is a product of multiple collaborations.* A diverse group of wise undergraduate and graduate women provided research support, critical readings, and widely varying narratives that will be included throughout the book. Rather than trying to summarize the powerful stories and experiences of college women, we undertook a

shared autoethnographic process where students got to name their own experiences and write their own stories. These narratives are included at the end of each chapter, not as an ideal for readers to aspire to (although many are worthy of emulation), but as an authentic expression of the lived experiences of unique individual college women and gender non-conforming people. Some of the stories are difficult to read as they describe incidents of sexual violence, harassment, and other challenges. Others are uplifting and life-affirming. *Where possible, I add a note warning readers of potentially triggering content.* Although, I tend to agree with feminist author Roxane Gay (2014), who describes the failure of trigger warnings to adequately protect people and their potential to limit civil discourse. Gay concludes "This is the truth of my trouble with trigger warnings: there is nothing words on the screen can do that has not already been done. A visceral reaction to a trigger is nothing compared to the actual experience that created the trigger." (p. 152).

4. *Throughout this book, you will likely encounter research and ideas that contradict your own life experience, values, and views.* My hope is that you will see yourself in the ideas and theories I am describing, but I also know there will be times when what I present will contradict your views and values. Feel free to yell at the book, or perhaps more productively, e-mail me and point out where I have been myopic, misguided, or just plain wrong. I will also present research studies that contradict each other, or that represent specific disciplinary or political perspectives, or that do not match your own experiences. One example is when I summarize existing studies about the gender wage gap, as there are thoughtful empirical studies that attempt to explain why the gap is bigger or smaller than conventional wisdom.

When I teach class and ask for feedback from students, I occasionally get responses that say my personal political beliefs and situatedness come through too strongly. These are balanced by an equal number of student responses saying that I am too neutral in my views and they wish they knew more about where I stand on particular issues. I am comfortable welcoming both pieces of feedback. I invite you to consider the tensions inherent in navigating multiple views and perspectives. What would it look like to invite many possible perceptions about an issue and see where there are overlaps and discrepancies? What if we first sought commonalities across differing views before arguing about points of divergence? What if, instead of agreeing to disagree, we spent more time learning about others' perspectives and working to establish common ground?

5. *This book acknowledges the social construction of ideas.* Anyone who has started to think about concepts of gender and leadership may realize that these are socially constructed ideas. That is to say, there is no concrete single manifestation of leadership or gender in the world. Rather, society and culture interact to create a host of meanings and associations about what is meant by the words "gender" and "leadership." The difficulty comes when certain views of what is deemed ideal (as in ideal performance of gender, or ideal enactment of leadership) come to be taken as the only truth. Much of the injustice in the world is created when socially constructed ideas come to be socially mandated. This happens because socially constructed ideas are embedded within larger social systems of power and inequality such as gender, race, ability, and social class, among others. The good news is that if ideas are socially constructed, then they are also subject to deconstruction and reconstruction. This text will offer some strategies for critically analyzing our understanding of both gender and leadership within broader social systems and contexts.

One example of how context matters is to consider the popular advice to women in leadership that they should "lean in" and work harder to earn a seat at the table and achieve goals (Sandberg, 2013). One might question how the larger social system functions to give people with privileged identities and backgrounds more opportunities and resources to "lean in" and that there are bigger systemic issues that need to be addressed in order to create equity in the workplace. Chapter 7 explores this debate further. My wish for you is that you consider who is served by these different perspectives. Which ones resonate most with your own lived experience? How might someone's experience of the same phenomenon be different from your own? Where is more research needed? I encourage you to seek and name your own positionality while acknowledging myriad views and perspectives. I invite the reader to form their own opinions and working philosophies of women and leadership and address the role of cognitive dissonance in learning.

6. *This book is a product of my own lenses and positionality.* I discussed some of my identities earlier in this section, but it may help to know a bit more about the origins for this book. As a professor of leadership studies, it was never my intention to author a book on college women and leadership development. After all, my own college experience was fraught with mistakes and missteps I would sooner forget rather than revisit and search for clues about women and leadership development. Suddenly I found myself assigned to teach a class on women and leadership and struggling

mightily to update the lessons I learned back in the early 1990s from the women's studies courses I took in college. I had been studying collegiate leadership development for more than 20 years but had not paid enough attention to the ways identities intersected with leadership research. Others have been doing this work in serious and thoughtful ways.

How the terminology and language had evolved! My first day of teaching the women and leadership class a decade ago, I invited students to introduce themselves. One student identified herself as "queer, gender nonconforming, omnisexual but with heteroromantic tendencies" and I knew I was way out of my depth. I learned early on in my teaching career that the absolute worst thing a professor can do is to pretend knowledge where none exists. I pride myself on being authentic in the classroom and learning as much from my students as they may learn from me. I took a big bite of humble pie and shared my predicament with the class by asking "What do those terms mean?" And then we all got on with the business of educating ourselves about gender identity and expression, fourth-wave feminism, critical theory, and modern forms of leadership. I have now taught this class more than 20 times, and I am still learning from my students. Throughout this decade of teaching, I was unable to find any single book that introduced concepts of gender and leadership to students in developmental, intersectional, and critically conscious ways. My students were inundated with articles and chapters from dozens of books and struggled to craft a coherent narrative about terms and concepts. One day, a student who was fed up with all the PDFs said, "Why don't you write a textbook for this class, Professor?" This book is my attempt to answer that call.

I have come to think of myself as a critical feminist and critical leadership scholar. Critical scholarship refers to people who do not try to distance themselves from the phenomena they are studying (in this case, gender and leadership). Instead, critical scholars accept that knowledge is embedded in the larger social and political world and think it is dangerous to deny or ignore that embeddedness. There is usually a tension in critical scholarship between describing the larger forces at work while also working to make change. *Critical scholarship* is by definition connected to critical practice. What does this mean for you the reader? It means that I have a penchant for using fancy philosophical words, but also remain strongly committed to making things understandable to anyone. It means I spend a lot of time examining and questioning the status quo and thinking about how power shapes the world and how to challenge dominant approaches that serve only narrow interests. It means self-reflection and reflective practice are essential to learning and growth. It means I value dialogue and deliberation. I say all of this as this textbook may not read like other textbooks with which you are familiar. Chapters include weighty peer-reviewed scholarship side-by-side with personal narratives, reflective exercises, poetry, and occasionally a bit of humor. Where possible, I directly quote a lot of original sources so that readers can experience the brilliance of pioneers in leadership and gender studies. These are intentional choices to allow the reader to access a wide variety of ways of knowing.

A Look Ahead

The following is a brief description of what to expect in the coming pages. Each chapter includes one or more autobiographical narratives from a college student. At the end of the book you will find a glossary of key terms used across the chapters, which may be helpful to your reading. Throughout the text, provocative propositions are presented for readers to keep in mind as they read. These overarching themes include: challenging binary conceptualizations of gender and complicating notions of difference; degendering leadership and moving from feminine to feminist approaches (Shea & Renn, 2017); addressing the intertwining nature of leadership efficacy, capacity, and enactment; and offering concrete strategies and tactics for enacting leadership in just, equitable, and humane ways.

Chapter 2, "A Critical Moment for Women and Leadership," offers a brief review of the social and historical contexts for women and leadership. This includes a review of the three waves of feminism and suggests the emergence of a fourth wave founded on intersectional approaches and global consciousness. Connections are made between waves of feminism and waves of thinking about leadership. The effects of systems of privilege and oppression on how people experience both feminism and leadership are explored, with an introduction to womanism and other reactions to white feminism, including poststructural and transnational feminism. Terminology related to gender and leadership is introduced, and the chapter reflects on Preskill and Brookfield's (2009) learning tasks of leadership.

In Chapter 3, "Who Am I to Lead? The Role of Identity, Intersectionality, and Efficacy in Leadership Development," concepts of identity and intersectionality are introduced (Crenshaw 1989, 1991). Students are asked to explore both their personal (roles and responsibilities) and social (racial, cultural, religious, sexual, [dis]abled, etc.) identities. Readers are invited to consider the effects of interlocking systems of power, privilege, and oppression and how these forces shape their lives and multiple social identities. The leadership identity development model (Komives, Owen, Longerbeam, Mainella, & Osteen, 2005) is reviewed, and readers are invited to think about their own motivations, capacities, efficacy, and enactment of leadership (Dugan, 2017).

Chapter 4, "How Did We Get Here? How Gender Socialization Shapes Women in Leadership," explores the way social, cultural, political, individual, and organizational dynamics shape the developmental experiences of girls and women. Concepts such as the Ophelia complex of postpubescent girls (Pipher, 1994), chilly classroom climates, queen bees and wannabes (Wiseman, 2009), crises of confidence, and leadership biases are presented. Issues of sexuality, appearance, and media influence are broadly addressed. Readers are introduced to Harro's cycle of socialization (Harro, 2013b).

Chapter 5, "Feminine or Feminist Approaches? Leading Across Campus and Communities," invites readers to consider their own contexts and communities for leadership. It includes examples and narratives about campus-based leadership, including efforts related to women's health and reproductive rights, body image and appearance, student debt, sexual violence and rape culture, Title IX, and more. This chapter reviews women-centric organizations such as women's centers and feminist organizations, women in cultural organizations, women in pride centers, sororities, student government, and sports. It also addresses how national organizations support women on campuses. The chapter concludes with advice about how to move from feminine to feminist approaches to campus and community leadership (Shea & Renn, 2017).

Switching gears, chapter 6, "What Difference Does Difference Make? The Effects of Stereotypes, Prejudice, and Discrimination on Gender Representation and Leadership," examines the empirical literature about women and leadership. It draws heavily on the leadership scholarship of Linda Carli, Alice Eagly, Crystal Hoyt, Barbara Kellerman, Deborah Rhode, and Janice Sanchez-Hucles, among others. It presents current research on gender and leadership traits, behaviors, and effectiveness, as well as on the effects of stereotypes, prejudice, and discrimination on women's underrepresentation in leadership. Research on wages and promotion are presented. The psychology of prejudice is briefly reviewed and readers are introduced to the idea of implicit bias.

Chapter 7, "Navigating Organizations and Systems: Metaphors for Women in Leadership," reviews the evolution of metaphors for women's leadership journeys, including concrete walls, glass ceilings, sticky floors, leaky pipelines, and labyrinths. The frequency of nonlinear career paths for women is discussed, as is the challenging nature of off-ramps and on-ramps to career development (Hewlett, 2007). This chapter briefly reviews and critiques *Lean In* ideology (Sandberg, 2013) and concludes with personal, organizational, and policy-oriented strategies for successfully closing the leadership gap (American Association of University Women [AAUW], 2016a).

Chapter 8, "Beware of Precarious Pedestals: Degendering Leadership," troubles the notion that women tend to lead in more participatory or democratic styles, whereas men tend toward autocratic or directive styles. Table 8.1 summarizes findings from research about gender differences in leadership. This chapter explores the nature and sources of power, and related concepts such as influence and empowerment. Concepts of the double-bind, positive marginality, and stereotype threat are introduced. The theory of culturally relevant leadership learning (Guthrie, Bertrand Jones, & Osteen, 2016) is presented.

Chapter 9, "Reimagining Women and Leadership: Strategies, Allies, and Critical Hope," examines the linkages between women's liberation and other social change movements. Diverse levers for social change are explored— including a taxonomy of civic action that describes differences among direct action, community organizing, policy levers, boycotting, and socially responsible personal behavior, among others (Owen & Wagner, 2010). It also addresses skills such as ally development, how to deal with nonfeminist others, how to avoid activist burnout, and how to maintain critical hope. The role of men and gender-nonconforming individuals in feminist leadership is discussed. The text ends with Love's (2013) idea of liberatory consciousness to encourage students to live their lives in oppressive systems and institutions with intentionality and awareness; maintain an awareness of the dynamics of oppression without giving in to despair and hopelessness; maintain awareness of roles played by those in the system without blame; and practice intentionality about changing systems of oppression.

A CRITICAL MOMENT FOR WOMEN AND LEADERSHIP

I change myself; I change the world.

—Gloria Anzaldúa, *Borderlands/LaFrontera: The New Mestiza,* 1987

Current Moment for Women and Leadership

If you are reading this book as part of a class, program, or reading group, you may have already faced questions from your friends and family asking why you want to learn more about women and leadership. They may ask you if you think women and men lead differently or if you think women lead better than men. They may comment that you must be a feminist if you are studying this topic, or may question if you want to exclude men from leadership. Your more "woke" friends may ask why leadership has to be gendered at all. What is the place for women in leadership in a world where many identify as gender queer, questioning, or nonbinary? How do systemic power, privilege, and oppression shape the way people view both gender and leadership? Rest assured that this volume will address each of these issues and help you formulate your own responses to these questions.

No matter what personal or political views you hold, most people can acknowledge that we are living in a critical moment for thinking about both gender and leadership. The news, and likely your social media accounts, is filled with stories about the #MeToo and Time's Up movements, issues of sexual harassment in the workplace, the attack on reproductive health and rights, issues of female representation in politics and across industries, pay disparities, sexual violence and rape culture, and the global status of women, to name a few. You likely have also read about people challenging traditional binary approaches to gender, such as parents deciding not to assign gender to their children at birth; people asking for options on government forms that reflect a third, nonbinary gender option; and the ongoing debate about access to gender inclusive bathrooms in schools. These issues are not new but have gained increased attention in recent years. Many suggest we are living in a moment of cultural reckoning where online organizing, renewed activism, and heightened awareness of discrimination are reinvigorating conversations about women's issues, feminism, and a dire need for inclusive and representative leadership.

Think about your own campus and community experiences. Are your teachers, peers, and friends talking about these issues? How are student groups like student or hall governments, sororities and fraternities, or cultural groups addressing issues of gender and leadership? What skills, knowledge, or abilities would be helpful to you as an agent of change in your communities? This book will invite you to consider these topics from your own campus context and to create your own personal approach to feminism, leadership, and change.

The "F" Word: Feminism

Before we discuss complex ideas like the social construction of both gender and leadership, let's talk about feminism. One of the barriers to discussing women and leadership is that not everyone is familiar with or has the same view of the basic tenets of feminism. Some view feminism as inherently anti-male and anti-family, others see it as closely tied to activism and politics and therefore too radical or extreme, uninformed people confuse it with lesbianism, and still others view it as a historically exclusionary endeavor practiced by white women from privileged backgrounds. In her book of essays *Bad Feminist*, author Roxane Gay (2014) states, "In truth, feminism is flawed because it is a movement powered by people and people are inherently flawed" (p. x).

Deborah Rhode (2014), a leading scholar on women and the law, summarizes recent public opinion polls about the idea of feminism in her book *What Women Want: An Agenda for the Women's Movement*. She reports that while over 75% of American women report that the women's movement has made life better and has been helpful to them, and about 80% agree broadly that the sexes should be treated equally, only about 25% of U.S. women surveyed identify as a feminist. Rhode describes the commonly heard refrain "I am not a feminist, but I care about women's issues" (p. 10) and ponders why so many people embrace the goals of the feminist movement but are reluctant to embrace the feminist label.

In her book *Feminism Is for Everybody*, activist scholar bell hooks (2000a) offers this definition:

> Feminism is the struggle to end sexist oppression. Its aim is not to benefit any specific group of women, any particular race and class of women. It does not privilege women over men. It has the power to transform all of our lives. (p. viii)

This approach to feminism is increasingly embraced by public figures such as actor Emma Watson (yes, of *Harry Potter* fame), who addressed this issue in her 2014 speech to the United Nations. She described feminism as the belief that men and women should have equal rights and opportunities, and that it refers to the theory of the political, economic, and social equality of the sexes. Watson then proceeded to outline why men are needed as feminist allies and also promoted the nonprofit group He For She (see www.heforshe.org). For those who think that feminism may be passé or an outmoded idea for a previous generation, I again turn to the wisdom of Roxane Gay (2014), who notes that "some women being empowered does not prove the patriarchy is dead. It proves that some of us are lucky" (p. 101). Gay's wise insight suggests that, while some may not experience overt sexism, there are still many people who experience gender oppression on a daily basis. This is especially true when one takes a global perspective. For the purposes of consistency in this book, we will use hooks's definition as a starting point for discussion, as it is widely embraced by many scholars of gender studies.

Just because someone holds a particular identity (e.g., identifying as a woman) does not mean they are necessarily familiar with the history, movement, and leaders of people advocating on behalf of that identity. Although this is not a textbook about the history of the women's movement (see my rant in chapter 1 about the dangers of glorifying *she*-roes), some familiarity with the social and historical contexts for women and leadership is warranted. It is important to know where we have been in order to decide where we are going.

Social and Historical Contexts for Women

You may be familiar with concept of three "waves" of feminism. The idea of waves came about as a result of a 1968 *New York Times* article by Martha Weinman Lear entitled "The Second Feminist Wave" where Lear attempted to link late 1960s gender activism to earlier women's liberation movements. The metaphor of a wave succeeds at showing it takes many iterations of action to make change. Others find the wave metaphor misleading as it suggests that gender activism in the United States is monolithic in nature and that there is consensus about the core ideas of feminism, which many dispute. In a 2018 article on the news blog *Vox*, contributor Constance Grady breaks down the problems with the metaphor of waves of feminism.

> The wave metaphor can be reductive. It can suggest that each wave of feminism is a monolith with a single unified agenda, when in fact the history of feminism is a history of different ideas in wild conflict. It can reduce each wave to a stereotype and suggest that there's a sharp division between generations of feminism, when in fact there's a fairly strong continuity between each wave—and since no wave is a monolith, the theories that are fashionable in one wave are often grounded in the work that someone was doing on the sidelines of a previous wave. And the wave metaphor can suggest that mainstream feminism is the only kind of feminism there is, when feminism is full of splinter movements. (para. 5)

It is now more common to talk about there being multiple *feminisms*, based on the intersectional identities of those involved, but more on that later. For now, let's look at the stereotypical summary of the three waves, and a possible emerging fourth wave.

First Wave

First-wave feminism typically refers to the suffragette movements in the United States and England in the late 1800s and early 1900s. In the United States, some date this wave as beginning with the Seneca Falls Convention in 1848 and ending with the passing of the 19th Amendment giving women the right to vote in 1920. Note that this is a primarily Western political phenomenon referring to mostly white people in the middle and upper classes. However, women of all class levels faced a wide variety of gender discrimination. Their movements were restricted to the home, they were not allowed to own property or vote, and many were not given access to education beyond primary schooling. In the late 1800s many women were part of reform movements such as those aimed at improving treatment of the mentally ill (Dorothea Dix), enacting prohibition (Carrie Nation and Frances Willard), and working toward the abolition of slavery (Harriet Beecher Stowe and Ida B. Wells). As a result of organizing on behalf of other disenfranchised groups, women began to examine their own disenfranchisement. In 1848, led by abolitionists Elizabeth Cady Stanton and Lucretia Mott, almost 200 women met in a church in upstate New York at the Seneca Falls Convention. A local newspaper, the *Seneca County Courier*, announced the meeting on July 14, describing it as "a Convention to discuss the social, civil, and religious condition and rights of women" (Woman's Rights Convention, 1848). Speakers included Sojourner Truth and Frederick Douglass. Attendees discussed their grievances and passed a list of 12 resolutions calling for specific equal rights—including, after much debate, the right to vote. Early feminism was directly related to the abolitionist movements, although it remained a predominantly white endeavor. In 1870, the 15th Amendment was passed guaranteeing Black men, including former slaves, the right to vote, although Jim Crow laws effectively curbed the execution of these nascent rights. Grady (2018) notes that Black women were even barred from some demonstrations or forced to march behind the white female demonstrators. In 1920, Congress passed the 19th Amendment granting women the right to vote, although it remained difficult for women of color to vote, especially in the South (Grady, 2018).

Second Wave

Second-wave feminism refers to the women's liberation movements in the 1960s and 1970s, predominantly focused on the quest for equal pay and reproductive freedom. Betty Friedan's *The Feminine Mystique* was published in 1963 and sold over 3 million copies. The book calls out the systemic sexism that teaches women that their place was in the home and that if they were unhappy as housewives, it was only because they were broken and perverse, rather than seeking creative and intellectual freedoms. Friedan called this "the problem that has no name" (p, 57). Second-wave feminism shifted the conversation from women's political equality to women's social equality. Grady (2018) describes the legislative and legal victories of the second wave, including the passing of The Equal Pay Act of 1963, which theoretically outlawed the gender pay gap; a series of landmark Supreme Court cases through the 1960s and 1970s that gave married and unmarried women the right to use birth control; Title IX, which gave women the right to educational equality and had a ripple effect on women's sports (and later sexual harassment, assault, and dating violence on college campuses); and in 1973, *Roe v. Wade,* which guaranteed women reproductive freedom. Women exerted more control on their finances, raised awareness about sexual violence and workplace harassment, and strove to name the systemic sexism ingrained in U.S. society at the time.

Working-class women and women of color often felt disenfranchised from the feminist movement, especially as many already worked outside of the home for necessity, and faced additional violations such as forced sterilization and double discrimination. In 1977, a Black feminist group in Boston called themselves the Combahee River Collective after guerilla action taken by Harriet Tubman in 1863 that freed more than 750 slaves and is the only military campaign in American history planned and led by women. The Combahee River Collective (1977) issued a Black feminist statement "actively committed to struggling against racial, sexual, heterosexual and class oppression and see as our particular task the development of an integrated analysis and practice based on the fact that the major systems of oppression are interlocking" (p. 210). Shortly after, writer Alice Walker coined the idea of a Womanist movement to address the needs of women of color in her short story "Coming Apart," which was featured in her 1983 collection of essays *In Search of Our Mother's Gardens: Womanist Prose*. Walker (1983) suggests that feminism cannot be considered apart from culture and thus Black feminists need their own approach, independent of white feminism. Audre Lorde, a Black feminist lesbian poet, tackled similar themes in *Sister, Outsider*, her collection of essays and poems in 1984.

Third Wave

There are many arguments about the timeline and characteristics of third-wave feminism. Most agree there was increased activism around gender starting in the early 1990s with the Anita Hill testimony during Supreme Court candidate Justice Clarence Thomas's confirmation hearings. After 24 women won seats in the House of Representatives and 3 more won seats in the Senate, 1992 was named "the Year of the Woman" (Grady, 2018, para. 50). Scholars like Kimberlé Crenshaw, Patricia Hill Collins, Susan Bordo, and Judith Butler made intellectual advances in feminist theorizing. Critics note that there was not a centralizing political or social reform goal of third-wave feminism, although writers like Naomi Wolf and Susan Faludi challenged notions of gender and femininity. Third-wave feminists made it okay to embrace female sexuality. Grady (2018) offers this description:

> In part, the third-wave embrace of girliness was a response to the antifeminist backlash of the 1980s, the one that said the second-wavers were shrill, hairy, and unfeminine and that no man would ever want them. And in part, it was born out of a belief that the rejection of girliness was in itself misogynistic: girliness, third-wavers argued, was not inherently less valuable than masculinity or androgyny. (para. 45)

Fourth Wave

Some pundits claim that the #MeToo and Time's Up movements are ushering in a fourth wave of feminism, others claim that the fourth wave has been here for a while. This fourth wave seems to be characterized by online activism and more intersectional approaches to gender liberation. One blogger described fourth-wave feminism as queer, sex positive, trans inclusive, body positive, and digitally driven (Sollee, 2015). Some have started using the spelling *womxn* where the x allows space for individuals who identify as genderfluid, gender-queer, gender nonconforming, or nonbinary to be included. There appears to be more global consciousness in the fourth wave. People are noticing that women across the globe face vastly different gendered expectations and continue to experience severe oppression in many places. There is a movement toward transnational feminism, which focuses on "intersections across nationality (including race and ethnicity), sex, gender, and class within the context of modern-day imperialism and colonialism" (Valoy, 2015, para. 7). Transnational feminism is also a reaction to Western thought, which some say overemphasizes gender roles as the only reason for women's oppression. It remains to be seen how historians will describe current actions to end sexist oppression.

Social and Historical Contexts for Leadership Studies

Just as it is important to develop a shared understanding of the women's movement, it is imperative to also be familiar with the stories most often told about leadership. We all hold assumptions that shape the way we think, feel, and experience leadership. In order to truly examine women's experiences in leadership, we need to know about not only the evolution of the women's movements but also how scholars have shaped our understanding of leadership. Each informs the other and is inextricably linked to how we understand and experience both gender and leadership. If you have signed up for a class or program focusing on leadership, then you likely hold some belief that aspects of leadership can be learned. Some of the foundational principles of modern leadership have a particular values orientation. A good way to start developing your own working philosophy of leadership is to reflect on your beliefs about the principles outlined in Box 2.1. The discipline of leadership studies is continuously evolving and we simultaneously see it in action. We see leadership play out in our lives every day; therefore, it is important to take the time to reflect on our own beliefs and values that shape our leadership philosophy. Although there are myriad ways to define *leadership*, this book makes use of the following definition that was developed with college students in mind and supports the change-focused approach of this textbook: "*Leadership is a relational and ethical process of people together attempting to accomplish positive change*" (Komives, Lucas, & McMahon, 2013, p. 95, emphasis added).

The principles presented in Box 2.1 reflect current thinking about leadership, but these views have significantly changed over time. The typical story of the evolution of leadership theories usually goes something like this: The earliest conceptions of leadership were focused on heroic men accomplishing

Box 2.1.
Principles of Contemporary Leadership

The following statements reflect current thinking about leadership. To what degree are these ideas similar to or different from what you have been taught or believe? How have you arrived at your beliefs? What are the implications of these beliefs for the theory and practice of leadership?

- Leaders are made, not born.
- You do not have to have a title or special position to be a leader.
- You do not have to have followers to be a leader.
- Having a charismatic personality is not required to be a leader.
- There is no one right way to lead an organization or a group.
- Leadership and management are different processes.
- Leadership is teachable.

Note. Adapted from Komives et al. (2013).

great feats, such as kings, warriors, religious leaders. Leadership was an inherited right that many believed had genetic components—"blue bloods" indicated aristocratic or noble heritage. In the 1700s the belief in a genetic component to leadership was strengthened with the rise of Darwinism and a new understanding of heredity (Bass, 1990). For most of early history, leadership focused on centralized control, power, and domination (Northouse, 2018). The leadership of women has mostly not been part of the equation. Yet we know they existed—think of Joan of Arc or Catherine the Great. With rare exceptions, women in leadership have been omitted from historical writings and teachings. Look at Exercise 2.1 and see if any of the names of historical powerful women are familiar to you. If these are new to you, you may ask why the stories of these powerful women are not more common knowledge.

As non-noble people also demonstrated leadership (e.g., William Wallace more commonly known as Braveheart) the story evolved that leadership may not only be about genetics and birthright but also have something to do with an individual's inherent traits, and that leadership was more about influence than domination. Certain people had specific personality traits that made them more likely to be leaders. In the early 1900s, research linked leadership to traits such as height, intelligence, and confidence (Bass, 1990; Komives et al., 2013). Trait research has had a recent resurgence among leadership scholars (Lord, DeVader, & Alliger, 1986; Stogdill, 1974; Zaccarro, Kemp, & Bader, 2004), but focuses on traits such as intelligence, determination, self-confidence,

Exercise 2.1.
Erased From History

The stories of powerful women have frequently been erased from history. This erasure process occurred in how people recorded history, and even in how monuments to great leaders were constructed. Statues to several of the following women were later altered to make them appear masculine. If you are not familiar with these names, consider searching for more information about these groundbreaking women.

- Enheduanna of the Sumerian City-State of Ur
- Trung Sisters of Vietnam
- Empress Wu Zetian of China
- Lady Murasaki Shikibu of Japan
- Empress Theodora of Byzantium
- Nur Jahan of Mughal India

Note. Adapted from Amanda Foreman's excellent BBC2 video series *The Ascent of Woman* (2016).

integrity, and sociability (Northouse, 2018). There is an offshoot of trait theory called influence theory that focuses on charisma and the idea that leadership is an influence or social exchange process (Riggio, 1988).

In the 1940s and 1950s, people started seeing some of the limits of trait-based approaches to leadership. The advent of psychological testing launched the field of career placement where individuals, such as GIs returning from World War II, could take a battery of tests and would be placed or matched with a specific job based on their results. Even when someone scored high on an assessment for leadership traits, they did not always exhibit leadership in the workplace. It turns out behaviors matter. By the late 1950s, the prevailing definition of *leadership* was "a behavior that influences people toward shared goals" (Northouse, 2018, p. 3). The seminal Ohio State and University of Michigan studies indicated that effective leadership behaviors involved paying attention to relationships (called consideration, or concern for people) and to tasks (called initiating structure, or concern for production) (Bass, 1990).

The effects of contexts or situations on leadership was not really considered until the 1950s and 1960s. Situational leadership (also called contingency theories) proposed that leaders should adjust their behaviors based on the situation, and that different situations call for different kinds of leadership. There are a variety of tools such as Hersey and Blanchard's (1969) situational leadership model that offer prescriptions for how people can best lead given different kinds of situations and the developmental level of their subordinates or followers.

This commonly told story of the evolution of thinking about leadership typically concludes with an explosion of leadership research in the 1980s and beyond. Scholars tend to describe older approaches to leadership as industrial theories, in that they focus on efficiency and effectiveness most suited to a manufacturing society. Since the dawn of the Internet age, it is generally acknowledged that we live in a knowledge economy. Theories of leadership designed for use in the knowledge economy are often called postindustrial theories. You may have heard of some more recent approaches to leadership: servant leadership, adaptive leadership, authentic leadership, relational leadership, shared leadership. And the vanguard of modern leadership includes research into chaos and systems theory, complexity theory, and other attempts to discern patterns in our complex world.

We will revisit some of these theories throughout the course of this book, but, just as how the metaphor of "waves of feminism" can be reductive and stereotyping, the story most often told about leadership faces similar critiques. Dugan (2017) notes the pervasiveness of "old" leadership theories in the world today stating that "these ideas continue to shape both formal and informal leadership as well as the application of theories to practice" (p. 61). The story is more nonlinear than the previous tale suggests. Dugan goes on to deconstruct the evolution of the leadership narrative by noting where it falls short. He asks why the story of leadership is mostly drawn from business, management, and psychology literature rather than other disciplines; that the story reflects a completely Western, U.S.-centric perspective on leadership; the story omits important conversations about culture, gender, race, ethnicity, sexual orientation, and other intersectional identities; and also omits inclusion of social context. Dugan suggests we instead evaluate theories based on how much they demonstrate concern for purpose, people, and process (and, I would add, planet).

> Women, people of color, and other minoritized groups are disassociated from the dominant narrative about leadership. Their stories are rarely told, their contributions delegitimized, and in the process, leadership becomes associated with the dominant majority. When examples of women, people of color, and other minoritized groups are connected to leadership, it is typically framed as an exception to the rule. (Dugan, 2017, p. 67).

Some suggest that we are ushering in an era of third- or fourth-wave leadership (Owen, 2015). Fourth-wave leadership invites conversations about ideology, hegemony, social location, power, and agency in leadership development.

It interrogates existing theories to examine whose voices have been omitted, and where indigenous voices and collectivist approaches to leadership have been co-opted by privileged Western scholars. Fourth-wave leadership connects concepts from critical theory to the study of leadership (see chapter 1), and acknowledges that, like gender, leadership is also a social construct. Having a sense of how you identify your own approaches to gender and leadership is helpful to situating yourself in the history and current contexts.

The Social Construction of Gender

How do you describe your own gender? Sex? Gender expression? Sexual orientation? For much of society, sex and gender are considered binary. Your sex is either male or female; your gender is man or woman; your sexual orientation is gay or straight. Fortunately, this narrow and bifurcating view of the world is being challenged. Turns out there is very little biological determinism involved in concepts of *sex* and *gender*. Rather, most of what we refer to when we talk about these terms is socially constructed. To say something is socially constructed indicates that its meaning is determined through social interactions, or the things we do and say with other people. Messages about the socially acceptable ways to enact gender begin before birth and are accelerated in childhood socialization, what we are taught by parents, religion, and peers, as well as lessons learned from the media, education, and other systemic forces. Box 2.2 outlines some of the terminology that will be used throughout this book.

Box 2.2.
Gender Terminology

The following definitions are adapted from the website of Gay & Lesbian Alliance Against Defamation (www.glaad.org) and the Human Rights Campaign (www.hrc.org).

Sex—The classification of a person as male or female. At birth, infants are assigned a sex, usually based on the appearance of their external anatomy, which is what is written on the birth certificate. A person's sex, however, is actually a combination of bodily characteristics including: chromosomes, hormones, internal and external reproductive organs, and secondary sex characteristics.

Gender Identity—A person's internal, deeply held sense of their gender. For transgender people, their own internal gender identity does not match the sex they were assigned at birth. Most people have a gender

(*Continues*)

Box 2.2. (*Continued*)

identity of man or woman (or boy or girl). For some people, their gender identity does not fit neatly into one of those two choices (see nonbinary and/or genderqueer). Unlike gender expression, gender identity is not visible to others.

Cisgender—A person whose gender identity and biological sex assigned at birth align (e.g., man and male-assigned). A simple way to think about it is: if a person is not transgender, they are cisgender.

Transgender—An umbrella term for people whose gender identity and/or gender expression differs from what is typically associated with the sex they were assigned at birth. People under the transgender umbrella may describe themselves using one or more of a wide variety of terms—including transgender. Use the descriptive term preferred by the person. Many transgender people are prescribed hormones by their doctors to bring their bodies into alignment with their gender identity. Some undergo surgery as well. But not all transgender people can or will take those steps, and a transgender identity is not dependent upon physical appearance or medical procedures.

Trans*—Used as shorthand to mean transgender—or sometimes to be inclusive of a wide variety of identities under the transgender umbrella. Because its meaning is not precise or widely understood, be careful when using it with audiences who may not understand what it means. Avoid using it unless in a direct quote or in cases where you can clearly explain the term's meaning in the context of your story.

Gender Nonconforming—A term used to describe some people whose gender expression is different from conventional expectations of masculinity and femininity. Please note that not all gender nonconforming people identify as transgender; nor are all transgender people gender nonconforming. Many people have gender expressions that are not entirely conventional—that fact alone does not make them transgender. Many transgender men and women have gender expressions that are conventionally masculine or feminine. Simply being transgender does not make someone gender nonconforming. The term is not a synonym for transgender and should be used only if someone self-identifies as gender nonconforming.

(*Continues*)

Box 2.2. (*Continued*)

Nonbinary and/or Genderqueer—Terms used by some people who experience their gender identity and/or gender expression as falling outside the categories of man and woman. They may define their gender as falling somewhere in between man and woman, or they may define it as wholly different from these terms. The term is not a synonym for transgender or transsexual and should only be used if someone self-identifies as nonbinary and/or genderqueer.

Questioning—Exploring one's own sexual orientation or gender identity; or an individual who is exploring their own sexual orientation and gender identity.

Gender Expression—The external display of one's gender, through a combination of dress, demeanor, social behavior, and other factors, generally measured on scales of masculinity and femininity. Also referred to as *gender presentation* (e.g., woman-ness, man-ness, femme, butch, androgynous, gender neutral).

Sexual Orientation—Describes a person's enduring physical, romantic, and/or emotional attraction to another person (e.g., heterosexual, homosexual, gay, lesbian, bisexual, pansexual, asexual). Gender identity and sexual orientation are not the same.

In her book *Gender Trouble: Feminism and the Subversion of Identity*, philosopher Judith Butler (1990) states, "There is no gender identity behind the expressions of gender; that identity is performatively constituted by the very 'expressions' that are said to be its results" (p. 34). If you are like me, you need to read that sentence a few more times to understand the meaning behind it. Here Butler is suggesting that there is no concrete biological reality of gender that causes us to behave in certain ways (more masculine, more feminine, etc.); instead, gender is constantly "performed" and performative. To put it another way, "gender is not something that one is, it is something that one does, an act . . . doing, rather than a being" (p. 191). So, what does it mean to perform gender? Gender is performed in the way one walks, talks, what one wears, and the meaning society ascribes to it. If gender performance does not match society's idea of binary gender (e.g., a girl who identifies as a tomboy, or a boy who is not assertive and does not like sports) there are often harsh and even violent consequences. This is especially true in Western cultures. There are places and spaces where the notion of a third and even fourth gender is a recognized part of the culture (see the Mashoga in Kenya; Ashtime in Ethiopia; Muxe in Mexico; Xaniths in Oman; Two Spirit in many indigenous communities). For more information about alternative approaches to gender and a detailed exploration of how gender ideology functions in society, check out the book *Gender: Ideas, Interaction, Institutions* by Wade and Ferree (2015).

The definitions presented in Box 2.2 are incomplete and evolving; they are shaped by powerful hegemonic forces of misogyny, racism, and colonialism. In "Night to His Day: The Social Construction of Gender," Judith Lorber (1994) describes how gender roles and norms are justified by religion and culture and often backed by the law. Think about cultural practices related to gender: female and male genital circumcision, the wearing of veils, foot-binding, breast augmentation, among others. Lorber goes on to state that gender is a major component of structural inequality, yet is often rendered invisible such that we cannot imagine another way. Gender creates distinguishable and unequal social statuses associated with rights and responsibilities. One word for this process of social, cultural, and ideological influence exerted by a dominant group is *hegemony*.

The Social Construction of Leadership

Just as there are norms around binary views of gender that have great consequences if challenged or violated, there are likewise norms about leadership. Ask people around you to describe attributes of leaders and you likely will hear words like *strong, decisive, commanding, persuasive, powerful*. How many of these qualities are stereotypically associated with men? Are these associations accurate, or are we socialized to view leadership this way? What happens if we reject traditional leadership norms? Muhr and Sullivan (2013) describe the problem:

> Attempts to understand—and in some cases rationalize—why leadership is gendered range from biological arguments that often cast men as more "natural" at leading than women to theories which highlight the socially constructed conditions that favor men in leadership. Rather than viewing gender as biologically deterministic, we see it as shaped by and through discursive practices, which construct certain expectations for the way people—both affectively and through their material bodies—ought to perform. These mandates permeate leadership studies, popular notions about leadership and follower's expectations for how leaders should perform. (p. 417)

Dugan (2017) suggests that any study of leadership must also grapple with the socially constructed nature of what leadership is, stating, "If leadership involves sense-/meaning-making, then perception is a powerful arbitrator of the reality we construct" (p. 29). How do we surface the taken-for-granted assumptions of leadership? Ask yourself: "Do people have to be strong to be leaders?" "What does it mean to be strong?" "Who decided that strong must look a certain way?" It becomes important to surface the taken-for-granted assumptions about leadership. What forces shape how we view, interpret, and explain the world around us? Davis and Harrison (2013) describe some of these forces, stating, "We need to interrogate the one size fits all policies and practices that obscure human differences, systems of oppression, history, and institutional contexts that lead to illusions of equality at the expense of genuine equity" (p. 25).

Critical Considerations

Leadership must learn to be responsive to global, national, and local concerns, and to work across sectors and disciplines, which require new approaches to inquiry and knowledge creation. We need new approaches to gender, leadership, and their intersections. One way is to challenge the legitimacy of dominant ideologies. This takes both critical thinking and critical theorizing.

You likely are familiar with the practices of critical thinking and critical reflection. Critical thinking is often considered a politically neutral enterprise that involves applying logic to a problem or situation. Critical reflection goes beyond critical thinking in addressing issues of the nature and sources of power: who really benefits and who is silenced by leadership efforts; which actions result in real change rather than the mere appearance of change; and the systemic and institutionalized nature of oppression (Owen, 2016). The power of linking leadership and critical reflection augments the transformative potential of leadership efforts—for individuals, groups, and communities. Brookfield (1995) offers sage advice:

> It becomes easy to lose sight of the political underpinnings, dimensions, and consequences of our reflection. But how we reflect and what we chose to reflect on are partisan questions . . . reflection in and of itself is not enough; it must always be linked to how the world can be changed. (p. 217)

Critical theory is a social theory oriented toward critiquing and changing society as a whole, in contrast to traditional theory oriented only to understanding or explaining it. It's about changing things, not just explaining them. Critical theory asks questions like: How do our own identities, subjectivities, and assumptions within dominant social, political, economic, and cultural systems and structures shape our approach to leadership? In interviews, Judith Butler often reminds us that critical does not necessarily mean destructive, rather a willingness to examine the assumptions and presumptions behind our thinking that can get in the way of a more livable world.

Preskill and Brookfield's (2009) Nine Learning Tasks of Leadership suggest implications for the development and enactment of critically conscious leadership. Table 2.1 poses questions for critical reflection about each of the learning tasks of leadership. You are invited to consider how you might enact these tasks as you explore ideas related to women and leadership development. The point here is to continue to unpack the many hidden assumptions and suppositions behind both gender and leadership. Davis and Harrison (2013) note, "Unless we are open to excavating the assumptions about how we know what we know, we will not generally ask the fundamental, and often hidden questions necessary for uncovering systems of injustice" (p. 19).

TABLE 2.1
Critically Reflecting on the Learning Tasks of Leadership

Nine Learning Tasks of Leadership	Questions for Critical Reflection
Learning how to be open to the contributions of others	What leadership knowledge, skills, and habits have you learned from collaborating with others? How open are you to alternative perspectives and creating space for dialogue and deliberation? What happened the last time you engaged in deep listening rather than putting forth your own perspective?
Learning how to critically reflect on one's practice	How often do you consider (and react to) issues of power, power relations, and equitable distribution of power in your leadership? Where does hegemony come into play (i.e., the dominance of one way of thinking)? To what extent are you aware of how you and those you serve may internalize ideas, beliefs, and values that may be undermining democratic outcomes? How do you support the agency of others? How are you supporting colleagues or community members in gaining meaningful control over their own work, learning, and lives?
Learning how to support the growth of others	How are you increasing the capacity of others to be active participants in the life of their community, movement, or organizations? Where are you seeing silence or withdrawal happen? What strategies do you use to stay curious about the lives of others? To ask constructive questions? To learn the stories of your collaborators?

(Continues)

TABLE 2.1. (*Continued*)

Nine Learning Tasks of Leadership	Questions for Critical Reflection
Learning how to develop collective leadership	Where are you challenging the myth of heroic, self-sufficient, and individualistic leadership? How are you working with others to create a shared vision? Are you willing to subordinate your own aims to the group's goals and interests?
Learning how to analyze experience	To what extent are your experiences shaped by forces under your control as opposed to forces that transcend your immediate circumstances? How does your understanding of your experiences change as you adopt different lenses for examining them? Which leadership experiences invite repetition and which encourage avoidance?
Learning how to question oneself and others	How do you move beyond asking rote questions to ones that invite discovery and wonder? How might you use questions to critique and assess shared accomplishments? How might you use questions to "unpack platitudes and deconstruct conventional wisdom" (Preskill & Brookfield, 2009, p. 130)?
Learning to live democratically	How is leadership (putting energies and talents toward collective goals) an inherent civic responsibility? How is leadership (participating fully and having an equal opportunity to influence the outcomes of deliberations) an inherent right? Where do you invite democratic dialogue, responsive to each community member's needs and concerns?
Learning to sustain hope in the face of struggle	How is hope a necessary precondition for social change? For leadership? How do you sustain hope over time? How do you use dissent to illuminate shortcomings and consequences of decisions? To what extent do you share examples of ordinary people doing extraordinary things?
Learning to create community	How does your community embody each of the principles described in this table? How are you harnessing the power of collective thought and action in order to transform society? How do communities invite redistribution of resources? Shared authority and accountability?

Note. Adapted from Preskill and Brookfield (2009).

The detailed exploration of the philosophical roots of critical theory could take a lifetime to unpack and is beyond the scope of this book. There are a few core concepts that we will revisit in the coming chapters that will be useful for you to know. First, it is important to have a working understanding of the concepts of ideology, hegemony, social location, power, and agency, and how these processes shape our approaches to leadership and learning. Brookfield (2005) defines *ideology* as the broadly accepted set of values, beliefs, myths, and explanations that appear to be true and desirable to a majority of the population. The function of ideology is to "maintain an unjust social and political order . . . by convincing people that existing social arrangements are naturally ordained and obviously work for the good of all people" (p. 41). Adams et al. (2013) describe *hegemony* as a subtler form of social control than ideology, whereby "dominated or subordinate classes of people consent to their own domination, as opposed to being simply forced or coerced into accepting inferior positions," which results in "the empowerment of certain cultural beliefs, values, and practices to the submersion and partial exclusion of others" (p. 28). Note that ideology typically functions through coercion and fear (e.g., the overt actions of white supremacists in Charlottesville, Virginia, in 2017), while hegemony functions through the silent acceptance of the status quo (e.g., the lack of outrage at the differential nature of sentencing for drug possession between cocaine and crack, where cocaine offenders, who are often white, received far fewer and lesser sentences). Dugan (2017) cautions: "The concept of hegemony is perhaps so powerful because of the depths of consciousness at which it operates as well as the way social systems reinforce it [as] a function of everyday life, but one that we rarely see and almost never name" (p. 37).

The second important concept of how we each experience the world, and our own experiences with ideology and hegemony, is *social location*. Social location refers to the position one holds in society based on a variety of personal and social identities. We will explore this concept more deeply in chapter 3, but readers can likely see how their unique combination of identities shape their experience of the world. These identities also manifest in different forms of power and feelings of agency. *Power* is directly related to leadership because they both involve the process of influence. In 1968, French and Raven offered important distinctions about the types and nature of power that are still in use today. They named six distinct types of power, and people can hold many of these simultaneously. *Legitimate power* refers to the power that comes from holding a title or position; the higher the status of the position, the more perceived power. *Reward power* is the ability to give positive or remove negative consequences, while *coercive power* is the ability to deliver negative consequences or remove positive ones. A person has *information power* if they have access to knowledge not available elsewhere or deemed important for a decision or task. *Expert power* comes from having unique knowledge, competencies, or skills. *Referent power* is derived from relationships, who a person knows, and their ability to draw on relationships as a source of support. A related concept to the types of power is the notion of having *agency*. Brookfield (2005) defines *agency* as "a sense of possessing power—or having the energy, intelligence, resources, and opportunity to act on the world" (p. 47). Someone may actually have access to different types of power but not feel agency to use them.

There are also key differences in the goals of leadership. Are you working toward equality, equity, or liberation in your change efforts? There is a popular Internet meme that tries to convey the differences between equity and equality. In the scene, three people of varying heights (tall, medium, and short) are standing on crates trying to peer over a fence in order to watch a baseball game. In the equality scenario, they all have the same number of crates, which is helpful for the middle person, but not for the shortest person, and not needed by the tallest person. The implication is that everyone receives the same amount of support, whether they need it or not. In the equity scenario, each person has the number of crates they need to see the game over the fence. The implied logic here is that some people need more support than others to have the same experience. Although it's a potentially helpful way to show the differences between equality and equity, there have been good critiques of this meme. The metaphor of the fence becomes troublesome when you think beyond the height of the people and start to ask why some people who want to watch the game need more support in the first place. When we start to think systemically about this, we move from a deficit approach where we blame victims for their own oppressions (how to help the short person see) to considering how we can change the context to be more inclusive overall (remove the fence entirely!). This is an example of liberation, where we remove hurdles to equal opportunity, equal rights, and human liberty. (See http://culturalorganizing.org for the image and the critique.)

The Power of Narratives

Obviously, this chapter has skimmed only the surface of some of the important considerations when thinking about gender and leadership. Think about this chapter as the beginning of developing an informed vocabulary necessary for having more complex conversations about the intersections of gender and leadership. One way to continue to make meaning of these important ideas

Exercise 2.2.
Authoring Your Own Story

There is a Native American parable about a person who says, "I feel as if I have two wolves fighting in my heart. One wolf is the vengeful, angry one. The other wolf is the loving, compassionate one." When asked which wolf will win the fight in his heart, the person replies, "The one I feed."

One of the implications of this parable is that the stories we tell ourselves, and that we tell about ourselves, matter. What stories are essential to your own experiences of gender and leadership? What do these stories reveal about your journey, values, and aspirations? Consider sharing your story with people close to you and see what connections you can find. How are stories sources of transformation and healing?

about the social construction of feminism and leadership, and about the nature of critical thinking, reflection, and critical theory, is to consider how these ideas connect to your own gender and leadership journey. The use of narrative, or telling stories, can be a profound tool for self-revelation, reflection, and healing. Stories are powerful because they allow others to access our thoughts, feelings, and experiences, and hopefully to find connections. They also allow us to make connections among experiences that we may not have realized before. Reflect on the questions in Exercise 2.2 to author your own story.

While narratives are powerful, counter-narratives can be transformative. *Counternarratives* refer to the telling of and listening to stories from those who have been historically marginalized (Zamudio, Russell, Rios, & Bridgeman, 2010). Inviting counternarratives creates empowerment and agency to those who may previously have been silenced, and can create understanding and connection across listeners. Surfacing counternarratives is not a new idea—indigenous communities have rich traditions of oral histories. For thousands of years, Aboriginal people have used stories to pass on ecological knowledge, historical events, and spiritual traditions, even when telling such stories was forbidden or outlawed. Latin communities have used testimony as a form of witnessing the oppression and social and political inequality faced by their people. Adams and Horton (1975) and colleagues founded the Highlander Folk School in the 1930s to use storytelling to solve community problems, which evolved to address civil rights and desegregation in the United States. For more on the power of narrative, see the companion manual to this book, *Women and Leadership Development in College: A Facilitation Resource* (Pigza, Owen, & Associates, in press).

Each chapter of this book concludes with short narratives or counternarratives written by college students about an experience in their lives that shaped their thoughts about gender and their approach to leadership. These narratives provide an authentic expression of the lived experiences of unique individual college women, men, and gender nonconforming people. As mentioned previously, of the stories are difficult to read as they describe incidents of sexual violence, harassment, and other challenges. Others are uplifting and life-affirming. Where possible, I add a note warning readers of possible triggering content, but know that I cannot predict what aspects of the stories will be most powerful to you. I invite you to experience the authors' words and see where they do or do not connect to your own experiences. The authors themselves were asked to select pseudonyms to protect their anonymity, as well as to describe their own identities, so the names and terms they use are their own.

We start with Katherine, a white, cisgender, heterosexual, middle-class, Christian female, who experienced pejorative comments from a teacher when she was labeled with a learning disability and who used that experience to motivate her own journey as an educator and leader.

Narratives and Counternarratives: Katherine's Story

It's Not Like She's Going to Set the World on Fire

I'm seven years old and in the teacher's conference room, a place filled with snacks and secrets. I remember my legs dangling off the seat as everyone talked about me, around me, but never to me. I heard things like:

"She's behind grade level."

"She's a sweet girl, but we're worried we are just going to have to lower our expectations."

"She's gifted and talented in some areas, but her scores are too low in reading and writing. It doesn't make sense."

"She's dyslexic."

After that statement the room grew silent. Then, my teacher cleared her throat, spoke over the room and said, "We can talk all day about what she's good at, but the reality is she's just a child with dyslexia. It's not like *she's* going to set the world on fire, or anything. Right?" Her eyes stared straight into my mother's.

I'm not sure what that means—to set the world on fire. My mom said not to mess with fire and I never had. I snapped my small head up to mother; by the look on her face I could tell that what was said wasn't good.

It reminded me of the face she made when my brother put a firecracker in my cast last summer on Fourth of July. She looked down at me, kissed me on the forehead, and grabbed me by my arm and said today was a mommy and daughter day.

I got to leave school early and we went and got ice cream. While in the car my mom was silent. I eventually asked over the sound of the radio humming in the background, "What does it mean, mommy? To set the world on fire? And, why can't I?" My mom looked down at the radio, back in the mirror, and grew silent again. Eventually she turned off the music, looked me in the eyes, and said, "My baby girl, there's going to be so many people in life who tell you that you can't. They'll say you're not smart enough, or strong enough. Don't listen to what she said. You are brave and will always be brave enough. Every day I want you to love so tightly, work so hard, and fight so endlessly to set the world on fire." And I have.

3

WHO AM I TO LEAD?

The Role of Identity, Intersectionality, and Efficacy in Leadership Development

When I dare to be powerful—to use my strength in the service of my vision, then it becomes less and less important whether I am afraid.

—Audre Lorde, *Sister, Outsider: Essays and Speeches*, 1984

O ne of the most challenging parts of the leadership journey is the old adage: Know thyself. As suggested in chapter 2, the dominant narrative of leadership paints leaders as extraordinary people who seem to have a prescient ability to predict the future, a charismatic communication style to convince you of that future, and the determination and persistence to make remarkable things happen. We also learned that the story most often told should be the story most often questioned and critiqued. In reality, leaders are human beings who, like all people, struggle with flawed and occasionally biased perception. They try to make sense of complex problems and issues with only partial information and struggle to make headway in uncertain and evolving contexts. This story of the faulty human leader who only has an incomplete vision for the future is seldom told. It is less catchy and compelling than tales of heroic individuals, and can trouble the binary images we have of great heroes and great villains. For example, my students often react when I mention that Martin Luther King Jr. had extramarital affairs, or that Adolph Hitler loved dogs. It requires higher-order thinking to go beyond dualistic notions of good and bad leadership. Leaders are complex and can exhibit contradictory and inconsistent values and behaviors. In order to embrace the tensions of opposites, people need to acknowledge the roles of context, complexity, and commitment in leadership.

Maxine Hong Kingston (1976) once said, "I learned to make my mind large, as the universe is large, so that there is room for paradoxes" (p. 35). Paradoxes are statements or propositions that appear contradictory at face value, but when investigated further may prove to be well founded or true. In Exercise 3.1, Cronin and Genovese detail some of the many paradoxes of leadership. For example, leaders are usually described as self-confident, yet we also value humble leaders who do not take all the credit. We want leaders who are visionary and have ideas about how to meet future challenges, but we also want leaders to be realistic and grounded in current fiscal, organizational, and social realities. So how do we determine the "right" way to lead? Or to take it even further, is there even such a thing as a "right" way to lead? And who gets to say what the "right" way is? As you might guess, there are no easy answers to these questions. Personally, I am skeptical of the many popular press leadership books that seem to offer easy solutions and quotable platitudes for becoming a "great" leader. These books tend to ignore the power of context and self-awareness in leadership. Part of the solution to leading in complex times lies in being deeply aware of your own talents, strengths, challenges, and limitations. How do your own identities, values, and capacities shape your efficacy for leadership?

Exercise 3.1.
Paradoxes of Leadership

In the book, *Leadership Matters*, Cronin and Genovese (2012) suggest some of the tensions inherent in leadership. Examine the seemingly contradictory statements in this exercise and see if you can think of examples of leaders or leadership situations that fit each side of the paradoxes. Which component of each paradox is most important in your own leadership?

COLD CALCULATION VERSUS SPONTANEITY: Leaders invent and reinvent themselves. Their leadership usually is intentional, not accidental. Yet people also want their leaders to be open, relaxed, authentic, sincere, spontaneous, and to somehow emerge from within rather than be imposed upon a group.

IS IT THE LEADER OR THE CONTEXT?: We want to believe that leaders make a significant difference—yet idealistic and romantic theories exaggerate the impact of leaders. Most of the time, leaders are agents of their organizations or are at least shaped by them more than they are agents of change.

(*Continues*)

Exercise 3.1. (*Continued*)

LEADER/FOLLOWER PARADOX: Leaders are supposed to lead, not follow the polls, yet they are often followers as much as they are leaders. One of the grand paradoxes of leadership is that leaders often follow, and followers often point the way or lead more than is appreciated. Change often comes from the bottom up rather than the top down. And it often comes from the young rather than the established elite.

MORAL VERSUS MANIPULATIVE: We want decent, just, compassionate, and moral leaders, yet at times we admire and need tough, assertive, cunning, manipulative, and even intimidating leaders.

PASSION VERSUS REASON: Leadership often calls for intensity, enthusiasm, passion, dramatization, and self-promotion—yet too much highly personalized volcanic energy can paralyze an organization. Too much of a "cult of personality" can create dependency or other organizational dysfunctions.

REPRESENTATIVE YET NOT TOO REPRESENTATIVE: Leaders must be representative—yet not too representative; they need to consult and engage followers, and they need to respond to them. Yet they also must educate, motivate, and unlock the best in everyone.

SELF-CONFIDENCE VERSUS HUMILITY: Effective leadership involves self-confidence, the audacity of hope, and sometimes even a fearless optimism. However, humility, self-doubt, and self-control are also essential.

UNIFIERS AND DIVIDERS: Leaders need to unify their organizations or communities through effective negotiation and alliance building, yet leaders also have to stir up and jolt their organizations out of complacency. In short, we ask them to be unifiers and dividers.

VISIONARY VERSUS REALISTIC: Leaders must be visionaries guided by ideas, ideals, and principles, yet we also want pragmatic realists guided by logic, evidence, and level-headed rational analysis.

Note. Adapted from Cronin and Genovese (2012)

Leadership and Self-Awareness

Some of the best learning cases for leadership development come from reflecting on one's own past successes and failures. Often a few memorable moments or critical incidents stand out as being exceptionally meaningful learning opportunities. Instead of trying to forget the painful things that happened, leaders should instead analyze and reflect on these experiences. Embracing learning from past experiences may offer insights about one's own role and preferences, decision-making, and also about how the larger system may influence leadership choices and opportunities.

In order to model this kind of vulnerability, I will share one of my own moments of learning from disaster, and believe me, I have plenty from which to choose. As the director of a center for leadership and service at the local university, I was invited to be part of a women in leadership panel for the local Junior League. I was given scant details about the event, just that there would be five panelists drawn from different sectors of business, health care, nonprofit, and educational leadership. I had often served on panels before with different community groups and enjoyed the format—a brief introduction of panelists, followed by some thoughtful questions posed to the group, and an energizing exchange of ideas and conversations among those on the panel. I usually prepared by jotting some random thoughts about the panel theme on an index card. Cue scary foreboding music. I arrived at the panel in my typical student affairs outfit (khakis and a polo) to an auditorium full of women dressed in three-piece suits and heels that cost more than my monthly salary. While all of us panelists sat on stage, there was a podium and microphone with a spotlight focused on it. The moderator introduced each of the panelists and announced we would each be giving 15-minute formal talks on how our philosophies of leadership were manifested in the larger sector we were representing. Upon hearing that I was to give a formal address that I was completely unprepared for, my brain started racing and my body was having its own reaction—stomach dropping to the floor, forehead breaking out in beads of sweat, shallow breathing. To this day, I thank the gods and goddesses that I was not called as the first presenter and had time to briefly compose some thoughts before the spotlight turned on me. I mumbled something about preferring a more ad lib approach, and started to recite the eight Cs of the social change model of leadership. Somehow, I made it through and one of the other panelists leaned over and said, "Good job—when I saw your index card, I was really worried for you." When later reflecting on this experience, I was able to see the fallacious tendency I fell prey to. I had drawn on my past experiences to inform my expectations of future experiences, which are likely to be not at all similar.

These critical moments often serve to clarify our values. I value spontaneity, but need to also learn the value of preparation. Values matter because they are standards that not only guide the behavior of individuals who hold them but also serve as their basis for judging the behaviors of others (Rokeach, 1973). Note how this is different from your interests, which refer to preferences you hold but do not use to evaluate others (e.g., soccer is an interest of mine, but not necessarily a value). Values are also different from needs. Needs definitely motivate behavior, but once they are satisfied, they are not enduring. *Ethics* describes values that are socially applied. Highly prioritized values can determine your life choices across multiple roles such as work/career, relationships, hobbies, spiritual pursuits. Your values may come into conflict, especially as they relate to life roles—for example, career values may clash with family values. When values clash or compete, the result can be ambivalence, procrastination, or stress and anxiety. This is especially true for women and will be discussed in more depth later in the book. The goal is to achieve congruence between what you value and your behaviors. (Use Exercise 3.2 to examine the congruence between what you value and your behaviors.) Values are also culturally influenced, and because of the values-laden nature of culture and processes of socialization, values may differ across gender, race, and ethnicity. Values determine short- and long-term goals and life satisfaction.

What happens when your values come into conflict with one another? For example, you claim to value security in life so you take a high-paying job that makes you miserable, violating your commitment to being happy in life. How might you reevaluate what matters to you? Almost all postindustrial leadership theories stress the importance of self-awareness. You may think you already know yourself pretty well. If you successfully gained admission to college, the odds are that the way you has lived your life has paid off fairly well for you so far. You had the skill, ability, and persistence to earn a certain GPA, the problem-solving ability to figure out how to apply to college and how to finance it, and the commitment to see your dream into reality. Hopefully you also realize that you still have many things to learn in life and that some of the most important will not come from a class or a book but will come from the experiences and relationships you have. How will you

Exercise 3.2.
How Congruent Are You?

Open your calendar or think back to how you spent your time over the past week. How much time did you spend on school, family, friends, spiritual pursuits, social media, groups, and organizations? If a stranger looked at where you spent your time, would they be able to infer what matters most to you? What does it mean for your own goal achievement and satisfaction if you are spending your time in ways that do not reflect your values? For example, I may say I value my family relationships but have not called or spent any time with them this week.

Exercise 3.3.
Learning From Change

When was the last time you changed your mind about something important to you, like a political belief, a religious value, or an opinion about a contested social issue? Can you recall what invited you to question your previously held views? How did you stay open to new information in light of your previously committed stance? If you cannot think of a time when you changed your mind, what does that indicate about your openness to new information and experiences? How might this affect your leadership journey?

know when you need to change or how to change? Exercise 3.3 will help you explore your own approach to learning from change.

Chapter 2 briefly reviewed the most commonly used theories and approaches to leadership (trait, style, behavior, situational, etc.) and mentioned that postindustrial theories of leadership (leadership for the knowledge era) have different characteristics than industrial leadership theories. One of the striking similarities across all postindustrial leadership theories is the focus on self-awareness. What follows is a brief introduction to some of the most popular modern leadership theories and a description of the role of self-awareness in each of these theories.

Adaptive Leadership

Adaptive leadership is the activity of mobilizing people to tackle tough challenges and to thrive (Heifetz, 1994). Heifetz suggests there are two types of challenges in the world—technical problems, where the solutions already exist in the world, and adaptive challenges, where answers are not known and thus require experiments, new learning, and adjusted behaviors. Tackling adaptive challenges requires self-awareness, including developing the ability to discern between conferred authority (power given by others) and actual leadership, as well as between technical and adaptive challenges. These processes involve ongoing learning, attention to personal and organizational values and missions, and the courage to act.

Authentic Leadership

Authentic leadership involves leading with purpose, meaning, and values, and developing authentic enduring relationships (George, 2003). Self-awareness is central to developing authenticity or genuineness in leadership. Authentic leaders practice certain behaviors that engender trust in others, including continually committing to their own learning in order to understand themselves as a person and how they and others see the world. George (2003) notes, "All of us have to develop ourselves to become good leaders. . . . The medium for developing into an authentic leader is not the destination, but the journey itself—a journey to find your true self and the purpose of your life's work" (p. 27).

Emotionally Intelligent Leadership

Emotionally intelligent leadership builds on Daniel Goleman's (1995) idea of emotional intelligence as the ability to "recognize and regulate emotions in ourselves and others" (p. 2). Emotionally intelligent leadership promotes a focus on three facets: consciousness of self, consciousness of others, and consciousness of contexts (Shankman, Allen, & Haber-Curran, 2015). The focus on consciousness of self is essential to developing emotionally intelligent leadership. It involves being aware of your abilities, emotions, and perceptions, and prioritizing "the inner work of reflection and introspection and appreciating that self-awareness is a continuous and ongoing process" (Shankman, Allen, & Haber-Curran, 2015, p. 10). Consciousness of self includes the following dimensions: emotional self-perception, emotional self-control, authenticity, healthy self-esteem, flexibility, optimism, initiative, and achievement.

Relational Leadership

The relational leadership model views leadership as "a relational and ethical process of people together attempting to accomplish positive change" (Komives et al., 2013, p. 74). The five components of relational leadership include being purposeful, being inclusive of people and diverse points of view, empowering those involved, being ethical, and recognizing that each of these elements is accomplished by being process-oriented. This model involves self-awareness about ways of knowing, being, and doing. It involves knowing yourself and others and developing new knowledge and competencies. It involves being open to difference and valuing other perspectives and approaches. Practicing relational leadership also requires actions such as active listening, civil discourse, and collaboration.

Servant Leadership

Servant leadership begins with the natural feeling that one wants to serve. That is, the effective leader is a servant first (Greenleaf, 1977). The goals of servant leadership are to enrich the lives of individuals, build better organizations, and ultimately create a more just and caring world. Servant leadership begins with the self-awareness and recognition that one has a disposition to be of service. More recent scholarship has emphasized characteristics of servant leaders, including self-awareness. Spears (2010) states:

General awareness, and especially self-awareness, strengthens the servant-leader. Awareness helps one in understanding issues involving ethics, power, and values. It lends itself to being able to view most situations from a more integrated, holistic position. As Greenleaf observed: "Awareness is not a giver of solace—it is just the opposite. It is a disturber and an awakener. Able leaders are usually sharply awake and reasonably disturbed. They are not seekers after solace. They have their own inner serenity." (pp. 27–28)

Social Change Leadership

The social change model of leadership development approaches leadership as a purposeful, collaborative, values-based process that results in positive social change (Higher Education Research Institute, 1996). The model views leadership as a process rather than as a position and explicitly promotes the values of equity, social justice, self-knowledge, personal empowerment, collaboration, citizenship, and service. Self-knowledge, the understanding of one's talents, values, and interests, is especially important as it relates to one's capacity to provide effective leadership. The model includes eight Cs essential to leadership: consciousness of self, congruences, commitment, collaboration, common purpose, controversy with civility, citizenship, and change. These values are clustered in three dimensions: individual, group, and community values. Within the individual cluster, the social change model focuses on personal values such as consciousness of self, or being aware of the beliefs, values, attitudes, and emotions that motivate one to take action; congruence, which refers to thinking, feeling, and behaving with consistency, authenticity, and honesty toward others; and commitment, or the passion, intensity, and energy that motivate the individual to serve and that drive the collective effort (Higher Education Research Institute, 1996).

Ways to Expand Your Self-Awareness

If you look online or in your local bookstore, there are myriad resources that fit the title of "self-help" or self-discovery. Some provide very useful tools and language for self-awareness, and some border on the ridiculous. The following are a few ideas for how to explore and expand your own self-awareness related to leadership.

Assessments and Quizzes

There are numerous assessments or quizzes that purport to reveal to you hidden facets of your own personality, typology, or leadership style. The best of these are based on empirical research and have established validity and reliability of the instrument. Some include peer evaluations of your performance and abilities, while others just rely on your own self-report. Many of these assessments have their roots in trait theory, so users should take caution in how they apply these results to leadership development. There is danger in using the results from these instruments to label people. Some of these charge a fee, and others are free. A few popular in collegiate leadership and education include:

- The CliftonStrengths Finder 2.0 (www.gallupstrengthscenter.com)
- The Dominance, Influence, Steadiness, and Conscientiousness Scale 2.0 (DiSC Classic 2.0) (www.discprofile.com)
- The Emotionally Intelligent Leadership Inventory for Students (www.amazon.com/Emotionally-Intelligent-Leadership-Students-Inventory)
- The Myers-Briggs Type Indicator (MBTI) (www.mbtionline.com)
- The Student Leadership Practices Inventory (SLPI) (www.studentleadershipchallenge.com)
- The VIA Survey of Character Strengths (www.viacharacter.org)

Community Engagement

Defined as "the collaboration between institutions of higher education and their larger communities for the mutually beneficial exchange of knowledge and resources in a context of partnership and reciprocity" (Carnegie Foundation for the Advancement of Teaching, 2015, para.14), *community engagement* is one of the best ways to learn more about yourself and your place in the world. One purpose of community engagement is to prepare educated and engaged citizens with strengthened democratic values and civic responsibility. You may experience community engagement as service-learning, community-based learning, participatory action research, experiential learning, and more. Dugan, Kodama, Correia, and Associates (2013) reveal that "involvement in community service experiences consistently emerge as strong predictors of leadership capacity" (p. 12). But more important than the act of doing is the quality of the interactions with community, and the nature of reflection and learning from the experience. The authors note that engagement with the community can potentially: develop self-awareness and group-related skills, deepen personal commitments to specific issues, build resilience for working in complex systems to create change, and disrupt assumptions about social systems and how they operate.

Critical Reflection

At the beginning of this chapter, I shared an example of my own learning from a past experience of mine (the scary panel) through reflection on my experience after it occurred. It is important to differentiate the processes of *general reflection* from those of *critical reflection*. Jacoby (2015) defines the latter: "Critical reflection is the process of analyzing, reconsidering, and questioning one's experiences within a broad context of issues and content knowledge" (p. 26). There are often political dimensions to critical reflection so that experiences and issues are examined in light of social and political forces and, hegemonic ideology, and link explicitly to further social action, concepts we reviewed in chapter 2 (Owen, 2016). More than just critical thinking, critical reflection addresses issues of the nature and sources of power; who really benefits and who is silenced by your leadership efforts; which of your actions result in real change; and the systemic and institutionalized nature of oppression. This is a powerful tool for self-awareness and self-development.

Dialogue Across Difference

Dialogue across difference and the related process of democratic dialogue, or sociocultural conversations, refer to the process of engaging with peers about differences (topics that elicit a wide range of perspectives) and across differences (e.g., with people with different backgrounds and beliefs). Research from the Multi-Institutional Study of Leadership (MSL) found that these dialogues are the single strongest predictor of socially responsible leadership capacity for college students across all demographic groups (Dugan et al., 2013). The authors note that sociocultural conversations may make such a vital impact on leadership development because they require students to clarify and articulate their own perspectives, seek a better understanding of others' world views, comprehend how personal values fit into larger social structures and perspectives, and discern how to work with different communities to initiate positive change.

Seeking Feedback

In her book *Dare to Lead*, author Brené Brown (2018) emphasizes the importance of being able to receive feedback for leadership learning. If we ever hope to master a task or role, we must be open to receiving feedback, yet this process requires us to be vulnerable and often uncomfortable, especially with critical feedback. Brown offers some strategies for receiving feedback. She recommends identifying a piece of self-talk that you repeat to yourself when facing the fear of feedback. Brown's is "I'm brave enough to listen" (p. 203). Leadership educator Kathy Guthrie from Florida State University taught me hers and I use it often: "Feedback is love." Brown further recommends that you take what works for you from feedback and leave the rest behind rather than ruminating over it or getting defensive. She invites us to stay present and reminds us that the ultimate goal in receiving feedback is "a skillful blend of listening, integrating feedback, and reflecting it back with accountability" (pp. 204–205).

Mentoring

The MSL study defines a *mentor* as "a person who intentionally assisted the student's growth or connects the student to opportunities for career or personal development. Students may be mentored by faculty, staff, employers, family members, community members, and/or peers" (Dugan et al., 2013, p. 10). Developing meaningful relationships with mentors and others can offer us deep insight into our own character, and are also correlated with the development of socially responsible leadership. Dugan et al. (2013) found that "not all mentoring relationships have the same effect on leadership development: students from different racial groups benefited from different types of mentors" (p. 10). Specifically, faculty mentors appeared as most important to the leadership development of African American/Black, Asian Pacific American, and white students. Mentors from student affairs or administration mattered to multiracial student leadership development, and peer mentors were important for Latinx students (Campbell, Smith, Dugan, & Komives, 2012).

Self-Authorship

On your way to expanding your own self-awareness, you might also engage in a more complex phenomenon known as self-authorship. As you likely have experienced, college is a time of profound transitions. Arnett and Tanner (2006) termed this period *emerging adulthood*, which they describe as a space in between adolescence and young adulthood. Even if you are a returning adult student, you likely have experienced transitions from one career path to another, and from the world of work to educational environments and back. Beyond merely getting a degree, some of the critical processes in this time of life involve you becoming more aware of your own identities, your abilities to connect with others, and your own capacity for meaning-making.

Baxter Magolda (2001, 2004, 2014) calls this process *self-authorship* and defines it as "the internal capacity to define one's beliefs, identity, and social relations" (Baxter Magolda, 2001, p. 27). The theory of self-authorship seeks answers to three core questions: How do I know? Who am I? How do I want to construct relationships with others? Self-authorship consists of four key phases. In phase one, students *follow formulas* and adhere to the plans laid out for them by others, even if they assure themselves that they also agree with and even created these ordained plans. In phase two, students experience a *crossroads*, where the plan they have been following does not necessarily fit anymore and new plans need to be established. This period is often accompanied by dissatisfaction with self and conflict "between external influence and the growing internal voice as young adults work to make their own way in the world" (Baxter Magolda, 2014, p. 28). When students finally find the ability to choose their own beliefs and stand up for themselves when facing conflict or opposing views, they enter phase three, often called self-authorship, or *becoming the author of one's own life*. When students become fully grounded in their self-determined belief system and develop a strong sense of self and mutuality in relationships, they are said to have entered phase four and have an *internal foundation* for self-authorship.

The process of self-authorship is essential for leadership learning. Baxter Magolda (2014) describes how more complex ways of knowing are essential in turbulent times:

> This transformational learning, or shifting toward more complex ways of meaning making that enable managing ambiguity, is the core challenge of a college education that prepares graduates for productive lives as citizens of the larger world. To thrive in the ambiguity that characterizes contemporary adult life, collegians need to develop self-authorship, or the internal capacity to determine their beliefs, identities, and social relations. (p. 26)

Abes and Hernandez (2016) interrogated the self-authorship model from the lens of underrepresented and underserved populations, noting that the concept of self-authorship focuses on the individual rather than the contexts in which individuals are situated. They state:

> Although context has long been considered relevant to development, researchers are specifically investigating how systems of oppression, such as racism, classism, and heterosexism, interact with development toward self-authorship. Focusing on systems of oppression shifts the inquiry away from the individual toward the social environments, such as racist, classist, and heteronormative contexts. (p. 97)

Their research reveals the potentially challenging nature of developing individual voice within an oppressive system and suggests additional considerations that would shift the theory of self-authorship away from a deficit perspective as well as welcome more collectivist and critical approaches.

Abes and Hernandez suggest that self-authorship be reconsidered to (a) validate those with marginalized identities as knowers; (b) value communal knowledge, relationships, and sense of self; (c) acknowledge the difficulty and risks associated with agency and authenticity for those with targeted identities; and (d) recognize the performativity of identity. Their fourth point about performativity reflects the discussion in chapter 2 about how gender itself is a kind of performativity. The authors go on to suggest that acts of resistance by students in oppressive systems should be validated rather than seen as oppositional to self-authorship. More thinking is needed about how self-authorship and critical self-authorship link to leadership. Is it necessary to be self-authored to engage in leadership? In liberation? Critical to conversations about self-awareness and self-authorship are the concepts of identity and intersectionality.

Identity and Intersectionality

Reflect on your journey toward self-awareness. To what degree do your personal and social identities shape your leadership journey? *Personal identities* refer to the unique constellation of roles and responsibilities that you inhabit. Are you a sister? A niece? An aunt? A mother? A supervisor? An assistant? The nexus of roles you inhabit shapes your relationships and experiences. Other powerful shapers of experience, some of which are listed in Exercise 3.4a, are your *social identities* (racial, cultural, religious, sexual, ableist, etc.). Hopefully you have done considerable thinking about your social identities and how they shape your experience in the world. Most of us hold both target and agent identities (Davis & Harrison, 2013). *Target identities* refer to those aspects of the self that are often subject to socialized forces of oppression. *Agent identities* are those aspects of you that align you with groups socialized to allow benefit from unearned privilege. You might also experience *internalized oppression*, where a person with target identities may start to believe the stereotypes and misinformation shared about them by people with agent identities. We will delve into this more deeply, especially as it relates to internalized gender oppression, in chapter 8. Many people are subject to *stereotyping*, where aspects of one's social identities (e.g., race or religion) are extrapolated for your entire identity. There are also aspects of your identity that are more visible to others (e.g., skin color, age) and those that may be hidden or concealed (e.g., ability, sexual orientation).

Davis and Harrison (2013) make the important observation that "identity is not just a private, individual matter but a complex negotiation between person and society" (p. 33). As discussed in chapter 2, identity is socially constructed and thus subject to the effects of one's positionality, dominance, and subordination. As people negotiate the world around them and interact with others, they absorb powerful messages. People may be unaware of, or unwilling to recognize their own privileged experience in the world. *Privilege* refers to "the unearned rights, benefits, and immunities granted to some solely based on particular aspects of their identity" (p. 35). I was reflecting on my own white privilege recently when I was hiking in a park and took a break on a sunny bench. The sun's warmth coupled with my tiredness from the hike enticed me to lay down and take a short nap. Because I am white, no one called the police on me for loitering or questioned my right to be in the park. There is often a *myth of meritocracy* around identity, meaning that people,

Exercise 3.4a.
Social Identities

Think about the following social identity categories, and write any descriptors you use in identifying these aspects of your own identities. Next, consider the reflections outlined in Exercise 3.4b.

Age:

Cognitive, developmental, or emotional ability:

Ethnicity:

Gender:

Language(s) spoken:

Nationality:

Physical ability:

Race:

Religion or spiritual affiliation:

Sexual orientation:

Socioeconomic class:

Exercise 3.4b.
Identity, Dominance, and Subordination

Which of the identities outlined in Exercise 3.1a do you think about most often? How have these identities played a role in how you see yourself as a person? Which do you consider least often? Why? Note that identities we consider *least* often are usually aspects of our identity that are dominant or privileged by society; our agent identities. Which aspects of your identities would you like to learn more about and explore more deeply?

Note. Adapted from "Voices of Discovery," Intergroup Relations Center, Arizona State University (n.d.) Visit servicelearning.msu.edu/resources/service-learning-toolkit for more information and to see the Service Learning Toolkit.

especially those from agent groups, may infer that all people exist on a level playing field and ignore how policies and practices differentially affect those with target identities. Simultaneously, people with agent identities may feel helpless to change who they are, rather than realizing it is systemic oppression that needs to be challenged. As Davis and Harrison wisely note, "We tend to conflate the personal with the institutional" (p. 39). As Exercise 3.4b suggests, the social construction of identity matters because the

> understanding identity as socially constructed interrupts the notion that individual hard work and character are the only forces at play in determining who succeeds and who doesn't, and who has access to vital resources and who has hurdles in the pursuit of life, liberty, and happiness. (Davis & Harrison, 2013, p. 33)

Intersectionality is an important concept when talking about multiple identities. Intersectionality refers to the effects of interlocking systems of power, privilege, and oppression and how these forces shape lives and multiple social identities (Crenshaw, 1989, 1991). The roots of the term *intersectionality* relate directly to feminism. Kimberlé Crenshaw wrote a paper in 1989 for the *University of Chicago Legal Forum* where she contends that viewing racism and sexism in isolation leads to Black women being theoretically erased and ignores the fact that Black women are multiply burdened. In a 2015 essay in the *Washington Post,* Crenshaw wrote:

> As a young law professor, I wanted to define this profound invisibility in relation to the law. Racial and gender discrimination overlapped not only in the workplace but in other arenas of life; equally significant, these burdens were almost completely absent from feminist and antiracist advocacy. Intersectionality, then, was my attempt to make feminism, antiracist activism, and antidiscrimination law do what I thought they should—highlight the multiple avenues through which racial and gender oppression were experienced so that the problems would be easier to discuss and understand. (para. 4)

Critics call intersectionality an extreme form of identity politics, but Crenshaw notes that the concept itself goes far beyond identity and indicts organizations and systems that exclude and oppress. In their book *Intersectionality,* scholars Patricia Hill Collins and Sirma Bilge (2016) describe how the concept of intersectionality has expanded in recent years and even coin the phrase *ornamental intersectionality* for people who use the word casually without understanding its roots in critical theory. Crenshaw (2015) describes the benefits of it being a more expansive construct:

> Intersectional erasures are not exclusive to black women. People of color within LGBTQ movements; girls of color in the fight against the school-to-prison pipeline; women within immigration movements; trans women within feminist movements; and people with disabilities fighting police

abuse—all face vulnerabilities that reflect the intersections of racism, sexism, class oppression, transphobia, able-ism and more. Intersectionality has given many advocates a way to frame their circumstances and to fight for their visibility and inclusion. (para. 5)

Intersectionality includes three core concepts as defined by Collins and Bilge (2016). These are the *interlocking matrix of oppression*, or the intersections of various social inequalities; *standpoint theory*, or the idea that knowledge is subjective and stems from your unique social position; and *resisting oppression and objectification*, which are the goals. As with all concepts presented in this introductory volume, the preceding is an extreme simplification of a complex set of ideas that merits further study. Exercise 3.5 invites you to consider intersectionality from a feminist lens.

Leadership Identity

If we have personal and social identities, visible and invisible, target, agent, and intersectional identities, how does this relate to leadership? Scholars have started to consider whether leadership itself might also be an aspect or form of identity, and if it is, how does it intersect with other aspects of one's identity?

The leadership identity development grounded theory (Komives et al., 2005) and related model (Komives, Longerbeam, Owen, Mainella, & Osteen, 2006) present a framework for understanding how individuals develop the

---

Exercise 3.5.
Linking Intersectionality and Feminist Liberation

Reflect on the following:
1. What are the unique intersections that you face?
2. What are the stories most often told about these identities and intersections?
3. What do you think are necessary strategies or tactics for women's liberation?
4. In what ways can women facing different intersectional oppressions effectively work together? What do you imagine would be required?
5. What is power? When did you learn what power was?
6. What do you think women (or other people) need to do, in order to be empowered?

Note. Adapted from R. Said (n.d).

identity of being collaborative, relational leaders interdependently engaging in leadership as a group process. This research emerged from noting that while some are very comfortable engaging in inclusive, collaborative group processes whether in positional or nonpositional roles, others are not. What is the process by which people become comfortable with nonhierarchical leadership? How do students move from thinking of leadership as only positional to considering that leadership can happen anywhere? These stages were revealed when students were asked "What did you used to think leadership was, and what do you think it is now?" This research revealed six stages of leadership identity, presented in Box 3.2.

Box 3.2.
Stages of the Leadership Identity Development Model

- *Awareness (Stage One).* The initial awareness that there are leaders "out there" who are external to one's self like a nation's president, a religious figure, a parent, or a teacher. This stage usually occurs in early childhood.
- *Exploration/Engagement (Stage Two).* A period of immersion in group activities and experiences; a time of learning to engage with others (e.g., a sports team, religious group, Scouts), which usually occurs throughout childhood.
- *Leader Identified (Stage Three).* When an individual views leadership as the actions of the positional leader of a group; an awareness of the hierarchical nature of relationships in groups. Students usually arrive at this point of view in high school and early college. This is the dominant narrative about leadership in the United States.
- *Key Transition.* The shift from thinking about leadership as person-centric and role bound (e.g., leaders do leadership) to thinking about leadership as an interdependent and collaborative process among people is often called the key transition. What invites this transition? It can happen when a person takes on a task that is too complex for any one person to do and the individual learns that they have to rely on others to accomplish goals. For example, you doing the entire group presentation may work in some cases, but you likely cannot produce a weeklong set of homecoming events alone. Learning about leadership, such as studying leadership theories and becoming familiar with the terms and language, can also help move people to more advanced stages.

(Continues)

Box 3.2. (*Continued*)

- *Leadership Differentiated (Stage Four).* The evolution of one's thinking where one sees leadership also as nonpositional and as a shared group process.
- *Generativity (Stage Five).* A person develops a commitment to developing leadership in others and having a passion for issues or group objectives that the person wants to influence.
- *Integration/Synthesis (Stage Six).* A stage experienced by relatively few involving acknowledging one's personal capacity for leadership across contexts and claiming one's identity as a leader without having to hold a positional role. At this stage, leadership identity is an integral part of one's being (Komives et al., 2005). See Rocco (2017) for further research on postcollege leadership identity development.

Note. Adapted from Komives et al. (2006).

Note that the leadership identity development (LID) model is stage-based and not age-based, especially after the leader identified stage (stage three). Students were at different ages when they shifted their identity and engaged differently in the leadership evident of the next stage, and many never move beyond stage three thinking. People usually experience stages one and two from a place of dependence on others, usually adults such as parents, guardians, and teachers. They may experience stage three from either a place of dependence (as a member of a group looking to the positional leader for guidance) or from a place of independence (where the student themselves is the positional leader giving direction to others). As people move through stages four, five, and six, they usually do so in an interdependent way, where they recognize the importance of connections among people.

In addition to the stages, there are developmental components that influence leadership identity including the role of adults in students' lives, the changing role of peers, opportunities for involvement, and time spent in reflective learning. At each stage people engage individual factors (their growing awareness of self, developing self-confidence, establishing interpersonal efficacy, developing leadership skills, and clarifying goals) and group factors (including their changing view of groups from friendship structures to organizations to systems, having meaningful group experiences, and maintaining a continuity of membership in key groups). The process of how people transition from stage three to stage four thinking is described here:

Leadership is learned in a group context and the dynamic reciprocity of the individual engaging in groups was critical to LID. As that engagement happened, the student changed their view of self with others beginning in a dependent mode when in a follower role, then feeling independent when in a leadership role, and finally recognizing interdependence with others. As their view of self changed, the student established different views of leadership moving from thinking of leadership as only the external other and always an adult, to holding a leader-centric view of leadership as anyone in a position, and as they valued interdependence they viewed leadership as happening in nonpositional roles as well as viewing leadership as a shared group process. (Komives, Longergeam, Mainella, Osteen, & Owen, 2009, p. 15)

All of this is a way of saying that relational leaders must acknowledge their interdependence with others engaged in the leadership process in order to be effective. As we reviewed in chapter 2, some call these "others" followers, collaborators, coconspirators, group members. Part of understanding the interdependence of the shared process of leadership is self-awareness of your own efficacy, capacity, and motivations for leadership.

Leadership Efficacy, Capacity, Motivation, and Enactment

As your own self-awareness deepens and your intersecting roles and identities become clearer, and as you develop a more accurate appraisal of your own gifts and limitations, you may feel more capable of leadership. Conversely, if you are like me, you may feel less capable of leadership the more you are aware of your flaws and eccentricities. It also happens that when students start leadership programs or courses, they are often very confident in their leadership abilities; however, as they learn more about the complexity of different leadership theories and approaches and are able to more accurately appraise their leadership abilities, their confidence often drops. This brings us to the important idea of leadership efficacy. Psychologist Albert Bandura (1997) coined the concept of efficacy to refer to an individual's beliefs that they can "organize and execute the courses of action required to produce given attainments" (p. 3). That is to say, do you believe you can do a particular thing? Efficacy is domain-specific, meaning that you can have high efficacy in one domain (e.g., I have high efficacy that I can bake an awesome cake) but low efficacy in other domains (e.g., I have low efficacy that I can run a marathon). Efficacy is different from confidence, which tends to refer to a more general level of a person's belief in themself. Bandura also evolved the concept of collective efficacy to refer to the beliefs of an entire group or organization about their shared capabilities.

Dugan (2017) conducted research on college students that reveals a startling picture about the intertwining nature of leadership efficacy, capacity, motivation, and enactment (Figure 3.1). He found that people may have all the *capacity* (competence, ability) for leadership in the world, but if they do not also have high efficacy for leadership (the belief that they can be successful in leadership), they are far less likely to act on their capacities (leadership enactment). To further trouble this finding, MSL research reveals that women score higher than men on seven of eight capacities for socially responsible leadership, yet women score significantly lower than men on efficacy for leadership (Dugan & Komives, 2010). Does this ring true with your own experiences or perceptions? Why might this be? Possible barriers to women's leadership self-efficacy can include perfectionism, the need to please, and the belief that one will be revealed as less than capable or as a fraud (called *impostor syndrome*). We will dive into these barriers in more depth in chapters 6 and 8.

These points bear repeating. Historically, college women score higher than men on their capacity for socially responsible leadership, yet significantly lower on their beliefs that they can enact leadership. Bandura defines four ways people can enhance their self-efficacy. These include enactive mastery experience (meaningful practical experiences), vicarious experience (learning through observing those around us), verbal persuasion (feedback and social support), and physiological and affective states (your socioemotional health and sense of well-being). Table 3.1 details specific ways people can enhance their leadership self-efficacy.

Figure 3.1. Cultivating leadership capacity.

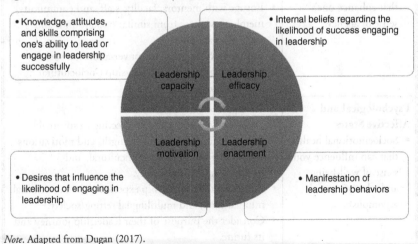

- Knowledge, attitudes, and skills comprising one's ability to lead or engage in leadership successfully

- Internal beliefs regarding the likelihood of success engaging in leadership

Leadership capacity

Leadership efficacy

Leadership motivation

Leadership enactment

- Desires that influence the likelihood of engaging in leadership

- Manifestation of leadership behaviors

Note. Adapted from Dugan (2017).

TABLE 3.1.
Ways to Build Self-Efficacy for Leadership

Ways to Build Self-Efficacy	How to Enhance Leadership Self-Efficacy
Enactive Mastery Experience • Meaningful practical experience depending on levels, structures, and complexity of tasks as well as structure of situation and skill development.	*Students can:* • Take on the responsibilities of formal roles and active involvement (e.g., student organizations; positional leadership roles). • Have the experience of peer-mentoring and student assistant roles. • Engage in sociocultural conversations (conversations about and across differences). • Develop knowledge of leadership vocabulary, theories, and approaches.
Vicarious Experience • Observing other people accomplishing tasks and learning about others' experiences. • Having role models who discuss effective strategies.	*Students can:* • Observe role models (e.g., educators and other students) who advocate for change on campus or in society. • Listen to stories of local, national, and international speakers. • View video clips of leadership stories across countries. • Compare themselves with other leaders who engage in activism.
Verbal Persuasion • Receiving feedback regarding individuals' capabilities. • Supportive comments that enhance one's sense of agency.	*Students can:* • Meet with other emerging leaders to learn from each other. • Develop formal and informal relationships from organizational involvements. • Engage with mentors, faculty, staff, and community members who are from similar backgrounds and those who are not. • Engage in dialogues and conversations on social networking sites about leadership (sociocultural conversations).
Psychological and Affective States • Socioemotional health that can influence your sense of well-being and what you can accomplish.	*Students can:* • Focus on well-being and connecting to spiritual (psychological) sources of strengths and motivations to lead in a multiracial, multicultural, and multilingual setting/society. • Reflect on their leadership experiences in a multiracial, multicultural, and multilingual setting/society. • Consider the purpose of their leadership journey and its future.

Note. Adapted from Owen, Hassell-Goodman, & Yamanaka (2017).

To develop your own self-efficacy for leadership you might join or volunteer for a leadership role or experience that will challenge you in new ways (enactive mastery); identify and pay close attention to the attitudes and actions of role models from whom you can observe various approaches to leadership (vicarious experiences); seek out positive and constructive feedback for your own leadership efforts (verbal persuasion); and pay attention to your mental health and well-being (physical and affective states). You may have heard many messages about the value of paying attention to your well-being in college, but research is revealing that how you manage stress and emotions makes a difference in your approach to leadership (Inceoglu, Thomas, Chu, Plans, & Gerbasi, 2018).

Howes (2016) conducted a dissertation study on female-identified college students to examine how they developed leadership self-efficacy. Findings not only echo Bandura but also reveal new insights related to how social and intersectional identities affect leadership self-efficacy. Howes's study revealed the following core concepts about how leadership self-efficacy is developed: (a) throughout their lives, people receive messages about leaders and leadership from societal norms, institutions, experiences, and interactions; (b) people and experiences mediate the effects of these messages; (c) leadership self-efficacy is shaped by internal processes; and (d) multiple identities influence the development of leadership self-efficacy (Howes, 2016). Participants successfully built leadership self-efficacy through receiving encouragement and affirmation, and engaging in leadership development experiences. Howes also explored how women were able to disrupt dominant narratives that had the potential to have a detrimental impact on their self-efficacy for leadership. She notes, "If students can learn to cope within unjust systems while attributing challenges to oppressive forces in the external environment rather than internalizing them, they will be more likely to navigate systems without harm to their [leadership self-efficacy]" (Howes, 2016, p. 217).

Thinking Beyond the Self: Predecessors, Instigators, and Inheritors

Navigating forces hostile to women's leadership development is not new. In their seminal study, *Women of Influence, Women of Vision*, Helen Astin and Carole Leland (1991) described how three different generations of women approached their work for gender justice. They described the value of *predecessors*, or those in generations before our own who advocated for women's rights or gender equity. Predecessors may or may not have used the language of feminism but were often the only woman in predominantly male groups and workplaces. They were familiar with the idea of being the first or only women in spaces and places, and often articulated the value of education as a path to equality. Astin and Leland labeled those engaged in activism around women or gender-related issues as the generation of *instigators*. This might refer to someone who is part of a gender-specific organization or group, who serves as a visible spokesperson and activist for gender equity, and who challenges the patriarchal structures of institutions directly. Instigators often use policy and government to try and codify equity for all. Astin and Leland label youth coming of age as the *inheritors*, or people who are recipients of a slightly more level playing field, but who still acknowledge there is work to do around gender equity. The inheritors are frequently mentored by predecessors and instigators, yet also serve as role models for generations still to come. They are the sustainers of the women's movement and work to create more inclusive and accessible feminisms.

There is value in reflecting on the people who come before and after you in the fight for gender justice. It is important to acknowledge that, although it may have changed forms or contexts, there are many who have shared experiences of discrimination, harassment, and rejection and risen to challenge systems of oppression. All three generational types are part of networked systems of people working to create change. Consider your own networks for a moment. Who would you label as a *predecessor* in your life, or someone who came before you and paved the way for you to have access to certain experiences and opportunities? If you had a chance to talk to that person or persons, what would you want to know about the struggles they faced and their wishes for future generations? Who would you label as an *instigator*, or someone who is currently working to dismantle systems of oppression? Consider interviewing an instigator about the root of their passion for social action and how they sustain hope in the face of interlocking oppressions. How might you learn from and be inspired by their experiences to make changes in your own life? Who is coming after you as an *inheritor*? Think about your younger siblings or cousins, or children of friends. What do you wish for them to experience about gender and leadership in their future? How are you acting as a mentor to them in their own journey? What wisdom can you share, and what conversations might you initiate to explore their own dreams and future aspirations? What are the ways you are clearing a path for those coming after you?

These reflection questions, coupled with those found in Exercise 3.6, invite you to explore the intersections of gender and leadership and their effects on goals, decisions, and paths. Hopefully this chapter caused you to think more about your own positionality related to leadership. How well do you know

Exercise 3.6.
Questions to Ask Predecessors, Instigators, and Inheritors

- What is their personal biographical background?
- What gender and cultural identities/experiences are most salient for this person?
- What are the gendered experiences that shape them as a leader?
- How did they discover purpose in their own life? Were they called to leadership and/or did they seek it because of convictions they held?
- How did they learn from the obstacles and challenges they faced?
- What has been the lasting impact of this person's leadership? What difference did they make—especially regarding women and leadership?
- What lessons (positive and negative) can be learned from this person's life and leadership experience?
- How does this person view leadership and were there any specific assumptions or beliefs that informed their behavior?
- How does this person communicate with people in their organization?
- How do they get the people in the organization to work harmoniously together toward common purposes?

yourself? How committed are you to your own values, beliefs, and perspectives? How do your personal and social identities shape your experience of the world? What can you do to increase your own self-awareness and self-efficacy for leadership? Do you see yourself as capable of leadership? Why or why not? Where are you on the journey toward self-authorship? What stage of leadership identity development most describes your current thinking about leadership? How would you evaluate yourself in terms of motivation for leadership, leadership efficacy, leadership capacity, and leadership enactment? It may be helpful at this point to craft something known as a leadership action plan, where you outline specific steps toward achieving your goals.

This chapter ends with Neta's poem about navigating intersectional identities and the power of labels. Neta rejects stereotypes ascribed to her and finds pride in her own identity.

Neta identifies as a Black cisgender woman.

Narratives and Counternarratives: Neta's Story

Little Black Girl

Little black girl
where is your "femininity?"
You responded just a little too aggressively.

Little black girl
where is your "humility?"
Stop bragging so much about your victories.

Little black girl
why are you so free?
Please curb some of that energy.

Little black girl
Fall in line
And don't you dare speak.

I felt the words
(Though figuratively)
As if they were meant to hurt me.

I felt the words
Via actions and interactions
Before I understood what gender and race meant to me.

I felt the words and instructions
As insults, reprimands
Before I could even own them as **my** identity
I felt the "labels"
And hardly ever separately.

Despite society's attitude
I am the black woman I want to be
And indeed, I am proud of me
Because I am the one who gets to define me.

4

HOW DID WE GET HERE?

How Gender Socialization Shapes
Women in Leadership

I just love bossy women. I could be around them all day. To me, bossy is not a pejorative term at all. It means somebody's passionate and engaged and ambitious and doesn't mind leading.

—Amy Poehler, quoted in Couric, *Glamour Magazine*, March 29, 2011

The conclusion of chapter 3 described the value of reflecting on your leadership predecessors, instigators, and inheritors. It was Marsha Guenzeler-Stevens from the University of Maryland, College Park, who first adapted Helen Astin's wise research into an interview assignment for a women and leadership course. I have used a version of this assignment in my classes for 10 years now and am always impressed by the wisdom and inspiration that comes from talking with others about our leadership journeys. As you can imagine, the *predecessors,* or those who came before us in the fight for gender equity such as a grandparent or a second-wave feminist, have seen profound changes in the world during their lifetimes. The *instigators* are those currently working for gender equality such as someone who is part of a gender-specific organization or group, and can speak to the struggle to achieve gender justice in an increasingly divided world. But perhaps the most interesting conversations my students have every semester are with those we label as *inheritors* of gender equity, or those from a more recent generation than even traditional-aged college students. This group often includes younger siblings or cousins, or neighborhood kids my students take care of after school. Occasionally, the college students will get permission to talk to a whole class of elementary or middle-school kids about their thoughts on gender and leadership. What emerges from these conversations often closely aligns with the research on gender socialization and youth leadership.

With young elementary-aged kids, gender norms and gender stereo-types abound. When asked to describe the difference between boys and girls, the young girls interviewed by students in my class often describe boys as "smelly," "rough-housing," and "into cars and trucks"; while the young boys interviewed described girls as "liking pink," "quiet," and "into dolls and playing house." When kids get a bit older, but are still in preadolescence, they tend to see more equality among boys and girls. My students ask these kids about how they defined leadership and who they considered a leader. In keeping with the findings from the LID study reviewed in chapter 3, interviewees often talked about political leaders such as the president, faith leaders such as Jesus or Muhammad, their parents, or sports and teen idols. One recent interview included a long statement from a fourth grader articu-lating the many reasons Taylor Swift was an ideal leader, including that she is good at speaking, helpful, and genuine. We might laugh, but that is a pretty good list! When asked if they saw themselves as leaders, the younger children almost all said yes, but the preteens and tween girls were much more likely to respond with no for reasons such as "I'm not talkative" or "I don't like being bossy" or "I like to stay in the background." Clearly there is work to do. This chapter examines how the experiences we have and the messages we receive growing up shape our approaches to leadership and gender. This chapter also includes two narratives detailing the power of formative experiences, gender socialization, and the persistence of memory.

Girls and Leadership

What messages did you receive as a child about gender? Were you told that girls should not climb trees or that boys do not cry? What about messages about leadership? Did you play the game "follow the leader" where you were "out" if you failed to obey? This chapter invites you to think about the ways you were socialized about gender and begins to explore the implications for leadership that will be addressed more deeply in ensuing chapters. Gender socialization begins before birth and continues across one's lifespan. How we are socialized shapes who we become.

In 2008 the Girls Scouts of America conducted a wide-reaching study about the leadership attitudes and experiences of girls. They conducted focus groups and interviews with 165 girls, boys, and mothers. There was no mention of nonbinary participants or perspectives in this research. They also surveyed over 4,000 girls and boys ages 8 to 17 weighted to reflect U.S. Census representation of racial and ethnic groups. This study posed ques-tions about how girls and boys defined leadership; their experiences with and aspirations for leadership; perceived barriers to leadership; qualities and skills associated with leadership; and questions about support systems and access to education about leadership. Findings show substantial gender differences in leadership aspirations. While a majority of girls surveyed see themselves as leaders, many are ambivalent about leadership itself. The study found "the conventional command-and-control model of leadership so prevalent in the culture does not resonate with their desire to make a difference in the world around them" (Girl Scout Research Institute, 2008, p. 7). Respondents who identified as girls preferred an approach to leadership that emphasizes personal principles, ethical behavior, and a commitment to social change. These findings echo that of Haber (2011), who studied college students' definitions of leadership and found that college women more often defined leadership as a collaborative and relational process resulting in positive social change, in contrast to men's definitions that often included more traditional, hierarchical, and command-oriented conceptualizations.

The study also identified issues with girls' efficacy for leadership, akin to what was described in the MSL findings in chapter 3, that noted "the greatest single barrier to leadership reported by girls is self-perception—a lack of self-confidence in their own skills and competencies" (Dugan et al., 2013, p. 7). While 92% of girls surveyed in the Girl Scouts study believe that leadership can be learned, only 21% believe that they themselves have the key qualities necessary for leadership. Girls exhibited a wide range of leadership identities—from strong aspiration to total rejection. Of girls who do not think of themselves as leaders, they attributed this to fear of being laughed at, fear of making people mad at them, fear of talking in front of others, seeming bossy, and not being liked by people. Thirty-nine percent of girls report being discouraged or put down when trying to lead, and 57% agree that girls have to work harder than boys to gain positions of leadership. Campaigns such as the #banbossy movement work to disassociate the idea of bossiness from girls and women exercising power and influence.

The study also looked at motivations for leadership and found that

> girls are more likely than boys to want to be leaders because they want to help other people (67% vs. 53%), share their knowledge and skills with others (53% vs. 45%), and change the world for the better (45% vs. 31%). Boys are more likely than girls to be motivated by the desire to be their own bosses, (38% vs. 33%), make more money (33% vs. 26%), and have more power (22% vs.14%). (Girl Scout Research Institute, 2008, p. 13)

These results also suggest that race and income are strongly correlated with leadership experience, in that those with higher incomes are more likely to have had leadership experiences. African American and Hispanic (a term used in the study) girls and boys exhibited more motivation and self-confidence about leadership than Caucasians and Asian Americans. In fact, Caucasian girls were twice as likely as African American and Hispanic girls to fall into the leadership "rejectors" category. The study concluded by calling for further research into the intersections of race, gender, and leadership. Overall, the Girl Scout study exposes a lack of environments and opportunities for girls to practice leadership at a young age. Taken in total, these findings suggest that there is far more work to do in promoting postindustrial definitions of leadership that are more appealing to girls; developing places and spaces where girls can practice leadership; addressing the fears and anxieties that might inhibit girls' leadership, especially related to perception by peers; and elevating girls from underrepresented populations as exemplars of leadership. So how did these feelings evolve? Use Exercise 4.1 to consider how childhood experiences shaped your views about gender and leadership. What childhood experiences shape these views? How might we counteract this data?

Exercise 4.1.
Looking Back

Reflect on the following questions and consider the effects of your early childhood involvements on the development of your gender identity and expression.

- What were your favorite toys and games that you played growing up? How were your gender identity and expression informed by these games and activities?
- How did your parents, guardians, or siblings shape your views about gender norms and expectations?
- Who were your best friends? What messages did you learn from them?
- How has your schooling played into your understanding of what it means to be a boy or a girl or a man, or woman, or to take a nonbinary approach to gender? Your religion?
- What messages did you receive from others regarding what it means to be a boy or a girl or a man or a woman? Did you receive any messages that acknowledged gender nonconformance? What messages did you receive about your looks, clothes, appearance? About how to act around others?
- Did you ever ridicule someone else for doing something you did not consider masculine or feminine enough? Were you ever subject to such ridicule?

Gender Socialization

Gender roles are culturally based stereotypes that influence and create expectations for appropriate behavior for people based on biological sex. Gender roles are influenced by the media, family, environment, and society. Moreover, a child's understanding of gender roles impacts how they socialize with their peers and form relationships, and can also greatly influence their own self-concept. Many young children have a firm sense of their gender identity, while some children can experience gender identity confusion. There are a plethora of psychological and sociological studies examining the effects of early childhood socialization on the development of gender identity (for e.g., check out studies in the scholarly journal *Gender & Development*). Although there are certainly other socializing forces that could also be addressed, in this chapter we will look at the effects of toys and games, family, school, peers, sports and organizations, religion, media, and society and culture on gender and leadership.

Toys and Games

Martin and Ruble (2010) did a meta-analytic review of studies of early childhood gender identity development funded by the National Institute of Child Health and Human Development. They found that most children develop the ability to label gender groups and to use gender labels in their speech between 18 and 24 months of age. By age four, most children have a stable sense of their gender identity. Strikingly, studies revealed that a knowledge of gender differences was related to increased play with strongly stereotyped toys (e.g., dolls for girls and trucks for boys). After two years of age, most children have developed basic stereotypes related to physical appearance, roles, toys, and activities and begin to relate certain abstract qualities with gender (roughhousing with boys, softness with girls).

As children grow older, the range of stereotypes about sports, occupations, school tasks, and adult roles expands, and the nature of the associations becomes more sophisticated (Sinno & Killen, 2009). By preschool, gender stereotypes may be so strong that children who play with cross-gender toys (e.g., a boy with a doll, or a girl with a fire engine) may be ridiculed (e.g., saying "Bob is a girl") or punished (e.g., ostracized) by their peers. Until approximately age 10, children may experiment with different gender identities in fluid ways. Some children have stable transgender identities (e.g., a person labeled as a boy at birth knowing that they were a girl since age three) while others may try on different gender identities throughout adolescence (e.g., a girl asking to be called Steve) and others do not experiment with gender identity until puberty approaches, or not at all.

Gender identity is not always "one or the other." We need to recognize that not every child is on the path to choosing a male or female gender identity. Many children (and adults) feel like they are both genders, neither gender, or go back and forth. They may have already arrived at their final destination, which is a space outside typical gender constructs. Or, they may still be figuring it out. We won't know until our child knows and can communicate this to us, and that may take many years. It is important for us to follow their lead, and let them figure out who they are at their own pace. (Gender Spectrum, 2019)

Family

When parents find out they are pregnant, one of the first questions typically asked is whether they are having a girl or a boy. Like it or not, gender-reveal parties are more popular than ever. Research about parents' socialization of gender in children noted that children's gender assignment becomes a powerful social identity that shapes children's lives (Leaper, 2014). During early child-hood, children spend much of their time in the home with their families and look to parents, guardians, and older siblings for guidance. Note that family does not just refer to genetic relations. These influences apply whether some-one is raised by grandparents, adopted parents, single parents, guardians, or extended family. These adults provide children with their first lessons about gender, including how they dress their child and the nicknames they give them. I have to confess to cringing a bit whenever someone calls their child "little man" or "daddy's princess." Leaper (2014) offers possible ways that parents might influence children's gender development including role modeling and encouraging different behaviors and activities in sons and daughters.

Parents and family members communicate about gender roles in a vari-ety of ways. Parents may set gender-role expectations about personality traits (e.g., boys are aggressive and girls are nice), career aspirations, and family roles. Parents and family members also serve as role models for gendered attitudes and behavior. Seeing mothers who go to work and fathers who are active in childcare and maintaining the household creates more egalitar-ian views of gender roles. Leaper also analyzed same-sex parent households and found that children raised by same-sex parents tend to be less likely to endorse gender stereotypes. However, when same-gender parents divided labor with one parent as the primary caregiver and the other parent as the primary breadwinner, their children were more likely to express stereotyped views about adult roles and occupations.

Parents are more likely to provide toy vehicles, action figures, and sports equipment for their sons; and they are more likely to give dolls, kitchen sets, and dress-up toys to their daughters (Kollmayer, Schultes, Schober, Hodosi, &

Spiel, 2018). Birthday parties often take on gendered themes. Research shows that fathers are slightly more likely to encourage gendered play than mothers, and that non-Western families may have much more stringent gendered expectations for both boys and girls. Some of these early messages about gendered expectations related to work shape how people later approach leadership.

School

In 1982, Roberta Hall and Bernice Sandler wrote a report for the Association of American Colleges Project on the Status and Education of Women called *The Classroom Climate: A Chilly One for Women?* that describes over 50 ways girls and women are treated differently from boys and men in the classroom. These differences in treatment start in early childhood and persist through college. Despite well-intentioned teachers and school systems, many of these issues still exist today. The report describes how teachers can, often unintentionally, lessen the self-esteem and vocational aspirations of women. Examples of this "chilling" effect include

- calling on men more frequently than women;
- creating doubt about women's accomplishments by attributing achievements to luck and men's achievements to talent and ability;
- responding more extensively to men's in-class comments with praise, criticism, or coaching;
- assuming that women who ask questions in class do not know or understand the material, but that men who ask questions are smart, curious, and involved; and
- praising men for their work and abilities and women for their appearance.

What are the possible effects of this persistent and pervasive discrimination? The cumulative effect of sexism in K–12 schools was described in Mary Pipher's book *Reviving Ophelia: Saving the Selves of Adolescent Girls* (1994). The book title references Shakespeare's character Ophelia, the daughter of Polonius and who falls in love with Hamlet and proceeds to lose her own identity and live only for Hamlet's approval. Ophelia is torn apart by her efforts to please and when Hamlet spurns her she lapses into madness and drowns herself in a river. Pipher's book describes what has come to be called the Ophelia complex, or the process during which, at adolescence, girls "become 'female impersonators' who fit their whole selves into small, crowded spaces. . . . Many lose spark, interest, and even IQ points as a 'girl-poisoning' society forces a choice between being shunned for staying true to oneself and struggling to stay within a narrow definition of female" (p. 4).

Pipher alerts about the rising levels of sexism and mental health issues that are affecting young women. She describes girls dealing with divorce, depression, eating disorders, drugs and alcohol, self-mutilation, sex, and sexual violence. She asserts that teenagers have been neglected by the feminist movement and require additional support.

Peers

Rosalind Wiseman (2009) published her groundbreaking research on the social behavior of adolescent girls and on the patterns of aggressive teen behavior in cliques in a book called *Queen Bees and Wannabes*. Wiseman developed names for a wide variety of social positions within cliques including, among others: queen bee, sidekick, wannabe/pleaser, bystander, target, and champion. *Queen bee* refers to a girl who "through a combination of charisma, force, money, looks, will, and social intelligence, reigns supreme over other girls and weakens their friendships with others, thereby strengthening her own power and influence" (p. 87). The *sidekick* is "the lieutenant or second in command, the girl who is closest to the queen bee and will back her no matter what because her power depends on the confidence she gets from the queen bee. Together they appear to other girls as an impenetrable force. They commonly bully or silence other girls to forward their own agenda" (p. 90).

The *pleaser/wannabe* will do almost anything to be in the group or to gain favor from the queen bee or sidekick. They often imitate the clothes, behaviors, and interests of the clique without really being in the group. Sometimes this group is referred to as "try-hards." *Bystanders* refers to girls who want to help those targeted by the queen bee or sidekick but who are not sure how to help or if it will make a difference. The *target* refers to girls who are the victims of the queen bee and her clique—they are often set up to be teased, humiliated, or excluded. Targets can be people both inside and outside of the clique. Insiders can also be targeted, especially if they challenge the queen bee.

Finally, Wiseman (1994) describes healthy girl *champion* who "can take criticism, doesn't make people choose friends, and doesn't blow someone off for a better offer. . . . she has friends in different groups and doesn't treat people differently when the groups are together. She can and will stand up to the queen bee in a way that treats them both with dignity" (p. 98). If these terms seem familiar, it may be because Tina Fey used Wiseman's work as the foundation for the movie and musical *Mean Girls*. The "plastics" in the film include each of the stereotypical roles as outlined previously with Regina George as the ultimate queen bee. In chapter 6 we will examine how these ideas are not limited to precollege environments. You may be just as likely to encounter queen bees, wannabes, and targets in the workplace and in other leadership contexts.

Exercise 4.2.
Queen Bees and Wannabes

Did you occupy any of the roles (queen bee, sidekick, wannabe/pleaser, bystander, target, champion) described by Wiseman in school? Were there other roles you observed? Who did you associate with and how would you describe your social status? Who in your school had high social status and how did you know? What did they look like and how did they act? Who in your school had low social status and how did you know? What did they look like and how did they act? What are the lessons you learned about gender and leadership from your adolescent experiences? Which lessons have you had to unlearn?

Use Exercise 4.2 to reflect on which of these roles you might have occupied. Were you ever teased in school and how did you handle it? What group, if any, were you in? How did you manage the bullies in your school if you did not agree with them? If you were the bully, what motivated your behaviors? Why is bullying considered by some to be a superficial rite of passage for girls? What do you think cliques and bullying teach girls? Do you see these experiences influencing the kind of woman she becomes? What are the implications for future stereotyping and prejudice formation? In what ways can extracurricular activities help girls combat the importance they place on cliques and their social status?

Sports and Organizations

Participating in individual or team sports is a significant experience for many girls and women. For many years, there were vast inequities in the availability of sports participation for women. The passage of *Title IX* of the U.S. Education Amendments Act of 1972 made it illegal for any organization receiving federal funds to exclude people from participating in any education program or activity on the basis of sex. Title IX has many implications for colleges and universities, including implications for the reporting of sexual assaults, and will be addressed in more depth in chapter 5. The National Coalition for Women and Girls in Education (NCWGE) reports the many benefits of participation in organized sports. Women and girls who participate in sports: have higher grades than nonparticipants; have lower school dropout rates; have lower pregnancy rates; are less likely to use drugs; are more likely to graduate college; and learn leadership skills that will help them all of their lives (NCWGE, 2017).

This link between participation in sports and the development of leadership skills and abilities is well documented. Specifically, students who participate in aspects of campus recreation such as club, intramural, or varsity sports demonstrate higher leadership capacity and efficacy than many of their peers (Dugan, Torrez, & Turman, 2014). Sadly, generational research on millennials and GenZers finds decreasing rates of participation in team sports or organized activity, where "interactivity trumps physical activity" (Seemiller & Grace, 2016, p. 14). Currently about 43% of the college students participating in sports are women (NCWGE, 2017). Read Calliope's story to gain one perspective on how female participation in sports shifts as one ages and reinforces both positive and negative messages about leadership and involvement.

Religion

Messages about gender from religious and spiritual practice can have a profound effect on the development of identity, efficacy, and self-esteem in girls and women. Most religious texts talk about gender in only binary ways, so people who identify as nonbinary are all but excluded from the documents of the most popular world religions. A recent report from the Pew Center on Religion and Public Life (2016), reveals that in the United States women are more likely than men to say religion is "very important" in their lives (60% versus 47%), and that American women are also more likely than American men to say they pray daily (64% versus 47%) and attend religious services at least once a week (40% versus 32%). This is especially true in Christian religions. The same study found more equitable religious practices among Muslim women and men.

Research reveals women as more valuing of religion and more consistent in their expressions of faith, yet the tenets of many religions limit leadership opportunities for women and relegate women to particular roles. Women cannot be ordained in many religions including the Roman Catholic Church, Latter-Day Saints, Orthodox Judaism, and others. Some women have managed to break through this "stained-glass ceiling." In 2006, the Episcopal Church's Bishop Katharine Jefferts Schori became the first woman to lead an entire branch of the worldwide Anglican Communion. The Evangelical Lutheran Church in America elected Reverend Elizabeth Eaton as its first female presiding bishop in 2013, and Reverend Sharon E. Watkins serves as general minister and president of the Disciples of Christ (Kuruvilla, 2014). Some scripture describes different roles and functions across gender, where men are the spiritual head of household and women are instructed to be obedient. Other religions teach about equality of the sexes. What messages have you received from your spiritual or religious practice? How do these messages shape your beliefs about gender and leadership?

Technology and Media

Like much of this text, this section could be a book unto itself. As cell phones and social media become ubiquitous, society struggles to understand the effects of rampant media consumption on youth and young adults. Wiseman (2009) notes how girls today live in two worlds simultaneously—the real world and the virtual world—and what happens in one impacts the other. In addition to concerns about safety and privacy online, social media increases the spread and intensity of gossip, humiliation, and drama. Wiseman (2009) calls social media a weapon of mass destruction and notes how technology can fan the flames of bullying, harassment, and paranoia, especially as "technology provides a constantly updated picture of everyone else's life" (p. 24). Then there is also the fact that the use of technology is addictive. If you do not believe me, see if you can read to the end of this chapter without checking your phone or surfing the web. A professor friend of mine offers students the chance to earn an automatic A on her course's final exam if students are willing to give up their cell phones for ten days. She has yet to find any takers.

Researchers are also looking at the effects of technology use on issues like body image, consumerism, and depression (Simon & Hoyt, 2012). Youth who spent more time on social media had almost two and a half times the risk of reporting eating and body image concerns than peers who spent less time on social media (Sidani, Shensa, Hoffman, Hammer, & Primack, 2016). Another study from the University of Pittsburgh School of Medicine showed that the more time young adults spent on social media, the more likely they were to have problems sleeping and report symptoms of depression (Levensen, Shensa, Sidani, Coldits, & Primack, 2017).

Other than going cold turkey, how can we educate youth about the dangers of technology and media over-consumption? Many parents and teachers talk to youth about the benefits and pitfalls of media consumption. The Geena Davis Institute (https://seejane.org) works to address media content. It is a research-based organization working within the media and entertainment industry to improve gender balance, reduce stereotypes, and create diverse female characters in entertainment. It offers lesson plans for addressing images of gender equality in schools, a learning series about challenging gender stereotypes in advertising, and research studies on gender in the media.

Movies also communicate messages about who is worthy and capable of leadership. The Bechdel test was developed by Alison Bechdel (1986) in her comic *Dykes to Watch Out For* and rates sexism in movies on three criteria: Do they have at least two women in the movie? Do these women talk to each other? And do they talk about something besides a man? Visit https://bechdeltest.com

to view a list of movies that do and do not pass this test.   Movies that failed to pass the test include *Harry Potter and the Deathly Hallows Part II, Slumdog Millionaire, La La Land, Toy Story 1 and 2, The Avengers, Avatar,* and the entire *Lord of the Rings* trilogy. Women are bombarded by messages telling them that they are invisible, decorative, and vulnerable.

Messages From Society and Culture

Addressing any of the gender socialization factors described in this chapter is complicated. It goes far beyond simply educating girls to watch out for peer pressure or be aware of technology use. This is because these issues are embedded in our larger society and culture. Even if we educate girls about these socialization factors in school, the fact remains that they are growing up in a sexist patriarchal world where they are continually exposed to messages that contradict any education or empowerment about gender equity. Especially if you hold marginalized identities, part of your socialization is based on messages society sends about your worth as a woman and as a leader.

Calliope identifies as a white, cisgender, heterosexual, middle-class, Greek Orthodox, female.

Narratives and Counternarratives: Calliope's Story

When you are a little girl and you are playing sports with the boys, you are fun and cool. When you get a little older, you get called bossy, but they still let you play. You get to high school, and now you are told you are trying too hard because you are trying to impress the boys. This is the trajectory for many young girls who play sports.

Fourth grade was awesome. Every day at recess, you get picked first for the kickball team. You kick home runs, get people out, and race to the bases before any boy could catch you. You loved running around in the sunshine and going inside when recess was over, sweaty and thirsty for water. You did not have a care in the world. You were doing what you loved because you loved it, not because you were trying to impress anyone.

In seventh grade, playing with the boys is a different story. There are fewer girls on the kickball field. The boys give you weird looks. You get called bossy when you say the same exact thing that your male teammate just said. You get called emotional when you object to a call, even though all your male counterparts are doing the same thing. When you come inside after gym, the teacher suggests you play on the blacktop with other girls while they jump rope.

High school is a whole new ball game. Where there may have been a few girls playing with the guys in gym, there are now none. When you make any attempt at playing with the guys, you get called a try hard, a slut, a show off, you get accused of trying to impress the boys. When you get named captain of your soccer team, people come up to you and ask if you're actually as "bitchy" in real life as you are on the field.

My gender was most salient when I was playing sports or being athletic. Boys are expected to show how muscular they are, how strong, how fast, how in shape they are. When I was muscular, I was called masculine. When I was fast, I was a show off. When I was in shape, I was obsessed and had an eating disorder. When I was playing sports, I was either treated as outstanding or impossible, no in between. I was forced to choose how I would be treated. I could not choose to just be me. To just be who I was and enjoy doing what I loved. There were always strings attached with my choices because I was a girl. Simply because I was a girl.

The Cycle of Socialization

Harro (2013b) developed a model to depict why it is so hard to counteract the forces of socialization. Many well-meaning people assume that if we just appreciate each other's differences and treat each other with respect then oppression would not exist. If only it were that simple. Harro describes how we are each born into a set of social identities (gender, class, religion, sexual orientation, race, culture, ability status, among others) that predispose us to "unequal roles in the dynamic system of oppression" (p. 45). We are then subject to powerful forces to play the roles assigned to us within this unequal system. Harro's model of the cycle of socialization, depicted in Figure 4.1, describes how socialization is pervasive, consistent, circular, self-perpetuating, and often invisible or unconscious and unnamed. We are socialized first by parents, relatives, and teachers, and later by our larger culture and institutions.

Even if we do recognize the messages, rules, roles, structures, and assumptions that surround us, they are almost impossible to counteract as there are enforcements in place to maintain the system. People who challenge the existing power structure are often labeled as troublemakers, experience discrimination or violence, or are institutionalized, imprisoned, or even killed. The reward for not making waves is that we are left alone to continue business as usual, but then the cycle continues. People often internalize the messages of oppressive systems so that the system itself does not have to do any work; people start to believe stereotypes about groups with which they identify and experience helplessness and hopelessness. Harro does suggest ways that

Figure 4.1. Harro's cycle of socialization.

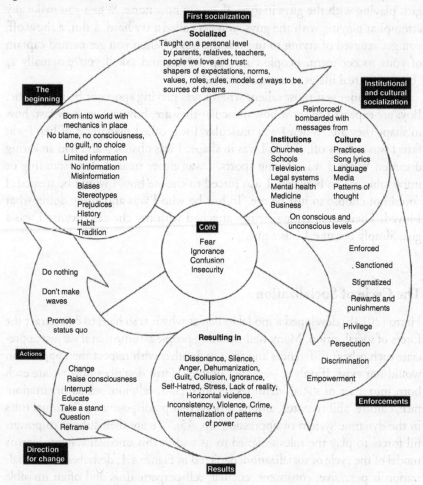

First socialization

Socialized
Taught on a personal level
by parents, relatives, teachers,
people we love and trust:
shapers of expectations, norms,
values, roles, rules, models of ways to be,
sources of dreams

The
beginning

Institutional
and cultural
socialization

Reinforced/
bombarded with
messages from

Born into world with
mechanics in place
No blame, no consciousness,
no guilt, no choice

Limited information
No information
Misinformation
    Biases
    Stereotypes
    Prejudices
    History
    Habit
    Tradition

Institutions   **Culture**
Churches   Practices
Schools   Song lyrics
Television   Language
Legal systems   Media
Mental health   Patterns of
Medicine   thought
Business

On conscious and
unconscious levels

Core
Fear
Ignorance
Confusion
Insecurity

Enforced

Sanctioned

Stigmatized

Do nothing

Don't make
waves

Promote
status quo

Rewards and
punishments

Privilege

Resulting In

Persecution

Discrimination

Empowerment

Actions

Change
Raise consciousness
Interrupt
Educate
Take a stand
Question
Reframe

Dissonance, Silence,
Anger, Dehumanization,
Guilt, Collusion, Ignorance,
Self-Hatred, Stress, Lack of reality,
Horizontal violence.
Inconsistency, Violence, Crime,
Internalization of patterns
of power

Enforcements

**Direction
for change**

Results

Note. Adapted from Harro, B. (2013b).

individuals can start to disrupt the cycle of socialization. You can see the off-ramp arrow in Figure 4.1. Actions like raising consciousness, education, questioning, reframing, interrupting, and taking a stand can all foster change.

Negative Effects of Gender Socialization

The effects of the socialization forces described in the beginning of this chapter are many. What follows are a few ways negative socialization about gender can show up in our daily lives. As depicted in Figure 4.1, the core of these messages spring from confusion, ignorance, insecurity, and fear, which keep us locked in the cycle of socialization.

Effortless Perfection

In 2003, a steering committee for the Women's Initiative at Duke University drafted a report naming the corrosive effect of effortless perfection on undergraduate women. Effortless perfection refers to the pressure people, especially women, feel to be smart, accomplished, fit, beautiful, and popular, all without exerting or displaying visible effort. This phenomenon can be directly linked to the gendered notions of agency and caring discussed earlier in this chapter. If it is unseemly for women to demonstrate too much agentic behavior, or to be seen as being a "try-hard," then the alternative is for women to act as if everything comes easily to them. The effortlessly perfect woman succeeds in all areas (personal, social, academic, career, health and beauty) and follows a "never let them see you sweat" mantra.

Of course, effortless perfection is an unachievable myth. Success, leadership, and achievement take hard work. Wiseman (2009) describes the illusion of the "perfect girl" about who

> everyone else thinks her life is perfect while she feels like a fraud and thinks that at any moment someone will pull back the curtain and expose her. She tries desperately to avoid making any mistakes and she is impossibly hard on herself. She finds fault with herself easily and never thinks she is doing enough. She runs herself into the ground trying to keep up with her image. (p. 203)

Impostor Syndrome

First described by psychologists Suzanne Imes and Pauline Rose Clance in the 1970s, *impostor syndrome* refers to a specific form of self-doubt. The desire to be seen as effortlessly perfect becomes especially anxiety producing when coupled with its sinister cousin, impostor syndrome, or the fear of being found out as less than worthy, or as a fraud. You can see how these phenomena work in concert to create stress and anxiety in women, whose self-talk may go something like this: "I must be perfect in all aspects of my life. I am definitely not perfect. People will discover I am not perfect and will no longer value me."

Research on the impostor syndrome, also called the impostor phenomenon, shows that women and people with other marginalized identities are especially hard hit by impostor syndrome. A 2013 study by researchers at the University of Texas at Austin found that Asian Americans were more likely than African Americans or LatinX Americans to experience impostor feelings. This correlates with the original 1970s findings that people who experience pressure to succeed when growing up are far more likely to suffer from impostor syndrome. Interestingly, the researchers also found that impostor feelings more strongly predicted mental health problems than did stress related to one's minoritized or marginalized status (Cokley, McClain, Enciso, & Martinez 2013). Ways to counteract impostor syndrome include: adopting a growth versus achievement mindset where you recognize progress on the way to goal attainment—not only the goal itself but also by reaching out to others through tutoring or mentoring to share your expertise and realize the value of what you do know; and seeking mentors or professional counseling to address irrational expectations for achievement.

Internalized Oppression

Internalized oppression can be defined as the internalizing, or believing, on the part of the target group, the lies and misinformation that the agent group disseminates (Adams et al., 2013). Internalized oppression is always an involuntary reaction to the experience of oppression. If society gives messages that Black women are unjustly angry, there is a possibility that a woman of color when facing real affronts will check herself and not speak out as not wanting to fit the stereotype. The story most often told influences the ways we do or do not see ourselves and sets expectations we hold of ourselves (internalized oppression) and others (stereotyping and prejudice). As Davis and Harrison (2013) explain, oppression itself is "deeply embedded, pervasively inconspicuous, and located in systems" (p. 42).

Microaggressions

In a 2010 blog for *Psychology Today*, Derald Wing Sue, a professor of counseling psychology at Columbia University, defined *microaggressions* as "the everyday verbal, nonverbal, and environmental slights, snubs, or insults, whether intentional or unintentional, which communicate hostile, derogatory, or negative messages to target persons based solely upon their marginalized group membership." These messages

> may invalidate the group identity or experiential reality of target persons, demean them on a personal or group level, communicate they are lesser human beings, suggest they do not belong with the majority group, threaten and intimidate, or relegate them to inferior status and treatment.

In Box 4.1, Sue offers numerous examples of microaggressions and suggests what they reveal about dominant ideology.

Box 4.1.
Examples of Common Microaggressions

Racial Microaggressions
- A white person clutches their purse or checks their wallet as a person of color approaches them. (Hidden message: You and your group are criminals.).
- An Asian American, born and raised in the United States, is complimented for speaking "good English." (Hidden message: You are not a true American. You are a perpetual outsider in your own country.)
- A group of people of color are seated at a table in a restaurant next to the kitchen despite there being other empty and more desirable tables located at the front. (Hidden message: You are a second-class citizen and undeserving of first-class treatment.)

Gender Microaggressions
- An assertive female manager is labeled as a "bitch," while her male counterpart is described as "an assertive leader." (Hidden message: Women should be passive and allow men to be the decision makers.)
- A female physician wearing a stethoscope is mistaken as a nurse. (Hidden message: Women should occupy nurturing and not decision-making roles. Women are less capable than men.)
- A person who identifies as transgender is questioned upon entering a gendered restroom. (Hidden message: Your gender identity is everyone's business.)
- Whistles or catcalls are heard as a person walks down the street. (Hidden message: Your body/appearance is for the enjoyment of others. You are a sex object.)

Sexual Orientation Microaggressions
- A person uses the term *gay* to describe a movie that they did not like. (Hidden message: Being gay is associated with negative and undesirable characteristics.)
- Two people hold hands in public and are told not to flaunt their sexuality. (Hidden message: Same-sex displays of affection are abnormal and offensive. Keep it private and to yourselves.)

(Continues)

Box 4.1. (*Continued*)

Religion, Ability, and Social-Class Microaggressions
- When bargaining over the price of an item, a store owner says to a customer, "Don't try to Jew me down." (Hidden message: Jews are stingy and money-oriented.)
- A blind man reports that people often raise their voices when speaking to him. He responds by saying, "Please do not raise your voice; I can hear you perfectly well." (Hidden message: A person with a disability is defined as lesser in all aspects of physical and mental functioning.)
- A person dealing with bipolar disorder is called crazy by a close friend. (Hidden message: It is okay to make fun of people's emotional well-being.)
- The outfit worn by a TV reality-show participant is described as "classless and trashy." (Hidden message: Lower-class people are tasteless and unsophisticated.)

Note. Adapted from Wing Sue (2010).

Social Pressure

The desire to fit in with a group of people is powerful and can motivate girls and young women to act in destructive ways such as changing their attitudes, behaviors, or values to conform to group expectations. It can also be harnessed to positive ends if group goals promote healthy or moral behaviors. Helping girls understand and articulate their own boundaries is essential to navigating the pressure inherent in any social situation.

Stress and Anxiety

Throughout their lifespan, people will experience challenging situations and relationships that can cause stress and anxiety. These incidents are often heightened in adolescence as young people face many complex challenges, often without having fully developed the skills necessary for coping with stress and anxiety. The National Institute of Mental Health (NIMH; 2019) describes the increase in anxiety disorders among youth in that almost 30% of all people have experienced some type of anxiety disorder in their lifetimes. Additionally, females (38%) are more likely than males (26%) to experience extreme anxiety. These disorders can include panic disorder, generalized anxiety disorder, agoraphobia, specific phobia, social anxiety disorder (social phobia), posttraumatic stress disorder, obsessive-compulsive disorder, and separation anxiety disorder (NIMH, 2019, para. 2). Stress affects everyone, but when it starts to interfere with work, school, or relationships it can require special treatment. Anyone experiencing severe or long-term, unrelenting stress can become overwhelmed and even hopeless. If you or a loved one is having thoughts of suicide, call the toll-free National Suicide Prevention Lifeline (www.suicidepreventionlifeline.org) at 1-800-273-TALK (8255), available 24 hours a day, 7 days a week. The service is available to anyone and all calls are confidential.

How Can We Support Healthy Gender Socialization?

Western society is built on a series of assumptions including hierarchy, competition, individualism, domination, capitalism, colonialism, and the scarcity principle (Harro, 2013b; hooks, 2000b, 2011). These societal values have implications for leadership, as discussed in chapter 2, and also for gender socialization. What are some strategies to counteract these values in raising girls and women? Recent research indicates there are things we can do to raise girls and women who view each other as allies and supports rather than as threats, and who feel capable of leadership (Fagell, 2018). A few practical interventions are described in the following sections.

Use Social Media for Good

Caroline Miller, a positive psychology expert, founded the #Share222 movement to encourage girls to share one another's achievements on at least two social media outlets, with the goal of replacing selfies and pictures from parties with shout-outs for friends who have achieved personal goals (Fagell, 2018). The hope is that girls will reciprocate kind gestures, leading to a positive cycle of friendship and support, rather than one focused on popularity and appearance.

Encourage the Use of Expansive Body Language

Assisting girls in developing presence can actually enhance their own sense of empowerment. Research shows that girls start to "shrink" themselves in middle school, learning to take up as little space as possible and call the least attention to themselves. Viewing examples of strong and proud girls, such as the *Fearless Girl* sculpture on Wall Street, which depicts a young girl defiantly confronting the Wall Street bull, can enhance girls' sense of space, and thus their sense of empowerment. Teach them about how to counteract man-spreading, or the practice of some boys and men involving spreading out legs and arms and taking up as much space as possible without thought about encroaching on the space of others.

Normalize Giving and Seeking Help

It is important to teach girls how to identify and access sources of support, and that doing so is an essential part of learning and growth. Girls who fear reaching out are less likely to get the resources they need when facing crises or difficulties.

Emphasize Mastery Instead of Performance

Instead of treating performances as a zero-sum or win-lose affair, help girls focus on achieving personal goals where they can be competitive rather than focusing on doing better than someone else. For example, the Girls on the Run program adopts this mentality of personal goal setting and social support, which helps teach girls that empathy and achievement can go hand in hand.

Identify Fierce but Kind Female Characters

In an age of rampant media consumption, it is important for girls to have role models who display both achievement and supportive behaviors. Disney has made efforts to develop more fully formed female characters such as Mulan, Merida, and Moana, who display strength and courage while also exhibiting kindness and compassion. This is in contrast to earlier Disney characters such as Ariel who trades her legs for a man, Belle who develops Stockholm Syndrome and falls in love with her captor, and Sleeping Beauty who is kissed against her will (for more feminist takes on Disney icons see www.jezebel.com/5925424/a-feminist-guide-to-disney-princesses/). Whatever your opinion, Disney's female characters provided early female role models where few existed, and their recent attempts to reframe princesses as protagonists is a step in the right direction. Other fierce female characters include Rey from recent *Star Wars* films, many of the female leads in Hayao Miyazaki's anime films such as Princess Mononoke, Arrietty, and others.

Encourage Them to Join a Team

Playing team sports can teach girls how to set aside ego and invest in one another's successes. In the LID study, many participants cited early team experiences as essential to their development of a relational approach to leadership (Komives et al., 2009). Sports that included both individual and team achievements such as swimming or track and field seemed especially powerful. Team involvement not centered on sports can be equally powerful, such as theater or community groups.

Developing Leadership in Girls and Young Women

Now that you have reflected on your own socialization to gender and leadership messages and been exposed to terminology describing some of the situations facing women as they navigate leadership experiences, it is important to think about concrete strategies for developing girls and young women's leadership capacity. Haber-Curran and Sulpizio (2017) offer four recommendations to consider when designing leadership education and development programs for girls and young women.

Haber-Curran and Sulpizio's (2017) first suggestion is to approach leadership not as a defined role or trait, but as a process or capacity that can be developed. As was revealed in the Girl Scout study (Girl Scout Research Institute, 2008), girls more readily identify with models of leadership that are inclusive, ethical, and process-oriented. When leadership is viewed only as a role, or as having a position of authority, girls and young women may opt out of leadership all together. Further, since women are underrepresented in traditional leadership roles, there are fewer role models for young girls and it can lead to the mistaken assumption that women are less fit to lead. As Haber-Curran and Sulpizio (2017) note, "Defining leadership as an authority role ignores the many women who practice leadership without authority" and "Establishing the thought pattern that anyone can lead is pivotal to women seeing themselves as capable of leadership in a variety of contexts" (p. 40).

Haber-Curran and Sulpizio's (2017) second recommendation is to address issues of gender expression with an emphasis on embracing feminine, masculine, and androgynous approaches to leadership. If girls are deeply affected by the socialization of gender, then leadership programs should include topics of gender identity and expression and acknowledge the complexity of messages about femininity and masculinity and leadership. Rather than linking leadership to a dichotomized view of masculine and feminine leadership styles, programs should "challenge rigid gendered standards" and "help learners explore their authentic self while developing their capacity to exercise leadership across a spectrum of leadership behaviors and approaches" (p. 41).

The third recommendation is that leadership programs should emphasize voice, power, and self-esteem and that "progress in women's leadership can happen when we explicitly name and focus on gendered aspects of leadership that negatively affect women" (Haber-Curran and Sulpizio, 2017, p. 42). This might include giving space for participants to discuss their own experiences with gender bias in leadership and to brainstorm ways to address bias in practice.

Haber-Curran and Sulpizio's (2017) fourth and final recommendation is leadership programs aimed at girls and young women foster engagement and include a mentorship component. They cite recent research that shows that high school leadership involvement, participation in leadership trainings, involvement in student organizations, participation in community organizations and community service, and holding leadership roles, all contribute to leadership development outcomes for women (Dugan et al., 2013; Dugan & Komives, 2010; Haber, 2011). Further, mentorship is especially important for the leadership development of girls and young women (Dugan et al., 2013). As discussed in chapter 3, the MSL defines a *mentor* as a person who intentionally assists a student's growth or who connects the student to opportunities for career or personal development (Dugan et al., 2013). Mentors can be drawn from a variety of places and include teachers, administrators, employers, family members, community members, and peers.

If you have had a mentor before, you may know that mentoring relationships do not just happen. They require commitment on both sides and time to develop. The MSL offers suggestions for developing effective mentoring relationships including: communicating with mentors about explicitly mentoring for leadership, which involves complex and open discussions that prepare students to negotiate authority relationships, navigate social systems, and build resilience; helping mentees understand the benefits related to mentoring and providing them with the information and skills necessary to establish these relationships on their own; developing mentors who have the ability to engage across difference in ways that support students from marginalized identities; and explicitly preparing mentors to acknowledge the ways in which power, privilege, and oppression are often embedded in leadership.

One example of a program that adopts each of the four recommendations previously mentioned is the organization Girls Inc. (www.girlsinc.org). Girls Inc (2014) offers a unique Bill of Rights for girls that suggests all girls have the following rights:

1. Girls have the right to be themselves and to resist gender stereotypes.
2. Girls have the right to express themselves with originality and enthusiasm.
3. Girls have the right to take risks to strive freely and to take pride in success.
4. Girls have the right to accept and appreciate their bodies.
5. Girls have the right to have confidence in themselves and be safe in the world.
6. Girls have the right to prepare for interesting work and for economic independence.

As you reflect on the ways you were socialized about gender and leadership, do you have insights about how you got to where you are today? That is to say, it may be helpful to think about the messages you received in your formative years and how these messages may still be informing your approach to gender and leadership.

Natalia, who identifies as a white, cisgender, pansexual, middle class, athe-
istic woman, shares her own story about how explicit and implicit messages
get internalized.

Narratives and Counternarratives: Natalia's Story

Mother Always Told Me

that I would be treated differently
than my brothers and not just by everyone
but also by her

My mother always told me

"when you're pumping gas
lock your doors and always
stay inside the car"

When I got my first car
I was afraid to go to gas stations
alone for six months

I still wait inside my car every time.

My mother always told me
"if you're home alone
don't open the door for anyone"

Just last week I hid a knife in
the sleeve of my bathrobe
as a maintenance man inspected our apartment

My mother always told me
not to go to North Avenue
dressed like *that*

Today I was nearly late for a meeting
as I assessed a man's potential
perception of my outfit

My mother always told me
not to scowl at men who smile at me
but never to smile back

Am I asking for it?

My mother never told me
what consent means, but she showed
me that fear was my first line of defense

5

FEMININE OR FEMINIST APPROACHES?

Leading Across Campus and Communities

Daring leaders who live into their values are never silent about hard things.

—Brené Brown, *Dare to Lead,* 2018

I f you are reading this book as part of a college course or program, you likely have powerful predecessors to thank for your institution admitting women. Even women-only colleges were founded, in part, as a reaction to the exclusionary gender practices of most of higher education. There remains much work to be done in creating inclusive curricula, policies, and practices that support all women. Our institutions have far to go to welcome people who identify as genderfluid, genderqueer, gender nonconforming, or nonbinary. If you are active on your campus, you have likely seen people raising issues related to women's health and reproductive rights, student debt, sexual violence and rape culture, Title IX, women in sports, women's centers and organizations, and more. This chapter offers a short summary of the history of women in higher education, and then proceeds to offer brief sketches of issues and organizations related to women and leadership on campus. As previously mentioned, we cannot assume that those who identify as women are aware of our own history, yet this knowledge is essential as we seek to create change. The chapter ends with a list of organizations dedicated to supporting campus women and a call to action from Shea and Renn (2017) about moving from feminine to feminist leadership on campuses.

History of Women in Higher Education

At the first Women's Rights Convention in the United States at Seneca Falls, New York, in 1848, attendees drafted a document called the *Declaration of Sentiments* that included an objection to women being barred from educational facilities and having "all colleges closed against her" (Stanton, Anthony, Gage, & Harper, 1922, p. 9). Early feminists appropriated antislavery abolitionist rhetoric and demanded equal rights for women including coeducation. Although coeducation existed in some places at the primary and secondary school levels, it was not until 1837 that Oberlin College became the first postsecondary school to admit women, and even then only a small number of African American women were included. The first women earned bachelor's degrees from Oberlin in 1841. Other small schools such as Hillsdale (1844) and Antioch (1853) soon followed, although they had to cease admissions during the Civil War (Micheletti, 2002). The University of Iowa (1855) has continuously admitted women since its founding. These institutions served only a tiny number of women, and women were a small fraction of those enrolled (Renn & Reason, 2012).

A post–Civil War boom in primary and secondary education led to a shortage of teachers, which in turn inspired more institutions to admit female collegians and more women to seek out a university education, especially women widowed in the war seeking to support themselves. Although many colleges still resisted admitting women, women were a vital part of the normal school movement, which focused on teacher preparation. Normal schools also often admitted nontraditionally aged students. Women also participated in junior and community colleges from their inception (Renn & Reason, 2012). In 1862 the Morrill Land-Grant Act subsidized the establishment of state colleges and universities to educate people in practical fields of study, encouraging taxpayers to demand equal access to state-sponsored institutions for their sons and daughters. In this era, most women were limited to home economics, teaching, or nursing curricula—often termed *ladies' courses*—and most colleges were only open to white, Christian, cisgender women. Many historically Black colleges and universities (HBCUs) such as Wilberforce (1856) and Fisk (1866) accepted women very early in their establishment for both financial and philosophical reasons (Micheletti, 2002). A second Morrill Act in 1890 provided limited funds for separate public institutions for Black students (Renn & Reason, 2012). Many elite colleges and universities such as Yale accepted female graduate students far earlier (1892) than they accepted female undergraduates (1969), mostly for economic reasons.

Early instances of coeducation were met with resistance. In 1873, a Harvard Medical School professor, Edward Clarke, argued that women endangered their reproductive health when using their limited energies to study, that women were not physically equipped for coursework, and that coeducation was a sin against man. Others argued that a female presence on campus would foster sexual immorality (hence why Catholic institutions were some of the last to adopt coeducation), distract men from their studies, and devalue college degrees (Micheletti, 2002). Partly in response to this hostile climate, independent nonprofit women's colleges were founded to offer women educational opportunities equal to men's. Many of these schools evolved from female seminaries and later were paired with men's colleges as part of the coordinate college system. Barnard (1889), Smith (1875), Mount Holyoke (1837), Vassar (1865), Bryn Mawr (1885), Wellesley (1875), and Radcliffe (1879) were given the name "the Seven Sisters" in 1927, because of their relative affiliations with the Ivy League men's colleges (Harwarth, Maline, & DeBra, 2005). Research on women's colleges recognizes the positive effects of their campus climates on learning effectiveness and other educational gains as compared to coeducational institutions (Kinzie, Thomas, Palmer, Umbach, & Kuh, 2007; Yates, 2001). Renn and Patton (2011) describe the benefits of these campuses:

> The presence of an all-women environment means that women's voices are heard and respected; issues important to women are unapologetically grounded in women's experiences; and students gain experiences by serving in leadership roles on campus, many of which are traditionally held by men on coeducational campuses. There is also a strong press towards positive peer influence. Finally, the mission of a women's college is deeply interwoven, linking history to current context in which the education of women remains at the core and intersects with every aspect of the campus environment. (p. 247)

Many institutional holdouts finally opened doors to women during World War II for financial reasons as men left for war. The post–World War II GI Bill resulted in a boom in college-going men, which led to some women-only colleges opening doors to men and eventually remaining coeducational, although some women also felt pressured to return to the domestic sphere to make room for returning veterans (Martínez Alemán, & Renn, 2002; Renn & Reason, 2012). In 1976 the U.S. military academies began admitting women (United States Military Academy [USMA], United States Naval Academy [USNA], United States Air Force Academy [USAFA], United States Coast Guard Academy [USXGA]). In 1979, women became more than 50% of undergraduate enrollments and now women compose upward of 57% of enrollments across all institutions of higher education (Renn & Reason, 2012). Columbia, the last single-sex Ivy League college, became coeducational in 1983. In 1996 the *United States v. Virginia* Supreme Court ruling required that state-supported single-sex military institutions, such as the Virginia Military Institute, allow the admission of women. Today more than 95% of female students attend coeducational colleges and universities (Micheletti, 2002). Vestiges of gendered approaches to higher education persist on many campuses. Some universities maintain single-sex housing, deans of women, sexist pageants or traditions such as ring dances, and male-only secret societies.

Just because universities admitted women does not necessarily mean there was equality on campus. Bastedo (2011) describes how the spread of feminism in the 1970s became a powerful force on campus resulting in people demanding that the study of women and women's issues be incorporated into the curriculum. He states, "Women's studies faculty and students alike, like those in Black studies, explicitly sought to change the curriculum of the university to rectify institutionalized sexism and misogyny in society" (p. 472). Renn and Reason (2012) note how the chilly climate for women (see chapter 4 in this volume) persists at many colleges and universities. This inhospitable culture often results in lower cognitive gains in the first year of college (Pascarella et al., 1997); a reluctance to enter science, technology, engineering, and math (STEM) majors (Sax, Bryant & Harper, 2008); and begs the question "If women are the majority and more successful in college, why is the climate still hostile to them?" (Renn & Reason, 2012, p. 101).

Many campus cultures can be characterized as *Guyland* (Kimmel, 2008), which is "an all-enveloping sociocultural milieu that promotes heteronormative masculinity at the expense of men and women's ability to express themselves authentically" (Renn & Reason, 2012, p. 101). It was not until 2014 that all women's colleges started admitting transgender women (Kellaway, 2014). Renn and Reason (2012) describe the climate for gender nonconforming individuals:

> Campus gender climate is dominated by a *Guyland* ethos and embedded in a system of genderism (Bilodeau, 2009) that mandates that everyone have a singular gender identity located at one of two binary poles (man, woman) . . . and race and ethnicity intersect with gender in college to amplify these standards and expectations. (p. 102)

This chapter will next explore a few of the critical issues facing women on campuses.

Women and Leadership on Campus: Issues

Institutionalized sexism is rampant, and campus and national policies often hamper progress toward creating more just, equitable, and sustainable campuses. Google the women's center or women's student organizations on your campus, or consider the campus culture audit presented in Exercise 5.1, to get a sense of the issues facing collegiate women today. The following sections include only some of the issues around which women are exercising leadership on campus. As you read these brief summaries, think about your own

Exercise 5.1.
Campus Culture Audit

In his book *Organizational Culture and Leadership*, Edgar Schein (2015) defines *culture* as:

> A pattern of shared basic assumptions that the group learned as it solved its problems of external adaptation and internal integration, that has worked well enough to be considered valid and, therefore, to be taught to new members as the correct way you perceive, think, and feel in relation to those problems. (p. 18)

Schein further describes different levels of organizational culture including:

- *Artifacts*—What are the visible products of the culture? What is the organization making sure you see, hear, feel? Look for both formal and informal artifacts. For example, how have students made the space their own?
- *Espoused values*—What does the organization say they value? Look for publicly stated mission, vision, values, publications, bulletin boards, recognition/awards, and so on.
- *Underlying assumptions*—What underlying assumptions seem to guide the organization? These may be hard to detect since they are mostly unconscious or taken for granted.

Given these definitions, what is the history of coeducation on your campus? Are pioneering women being honored on your campus? If so, how? What vestiges of gendered approaches still exist on your campus? What spaces or places do you find affirming to women's experiences and leadership? To genderqueer and nonbinary individuals? Where do you see gendered messages in the artifacts, espoused values, and underlying assumptions of your campus? Do you belong to any organizations that focus on gendered experiences? Why or why not? Where are women leading and making a difference on campus?

knowledge, skills, attitudes, and experiences in relation to these topics. How have or how have you not demonstrated leadership in these domains on campus? What motivates you to or holds you back from being active in these areas? What resources and supports are available if you want to learn or do more?

Sexual Harassment, Sexual Violence, and Security

Sexual harassment and sexual assault are ever-present factors on college campuses. The National Sexual Violence Resource Center (NSVR) reports that 20%–25% of college women and 15% of college men are victims of rape during their time in college, that 27% of college women have experienced some form of unwanted sexual contact, and that nearly two thirds of college students experience sexual harassment (NSVR, 2019). These statistics do not include the frequent violence that transgender individuals are subject to on and off campus (Nicolazzo, 2016). Sexual violence and assault impede survivors' ability to participate fully in their education. The American Association of University Women (AAUW) outlines where work is needed: "Educational equity for women and girls requires fair, responsive, fully developed campus sexual assault policies; knowledgeable administrators; and ultimately an end to sexual violence on campuses" (2016b, para. 2).

As described in chapter 4, Title IX of the Education Amendments of 1972 is the federal law that prohibits sex discrimination in education. In addition to the policies related to gender parity in sports, Title IX protects students from unlawful sexual harassment in all of a school's programs or activities, whether they take place in the facilities of the school or at a class or training program sponsored by the school at another location, and protects both male and female students regardless of who the harasser may be, and there is no timeline for reporting (AAUW, 2016b). Title IX requires that colleges and universities develop and enact policies against sex discrimination and implement grievance procedures providing for prompt and equitable resolution of student and employee discrimination complaints. These policies must include the following: a definition of *sex discrimination* and *sexual violence*; a published statement that the school does not discriminate; a detailing of procedures for students to file complaints when sexual harassment, discrimination, or violence takes place; and the appointment of a Title IX coordinator to oversee these activities, review complaints, and deal with patterns or systemic problems (AAUW, 2016b).

The Jeanne Clery Disclosure of Campus Security Policy and Campus Crime Statistics Act (more familiarly known as the Clery Act) is a federal statute requiring colleges and universities participating in federal financial aid programs to maintain and annually disclose campus crime statistics and security information (Clery Center, 2019). Sexual assaults that are reported to local law enforcement are included in these disclosures, along with crime reporting; campus facility security and access; law enforcement authority; incidence of alcohol and drug use; and the prevention of/response to sexual assault, domestic or dating violence, and stalking. In 2013, Congress reauthorized the Violence Against Women Act and included provisions to improve campus safety. Schools are now required to report additional crime statistics, update procedures following an incident of sexual violence, and provide prevention and bystander intervention training to all students and employees (AAUW, 2016b). The U.S. House of Representatives passed another reauthorization of the Violence Against Women Act (VAWA) in April 2019, but the act remains stalled in the Senate. The latest version of VAWA does not include measures to deter female genital mutilations, honor killings, sex trafficking or forced child marriages. The Violence Against Women Act is up for reauthorization in 2019.

When schools and administrators fail to take appropriate action, students can experience a phenomenon called institutional betrayal (Linder & Myers, 2018). Institutional betrayal can include failing to prevent abuse, normalizing abusive contexts, creating difficult processes for reporting, failing to adequately respond to instances of harm, supporting cover-ups and misinformation, and punishing victims and whistleblowers (Smith & Freyd, 2014). Students from marginalized groups (e.g., queer and trans* students) may be more vulnerable to their stories being ignored, minimized, or delegitimized by the institution (Linder & Myers, 2018). Linder and Myers caution that "failing to acknowledge the relationship between sexual violence and oppression (including racism, classism, trans* and homophobia, and ableism) results in incomplete strategies for prevention of sexual assault" (p. 14).

Sexual assault and rape are the most underreported crimes on campus. If you or someone you know is a survivor of sexual violence, it is important to connect to resources that can offer psychological and medical services; advocacy and information on reporting and legal rights; and most importantly, services that let survivors decide what next steps, if any, should be taken. The Title IX coordinator on your campus may be part of the dean of students' office, the student support and advocacy center, the counseling center, the university police, or the women's center. You might access national groups like the Rape, Abuse & Incest National Network (RAINN), which is the nation's largest anti–sexual violence organization. RAINN operates the National Sexual Assault Hotline (800-656-HOPE) in partnership with more than 1,000 local sexual assault service providers across the country (www. rainn.org). Or contact the National Sexual Violence Resource Center (www.nsvrc.org). At the very least, if someone shares their experience with you, the most important thing you can do is listen to them, believe them and not question or dismiss

Box 5.1.
Sexual Violence Awareness-Raising Programs on College Campuses

- *Clothesline Project.* Have people affected by sexual violence decorate a shirt and hang it on a public clothesline as a testimony to the problem of sexual violence.
- *Denim Day.* Wear jeans on April 23 to protest and raise awareness of the misconceptions that surround sexual assault.
- *International Day Against Victim-Blaming.* Use the hashtag #EndVictimBlaming on April 3, the online day of action to speak out against victim-blaming and to support survivors, and get involved through social media.
- *It's on Us.* Pledge your commitment to help keep all people safe from sexual assault. This growing movement reframes sexual assault in a way that inspires everyone to see it as their responsibility to do something, big or small, to prevent it.
- *NotAlone.gov.* This is a White House project that includes information for students, schools, and anyone interested in finding resources on how to respond to and prevent sexual assault.
- *Slut Walk.* Participants protest against explaining or excusing rape by referring to any aspect of a woman's appearance and call for an end to rape culture, including victim-blaming and slut-shaming of sexual assault victims. The rallies began on April 3, 2011, in Toronto, Ontario, Canada, after a Toronto Police officer suggested that "Women should avoid dressing like sluts" as a precaution against sexual assault. Subsequent rallies have occurred globally.
- *Take Back the Night.* Take part in this after-dark march that is popular on college campuses, and make a statement that women have the right to be in public at night without the risk of sexual violence.
- *V-Day.* Hold a performance or a film screening to raise awareness about violence against women and girls.
- *White Ribbon Campaign.* Wear a white ribbon, and make a personal pledge to never commit, condone, or remain silent about violence against women and girls.

Note. Some sources adapted from www.aauw.org/2016/04/04/fight-campus-sexual-assault/

their experience, assure them that it is not their fault, and help connect them to resources and support if they so desire. Box 5.1 details how some college campuses seek to raise awareness about sexual violence.

Women's Health and Reproductive Rights

When I was in college in the 1990s there was a story circulating around campus that the university health center thought every woman who walked through its door was pregnant. If you went to the health center for a sore throat, you were given a pregnancy test. Rash on your arm? Pregnancy test. Broken leg? Pregnancy test. Looking back on this, rather than being appalled, I marvel that we had that much access to reproductive support services on campus. Issues of women's health and reproductive rights have become a hot-button issue on campuses as students demand access to contraception, testing for sexually transmitted infections, day-after or emergency contraceptive pills, gynecological health exams, and an environment that is nonjudgmental and respectful of each individual and their gender and sexual diversity.

Student leaders have also begun advocating for menstrual equity and passing legislation in student government associations demanding access to free menstrual hygiene products on campus. Chanting "Hey hey! Ho ho! Period poverty has got to go!," activists make the point that many women pay a "pink tax." They argue that menstruation should be a health issue and that hygiene products should not be taxed as luxury items (Smith & Strauss, 2019). Students at Ohio State University formed a campus chapter of a national group called Period, which is the world's largest youth-run nonprofit group working to shatter stigma associated with menstruation. The students have successfully lobbied the administration to stock campus bathrooms with free menstrual hygiene products. Many other universities such as Brown, Cornell, and Emory have followed suit. Nationally, the House of Representatives passed H.R. 972 (the Menstrual Equity for All Act of 2017), which allows individuals to use their own pretax dollars from their health flexible spending accounts to purchase menstrual hygiene products. An updated version of the bill going before the House has expanded access including:

- allowing individuals to use their own pretax dollars from their health flexible spending accounts to purchase menstrual hygiene products;
- giving states the option to use federal grant funds to provide students with free menstrual hygiene products in schools;
- ensuring that inmates and detainees incarcerated in federal (including immigration detention centers), state, and local facilities have access to free menstrual hygiene products;
- allowing homeless assistance providers to use grant funds that cover shelter necessities (e.g., blankets and toothbrushes) to also use those funds to purchase menstrual hygiene products;
- requiring that Medicaid covers the cost of menstrual hygiene products for recipients;

- directing large employers (with 100 or more employees) to provide free menstrual hygiene products for their employees in the workplace; and
- requiring all public federal buildings, including buildings on the Capitol campus, to provide free menstrual hygiene products in the restrooms.

Students continue to activate around these issues on campus and have expanded their goals beyond access to contraception and hygiene products to include adding sections about sexual health education to required classes, reducing the stigma associated with sexual well-being, and offering emergency contraception and pregnancy tests at little to no cost.

Body Image, Eating Disorders, and Appearance

Most college students worry about their appearance and struggle with body image at some point. Especially in the age of social media when comparisons are just a click away, it can be challenging to maintain a healthy body image. Body image is what you believe about your own appearance including memories, assumptions, and generalizations. The National Eating Disorder Association (NEDA, 2019) states that body image can also include how you feel about your height, shape, weight, and how you sense your body as you move. These issues can be compounded by changes in weight or appearance that may occur as students transition to college. As students are trying to figure out their own identity and personal development, it can be exciting and stressful to navigate shifting body images. Here are a few stressors in the college environment that may impact body image: physical and emotional separation from family; prioritizing academic performance above physical and emotional health; transition related to food and housing such as moving on or off campus, changing to or from campus meal plans, or roommate issues; beginning or ending significant romantic relationships or friendships; and graduation and job searching (University of Michigan University Health Services, 2019). Because girls and women face the extra pressure to fit societal beauty norms, any deviance from the norm can result in guilt, shame, and discrimination.

Eating and body image issues are often connected. People with a negative body image have a greater likelihood of developing an eating disorder and are more likely to suffer from feelings of depression, isolation, low self-esteem, and obsessions with weight loss (Stice & Shaw, 2002). Some studies show that concerns about body image can occur at ages as young as six years old, and more than 50% of elementary school girls are concerned about weight (Cash & Smolak, 2011). It is no wonder that by college, almost half of girls and almost one third of boys use unhealthy weight control behaviors such as skipping meals, fasting, smoking cigarettes, vomiting, and taking laxatives (Neumark-Sztainer, 2005). There are also cultural pressures around beauty such that women of color may face colorism, also called shadism, where people with darker skin tones are subject to more prejudice and discrimination. This is illustrated by the "paper bag test" in the late 1800s and early 1900s where people with skin darker than a paper bag were not allowed to work in many establishments. Transgender individuals experience eating disorders at rates significantly higher than cisgender individuals (Waldron, Semerjian, & Kauer, 2009). Table 5.1 describes some of the risk factors and resources related to eating disorders.

Fortunately, the body positive movement has made some inroads to promote body acceptance, and a healthier body image for all ages, genders, races, sexual orientations, and abilities. NEDA (2019) notes that

> While we all may have our days when we feel awkward or uncomfortable in our bodies, the key to developing positive body image is to recognize and respect our natural shape and learn to overpower those negative thoughts and feelings with positive, affirming, and accepting ones. (para. 3)

Stress, Anxiety, Perfectionism, and Well-Being

Other critical issues facing women on campus are related to our experiences with stress, anxiety, and well-being. Women are nearly twice as likely as men to be diagnosed with an anxiety disorder in their lifetime (National Institute of Mental Health, 2019). The term *anxiety disorder* can refer to any psychiatric disorders that involve extreme fear or worry and includes generalized anxiety disorder, panic disorder and panic attacks, agoraphobia, social anxiety disorder, separation anxiety, and specific phobias. Because of the transition to independence as well as juggling multiple academic, social, and financial commitments, the college experience can also promote stress and anxiety. One common form of anxiety experienced by women is related to academics. Despite earning overall higher grades than men, women still report less academic confidence in their skills and often drastically underestimate their academic abilities (Pascarella & Terenzini, 2005). This may be due to lack of self-efficacy, self-confidence, or impostor syndrome, all of which have been addressed in previous chapters, in addition to the chilly climate and systemic sexism that persist at many institutions.

College women also suffer from anxiety about finances, student loan debt, and their financial future. A recent report from the AAUW reveals that women take on larger student loans than do men (partly because of women's higher college-going rate) and, because of the gender pay gap, they have less disposable income with which to repay their loans after graduation, resulting

TABLE 5.1.
Developing a Healthy Body Image

Risk Factors For Eating Disorders *Adapted from National Eating Disorders Association (NEDA)*	Tips for Developing a Healthy Body Image *Adapted from* Bodylove: Learning to Like Our Looks and Ourselves, *by Rita Freedman* (2002)
Biological • You have a close relative with an eating disorder. • You have a close relative with a mental health condition like anxiety, depression, or addiction. • You have a history of dieting. • You have a negative energy balance, or burning off more calories than you take in. • You have Type 1 (insulin-dependent) diabetes. Over 25% of women with diabetes also suffer from diabulimia, or intentionally skipping insulin injections to manage weight. ***Psychological*** • You seek perfectionism or set unrealistically high expectations for yourself. • You have body image dissatisfaction and an internalization of the appearance ideal. • You have a personal history of an anxiety disorder. • You exhibit behavioral inflexibility or always following the rules and feeling like there is one "right way" to do things.	• Be realistic about the size you are likely to be based on your genetic and environmental history. • Stay active (walking, dancing, yoga, etc.), regardless of your size. • Expect normal weekly and monthly changes in weight and shape. • Work toward self-acceptance and self-forgiveness; be gentle with yourself. • Ask for support and encouragement from friends and family when life is stressful. • Decide how you wish to spend your energy: pursuing the "perfect body" or enjoying family; friends; school; and, most importantly, life. • Look for student organizations on your campus that promote body acceptance. You might also check out the women's or health centers for support. • Read more at the NEDA website: www.nationaleatingdisorders.org • Consider The Body Positive campus leadership program: www.thebodypositive.org/campus-leadership • Check out Joy Nash's Fat Rant on YouTube: www.youtube.com/watch?v=yUTJQIBI1oA

(Continues)

Table 5.1. (*Continued*)

Social	
• You suffer from weight stigma or internalizing the message that thinner is better. • You've experienced teasing or bullying, especially weight shaming. • You experience appearance ideal internalization. • You experience acculturation; especially people from racial and ethnic minority groups may be at risk for trying to adapt to Western ideals of beauty. • You have limited social networks, leading to loneliness and isolation. • You've experienced historical trauma.	

in it taking more time for women to pay back their student debt than men (AAUW, 2018). As a result, the U.S. Department of Education reports that women hold nearly two thirds of the outstanding student debt in the United States, almost $900 billion as of mid-2018. On average, African American women take on more debt than members of any other racial group (AAUW, 2018). People rarely talk about college debt as a women's issue, but these figures suggest that it is.

Women also suffer from perfectionism at a much greater rate than men, up to 25% more (AAUW, 2014). Perfectionism often stems from the fear of being judged. One way to avoid being judged is to be as perfect as possible so no judgment comes your way. When women strive for excessively high standards and apply rules of conduct in a very rigid manner, social interactions can become very stressful. To maintain control, perfectionists may become hypervigilant about their own imperfections and behaviors, a process called self-monitoring, which can limit enjoyable interactions with others. This maladaptive perfectionism inhibits people from being themselves, which in turn hinders authentic connections that lead to belonging and acceptance (Chandler, 2011). Perfectionism can also distort one's thinking by only seeing one's self as flawed and making unfair comparisons to others. Perfectionism can have real costs as women limit their opportunities for connection and even leadership. One study showed that women only apply for a job or promotion if they meet close to 100% of the outlined criteria, while men will apply if they only meet 50% of those same criteria (AAUW, 2014).

So how can college women address issues of stress, anxiety, and perfectionism? One set of strategies is the regular practice of self-care. Psychologist Brené Brown (2010) states that "Owning our story and loving ourselves through that process is the bravest thing we will ever do" (p. ix). In her books *The Gifts of Imperfection* (2010), *Daring Greatly* (2012), *Rising Strong* (2015), *Braving the Wilderness* (2017), and *Dare to Lead* (2018) Brown tackles issues such as self-care, compassion, connection, resilience, and whole-hearted living. If this section reads like an advertisement, it in some ways is. I cannot tell you how meaningful Brown's work has been to me personally in developing courage, compassion, and connection. In addressing self-care, Brown (2010) describes Kristin Neff's work on self-compassion, which includes these three elements:

- Self-kindness: Being warm and understanding toward ourselves when we suffer, fail, or feel inadequate, rather than ignoring our pain or flagellating ourselves with self-criticism.
- Common humanity: Recognizing that suffering and feelings of personal inadequacy are part of the shared human experience—something we all go through rather than something that happens to me alone.
- Mindfulness: Taking a balanced approach to negative emotions so that feelings are neither suppressed nor exaggerated. (pp. 59–60)

Lia discusses the challenges of maintaining a healthy body image. Lia identifies as an Asian American, middle-class, cisgender woman.

Narratives and Counternarratives: Lia's Story

From as far back as I can remember, I have always been concerned with the way I see myself. As a young girl I was always taught to "put myself together" when leaving home, even if it was to run a quick errand with my mom where I would stay in the car and not be seen. As I got older, I was given heat tools to tame my curly hair, makeup to cover those troublesome spots, and Spanx to hold in as much of my body as possible. Growing up I never worried about my weight until I was taught by my family to be embarrassed by how I looked.

I have a severe skin condition that was treated by steroid injections until I was 20. Although these injections were a temporary relief for my condition, they were a catalyst to my weight gain. Around my senior year of high school, I was also diagnosed with polycystic ovary syndrome, which unfortunately also causes weight gain. As I grew older and gained more weight, I would wear large hoodies to hide my arms and my weight. My grandmother, whom I love dearly, would tell me how pretty my face was, but that I would be prettier if I was skinny. She would then proceed to name friends of mine who I should strive to look like.

How does one juxtapose the love from a trusted person to the understanding that they wish you were different? I am still not sure how. Even today, I wear clothing strategically to tuck away what seems like too much. When I see others looking at me, I manage to convince myself that they are seeing all my flaws. When I see them laughing, I think it's about me. My negative body image was created for me and not by me. I think that is what hurts the most.

Women and Leadership on Campus: Organizations

This section includes spaces and places on college campuses where women often exercise leadership. Although not limited to these kinds of groups and organizations, involvement in woman-centered experiences can be an affirming way to find support and create change on campus.

Women's Centers and Feminist Organizations

Women's centers were first established on college campuses in the 1960s primarily to support women with children returning to school. These centers quickly evolved during the late 1960s and 1970s to support the second-wave feminist activism of that time. Today's women's centers provide a wide variety of services and programs including: leadership development activities, networking and empowerment programs, support for activism, connections to public health concerns and issues of sexual and domestic violence, essential services to mothers including childcare and lactation rooms for breastfeeding, support for women faculty and staff, and curricular and cocurricular programming (Marine, Helfrich, & Randhawa, 2017). Many women's centers are adopting more gender inclusive practices by intentionally welcoming people of all genders including men, and people who identify as trans*, genderqueer, and nonbinary. Some prefer the spelling of women as womyn or womxn to challenge the etymology that implies that a woman's identity is inherently reliant on a man (the term *woman* literally meaning "of man"). Choosing a different spelling of woman is one way to recognize that women, womyn, or womxn, have multiple identities and roles that are independent of their relationship to men.

There are questions about how women's centers can expand their services to a much wider audience, frequently without additional staffing and resources, while also maintaining core missions. Although most women's centers claim to be inclusive spaces, there are often questions about how inclusive they are in practice. As Marine and colleagues (2017) note:

> The erasure and silencing of many women within feminist movements, answered by the urgency of intersectional theory, renders any feminist project—such as women's centers and their daily operations—essential locations for examining the outcomes of theory to practice for whether they are truly inclusive of all women, even as they are opening their doors to those of other genders. (p. 48).

Women's centers serve a vital function on many campuses yet should also embrace taking a critical look at their own culture and operations.

Many campuses also have a wide variety of student organizations that focus on women, such as the college feminists, women in leadership, women in STEM, and other groups affiliated with national women's organizations. These groups offer important access for women to assume leadership roles and increase gender-based activism and advocacy on campus. When gender-based groups come together they can form a larger coalition to leverage resources and create more change on campuses.

Cultural Student Organizations and Sister Circles

Women of color have long been marginalized within mainstream feminist movements. Intersectionality theory suggests that feminists must understand the ways that women's differing social identities affect their opportunities and choices. How can women of color achieve equity within a social system that depends on subordination of some for the benefit of others (Collins, 2003; Crenshaw, 1991; Crenshaw, Gotanda, Peller, & Thomas, 1995)? One place women of color have found belonging on campus is in cultural student centers, organizations, and circles. Multicultural centers go by many names on campus and typically have stated missions to address diversity, equity, and inclusion and to center the experiences of students of color. At times, heterosexual and patriarchal norms can be replicated in multicultural offices and programs, leading women of color to seek spaces that recognize the intersections of both race and gender in students' experiences.

Spaces that center both race and gender, often called *sister circles*, are vital sources of support and belonging for many women of color. Croom, Beatty, Acker, and Butler (2017) note that

> similar to Black Greek-letter sororities, these spaces have been constructed through communities of Black womyn to respond to racist and sexist aliena-tion and isolation experienced within the larger campus community . . . [and] . . . these counter-spaces ostensibly serve as sites where students can not only engage in productive academic and social identity development processes, but also grapple with intersectional analyses of systemic oppression occurring in the context of their respective campus environments. (p. 217)

There is a need for more research exploring the leadership learning and development that occurs in these spaces.

Pride Centers

Similarly, women who identify as lesbian, gay, bisexual, transgender, queer, questioning, intersex, allies, asexual, or pansexual (LGBTQQIAAP) might seek out programming, resources, and support that center around their own experiences. Most pride centers are fluent in how students experi-ence intersectional aspects of their identities while on campus. The LGBT Center at Brown University (2018) offers the following statement of support:

> We recognize that sexual orientation and gender identity and expression work through and are influenced by race, ethnicity, gender, culture, age, disability, class, faith and other social characteristics. In keeping with the ideals of Brown University we commit to justice, equality, and respect for all persons in all of our endeavors.

Scholarship has shown that for LGBT students, LGBT student organiza-tions provide a supportive community that invites active exploration of their sexual identities (Hughes & Hurtado, 2018; Renn, 2007). Centers are also hubs for leadership development and campus activism, and serve as a place for people to interact with others of different sexual orientations (Hughes & Hurtado, 2018).

Sororities

Perhaps some of the longest standing women-only organizations on campus, the first Greek-letter sororities (or as they were first termed, *women's fraterni-ties*) were founded in the 1870s. Early sorority mission statements focused on academic support for women while maintaining Victorian ideals of womanhood by monitoring the social activities of their members (Turk, 2004). At this time, many other campus organizations like literary societies, student government, and other social clubs restricted membership to men. Twenty-six national sororities are members of the National Panhellenic Conference (NPC), which works to support the work of member chapters, especially as it relates to philanthropic work, recruitment, and alumnae development. NPC's (2019) website describes the activities of the modern sorority as "supporting victims of sexual assault, to leading bystander intervention programs, to fighting for body-positive campus cultures, sorority women are at the forefront of solving some of the most pressing challenges facing collegiate women today" (para. 1).

Black Greek-letter organizations evolved in the early 1900s to meet the needs of students of color. The National Pan-Hellenic Council (NPHC, 2019) is a collaborative organization of nine historically Black/African American fraternities and sororities. NPHC organizations work toward unanimity of thought and action as far as possible in the conduct of collegiate fraternities and sororities. The primary purpose of NPHC is camaraderie, academic excellence, and service to the community. Scholarship on the experience of women engaged in Black Greek-letter sororities shows that membership is correlated with productivity in the classroom (Turner, 2001) and leadership skills such as enhanced self-efficacy, civic engagement, character development, academic performance, and personal development (Benson & Saito, 2000). Many schools also have multicultural Greek councils that include Latinx sororities and other cultural organizations. The National Multicultural Greek Council (NMGC, 2019) is an umbrella council for a coalition of multicultural Greek-letter organizations established in 1998. The purpose of NMGC is to provide a forum that allows for the free exchange of ideas, programs, and services between its constituent fraternities and sororities; to promote the awareness of multicultural diversity within collegiate institutions, their surrounding communities, and the greater community-at-large; and to support and promote the works of its member organizations.

In some places, single-sex organizations on campus are being scrutinized. In 2016, as an effort to end the exclusionary nature of finals clubs and other male-dominated spaces, Harvard announced all campus-based organizations must be coeducational. Unfortunately, this ruling also applied to fraternities and sororities and has resulted in several lawsuits alleging discrimination (Field, 2018).

Women in Student Government and Sports

While frequently leading in other types of student organizations, women in leadership roles in student government are surprisingly rare. The American

Student Government Association (ASGA, 2019) estimates that about 40% of colleges, including community colleges, have female student body presidents. When you look at only top-ranked colleges and universities that number shrinks to only about one third having female student body presidents. Studies reveal that it is not because women are not receiving more votes than male candidates, but rather that women are not running in the first place (Lawless & Fox, 2013).

In their report *Girls Just Wanna Not Run*, Lawless and Fox (2013) suggest that women are less likely to be exposed to politics by their friends and family than men are, they receive less encouragement to run for student and political office, and they suffer from a lack of role models in campus and community leadership positions. A troubling related outcome of this finding is that holding student leadership positions is often the foundation for holding higher political offices. Of women currently serving in Congress, 53.7% had been involved in student government leadership in high school or college or both. Organizations such as Elect Her, are working to give more women the skills and opportunities to run for elective offices, both on campus and in communities.

One study (Zimmerman, 2017) looked at how women who run for student government president navigated the leadership labyrinth on campus. Results suggest that precollege and early college experiences are important for women. Specifically, the women in this study gained important leadership insights from competitive sports in high school and experiences with activism early in their college careers. Study participants discussed going through a process of validating their internal sense of self as a leader with others while navigating varying levels of confidence about their perceptions of themselves and external perceptions of them as leaders.

Chapter 3 addressed the importance of participation in women's sports teams as a precursor to leadership. The Lawless and Fox (2013) study revealed that men were significantly more likely than women to play sports in college and to have played sports when they were younger. Women were also roughly one-third less likely than men to self-assess as "very competitive" and to report that winning was "very important." The report states the following:

> Overall, our results suggest that playing organized sports either provides an opportunity to develop, or reinforces the propensity toward, a competitive spirit. These characteristics relate to running for elective office later in life, and this effect is evident in both female and male college students. Because men are still substantially more likely than women to play sports and to exude competitive traits, however, they are also far more likely to find themselves in a position to direct that competitive drive into politics. (p.11)

Kate identifies as a white, bisexual, middle-class, able-bodied, butch woman in her 20s. She describes the joys and challenges of being butch on and off-campus.

Narratives and Counternarratives: Kate's Story

I feel my gender most when someone else does not accurately recognize it. I can recall pretty much every time someone has mistaken me for a man. I am probably giving myself too much credit here—the "man" I unwittingly pass for has probably just had his bar mitzvah. I remember the first time an older man at a grocery store slid past me with an "Excuse me, young man." I was stoked, and then I felt guilty. Who was I to be going around passing for a man? The same privilege was not always afforded to the guy I was dating at the time. And in some ways that was my fault. We would be seated at restaurants with a "Right this way, ladies," trailing obediently behind the hostess. Carnies at Coney Island would call out to us, "Hey honey, win a bear for your girl!" My butchness reflected off him like sunlight off the moon—waiters, carnies, and passersby concluded that someone they had *thought* was a man must just be a very butch woman, holding hands with another butch. Never mind his beard.

Of course, when I wasn't around, he would pass just fine. I'm sure he does now that I am never around. I shared this story at a support group organized for trans women, but to which everyone was welcome. I found myself in that circle of hard plastic chairs after trying and failing to sign up to volunteer at an organization assisting transgender people with housing insecurity. The woman I talked to suggested I stay for the group downstairs, so I did. About an hour into the meeting, the group landed on the topic of passing, and one woman mentioned how the people you are with affect how you pass. I let a little bit of my guilty story slip out, and the group paused to consider this new perspective. Two of the women sitting nearest to me leaned over and grinned at me, admitting that they had assumed I was a trans man. I smiled about that for a long time. I do not always know how to explain that. One week later, a security camera recorded a man walking into that room, knocking a woman unconscious, and leaving. I never went back.

Sometimes being misgendered makes me angry. I took many, many deep breaths before responding to a student who asked me when I was going to "transition into a man," and I've spent hours in a huff after leaving restaurants that greeted me with a "sir." I am a woman, after all, whether womanhood wants me or not! Other times, though, I'm giddy with the feeling of being understood. Not entirely, of course, but my masculinity is so often overlooked or hidden out of necessity, that it's nice to see it reflected at me in one way or another. Besides, what is butcher than being mistaken for a man?

National Organizations Supporting Women on Campus

In addition to the aforementioned gendered spaces on campus, there is a wide variety of national women's organizations that sponsors campus chapters that focus on gender and leadership development. Table 5.2 includes some of these.

TABLE 5.2
National Organizations Supporting Women on Campus

Title	Resources
American Association of University Women (AAUW)	The AAUW was officially founded in 1881 and works to instill gender equity in academia. Its nationwide network encompasses 170,000 members (including students), 1,500 branches, and over 500 college and university partners. In addition to offering scholarships, it helps facilitate salary negotiations, campus leadership programs, STEM education advocacy, legal and public policy funding, and more.
American Council on Education (ACE) Women's Network	The ACE Women's Network facilitates the networking of women interested in pursuing leadership opportunities in higher education. A four-part structure—Network Executive Council, independent state-based networks with state chairs, presidential sponsors, and institutional representatives—fosters these connections; allows for sharing of best practices, particularly at the State Chairs Annual Conference; and enables local leadership training by the state networks.
Association for Women in Science (AWIS)	AWIS was founded in the 1970s and works to eliminate job discrimination, lower pay, and professional isolation for women working in the sciences. Over 20,000 members and chapters are part of the AWIS community.
Institute for Women's Policy Research (IWPR)	IWPR mostly concentrates on issues related to poverty, welfare, employment, earnings, health, and family. It collaborates with policymakers and public interest groups in its research and efforts to disseminate research findings; one of its most recent reports is titled "Mothers in College Have Declining Access to On-Campus Child Care" (IWPR, 2016).

(Continues)

Table 5.2 (*Continued*)

Title	Resources
National Coalition for Women and Girls in Education (NCWGE)	This coalition is a nonprofit partnership among over 50 groups dedicated to bettering the academic opportunities for women. It closely monitors public issues and legislation that concern women's equal rights, everything from athletics and pregnancy to technical and STEM education.
National Organization for Women (NOW)	The largest organization of feminist activists in the United States, NOW has 500,000 contributing members and 550 chapters in all 50 states and the District of Columbia. Since its founding in 1966, NOW's goal has been to take action to bring about equality for all women. Interested students can bring activism to their schools and colleges by starting campus NOW chapters and Campus Action Networks (CANs).
Academic Associations (partial list)	• American Medical Women's Association • Association for Women in Communications • Association for Women in Mathematics • Association for Women in Science • Association for Women in STEM • Financial Women's Association • Her Campus/ Journalism • Society of Women Engineers • Women Impacting Public Policy • Women in Tech

Moving From Feminine to Feminist Approaches to Leadership on Campus

Shea and Renn (2017) issue a call to action around gender and leadership on campuses. They describe how individuals, groups, and organizations may knowingly or unknowingly impose gendered notions upon leadership. They call for a shift from *feminine* to *feminist* leadership as a way of addressing larger social change. In reaction to early studies of women and leadership that examined how women lead organizations differently from men, it is important to not think, talk, and exercise leadership in these comparative and binary ways. There is a reason this book title refers to women *and* leadership, rather than women's ways of leading. When people talk about feminine leadership styles, they are reinforcing essentialist and heteronormative ways of being. This includes conversations about hierarchy versus collaboration, assertiveness versus nurturing, which reinforce binary thinking and can promote gendered approaches to leadership. In chapter 8, we will look deeper into the dangers of precarious pedestals and the ostracization that can occur if we try and promote a narrow version of what constitutes women's leadership. Instead, Shea and Renn suggest we shift from feminine to feminist ways of leading as ways to transform organizations while addressing pervasive sex and gender inequality. The authors also add, "Feminist leadership is both a philosophical stance and a way of leading that can be employed by any gender, including cisgender men" (p. 84).

Shea and Renn (2017) describe three interconnected tools of feminist leadership including using and subverting power structures, complicating difference, and enacting social change. First, feminist leaders use and subvert power structures primarily through counteracting powerlessness and fostering empowerment. As you engage in leadership on your campus, how are you speaking truth to power? That is, how are you naming and challenging oppressive structural power inherent in campus and organizational hierarchies? How do you work to balance power inequities by empowering others and seeking shared and reciprocal power? Shea and Renn remind women in leadership not to "shy away from power, but instead use it to their own advantages to create equity" (p. 87).

Second, feminist leaders complicate difference. This means troubling dualistic notions of both gender (man/woman) and leadership (leader/follower) where they arise. It means inviting intersectional approaches into the spaces where you exert leadership. Feminist leaders also understand that people practice different approaches to feminism and seek ways to cross boundaries and find commonalities among differences. Shea and Renn (2017) encourage us that "the ways in which feminist leaders complicate these gender binaries bring forth a more universally accessible style by leaders of any gender including men, trans* and genderqueer leaders, and women" (p. 87).

Third, feminist leaders enact social change. Feminist leadership must examine the linkages between women's liberation and other social change movements, and find ways to contribute. Shea and Renn (2017) state, "It is not enough to just talk about justice and equity; feminist leaders engage in advocacy and activism to counteract injustice" (p. 88). The remaining chapters of this book are designed to encourage this shift from feminine to feminist approaches to leadership. Chapter 9 examines diverse levers for social change and how to cultivate skills such as ally development, dealing with nonfeminist others, avoiding activist burnout, and maintaining critical hope.

TRIGGER WARNING: Please take note that the following story describes an incident of sexual assault. Readers are encouraged to make their own choices about when and how to engage with this powerful narrative and to seek campus and community resources if needed. This narrative is offered to demonstrate the wide-ranging and lasting effects of sexual violence on trust, confidence, and relationships.

Lynn identifies as an Asian American, cisgender, heterosexual, middle-class, college student.

Narratives and Counternarratives: Lynn's Story

At the age of 14 I learned what it meant to be a woman. I was a straight A student with multiple city championships in debate and a long list of friends. Out of the many friends I had, Sarah was the closest friend to me at the time. She was the kind of friend that I cherished enough to wear the cheap matching friendship necklaces with that would turn green after a few days. It was the summer before high school, and I couldn't wait for summer adventures with my best friend.

Sarah had her cousin spend the summer with her every year; however, I had never met him because I was never allowed to visit other friends' homes, as I grew up under a very strict ethnic household. Eventually I convinced my mother to let me visit Sarah's home, which is when I met her 19-year-old cousin Brad. I remember meeting him and instantly experiencing my first crush. He had the most striking green eyes and a smile that was a combination of mystery and warmth. At 14 I didn't know too much about boys, other than that they made gross jokes and did not always understand the concept of deodorant. I spent the summer with Sarah and Brad, always visiting her house and slowly but surely getting to know Brad. Eventually I started talking to Brad outside of Sarah's home, making the most of my first-generation iPhone. Each time he texted me my heart would skip a beat, each time he called I felt like I was literally going to faint. One day he told me I was cute.

Soon after, my parents went for a shopping trip to Costco, which would always take hours. I had always been allowed to have one friend over while my parents were gone, and so I had Brad over. I was a very innocent 14-year-old. I had never had "the talk" about the birds and the bees. I had never even had my first kiss since my dad scared me by telling me that if I ever kissed a guy, I would get these horrible and disgusting bumps on my lips. Looking back, I am shocked how well Dad's fiction worked on me. Anyway, Brad came over and we listened to pretty terrible music, but I pretended to like it because my crush was into it. I thought that we would just hang out, maybe even watch a movie.

This was the day my life would change. Listening to music turned into my first kiss. I remember thinking to myself "Okay this is not so bad." But then suddenly it was more than my first kiss, and I didn't know what was happening and I knew even less about what to do. What felt like butterflies from in my stomach turned into a hurricane of anxiousness. I pulled away because I was nervous and knew something was not right, but it was too late. It was like every conscious thought I had was 10 seconds too late. He pinned me down to my twin-sized bed. I gave up fighting and felt my work-out shorts slide down, and all I could think about were my little brothers playing video games in the next room. If I screamed, I feared he would hurt or scare them. Instead of screaming, I froze. I remember looking up into his eyes. The green eyes that used to feel familiar looked distant and wicked. The smile that was once filled with warmth disappeared and consumed me with anguish. I stared into those eyes for what felt like hours, but realistically was only a few minutes. By the time he was finished I felt nothing. When he left, he took more than just my innocence. He robbed me of my confidence, my joy, and my trust. I was 14 and felt numb.

When I look back at that day, I have so many regrets. I did not know what being a woman could entail. I did not know what to avoid or that wearing my old gym shorts would mean I was asking for it. I learned what it meant to be a woman in a matter of minutes. I learned that my kindness would be used against me and that my outfits would suggest that I wanted to be more than a friend. I learned that consent was always questionable and that my gender would define the types of relationships I would have. I learned that having sex as a woman (consensual or not) meant I would be looked at differently. My parents told me that having sex was an adult thing to do, and ever since they found out I had sex they treated me differently. They called me things I swear to never call another human being, and they accused me of things I would have never dreamed to do. To this day they still do not know about the assault. They think I was just a stupid girl who consented and made a mistake.

It has taken me a long time to learn to trust others. I had to relearn how to genuinely laugh and be passionate. Sometimes I forget how to feel, but I will always remember what hurt me the most. This experience was a pivotal moment for me because it led me to immerse myself in the importance of women's equality and autonomy ever since. This was the moment I wanted to become an advocate for myself and for other women.

6

WHAT DIFFERENCE DOES DIFFERENCE MAKE?

The Effects of Stereotypes, Prejudice, and Discrimination on Gender Representation and Leadership

You gain strength, courage, and confidence by every experience in which you really stop to look fear in the face. You must do the thing you think you cannot do.

—Eleanor Roosevelt, *You Learn by Living: Eleven Keys to a More Fulfilling Life*, 1960

Now that we have explored our own socialization to gender and leadership, let's take a broader look at the status of women today. This chapter describes the structural representation of women in various career fields. The term *structural diversity* refers to the number and proportional representation of various groups of people present in a given organization, system, or community. Scholars differentiate between structural diversity and the creation of inclusive and equitable climates. An organization might be high on representations of diverse kinds of people, yet still low on interactional diversity where people engage each other across difference and work to create a just, equitable, and inclusive place for all people. After presenting statistics about gender representation and leadership within each industry or section, the chapter goes on to look at potential contributing factors for underrepresentation. Where possible, organizations working to support women in these career sectors are included.

After examining the state of women's representation across various industries and sectors, this chapter will examine the effects of women's under- or nonrepresentation on various factors such as wages, promotions, and access to power and authority. Next it explores sources of the continued resistance to women in leadership, including the existence of stereotypes, prejudice, and discrimination. The psychological effects of discrimination on women are described as including stereotype threat, double standards and the double bind, and the development of implicit bias. The chapter concludes with recommendations about how to combat stereotypes, prejudice, and discrimination.

Where Are We Now? Women's Representation

Warning! What you are about to read is a very disheartening look at women's representation and status across diverse sectors and career fields predominantly in the United States. I wanted to label this section "the doom and gloom" outlook on women and careers. If you have yet to experience gender discrimination in your life, it may be because much of our educational experiences seem relatively equitable when compared to postcollege life. These numbers are not meant to discourage you or dampen your aspirations. Rather, it is important to understand why women remain underrepresented in leadership positions, the effects of this underrepresentation, and what strategies we can use to combat prejudice and discrimination. You will notice that many of the statistics cited refer to positional leadership roles. This is not to discount the many women influencing organizations in nonpositional ways (e.g., using their knowledge or referent power) but does represent one way to assess gender inclusiveness across industries. So, take a deep breath, and let's look at the status of women as we enter the 2020s.

Corporations and Entrepreneurs

A recent Pew Research Center (2018) report, *The Data on Women Leaders*, found that female CEOs of Fortune 500 Companies reached an all-time high of 6.7% in 2017 with 32 women heading major firms, yet this number fell to less than 5% in 2018 as several top women leaders resigned positions. The share of women sitting on the boards of Fortune 500 companies has risen from 9.6% in 1995 to 22.2% in 2017 (Pew, 2018). Across the globe, women hold less than 25% of senior management roles and that number appears to be declining, and in the United States, only 4% of executives in Standard & Poor's companies are women of color (Catalyst, 2018b). Catalyst, a research and think tank focused on women in the workplace, also lists the industries most lacking women among hires for leadership roles: manufacturing, energy and mining, software and IT services, finance, real estate, corporate services, and legal fields. The report indicates that many industries still suffer from a "think manager, think male" mindset, or that "women take care while men take charge." One report shockingly revealed that there are more men named John in top leadership positions, such as CEOs, than there are women holding those same roles (Miller, Quealy, & Sanger-Katz, 2018).

In the United States, women represent nearly half (46.9%) of the labor force but compose only slightly over one third (39.8%) of managers. This occurs even though women enroll in and graduate from college at a higher rate than men, as discussed in chapter 5. Of these woman managers, 33% are white women, followed by Latinas at 4.1%, Black women at 3.8%, and Asian American women at 2.4%. Women make up the highest share of managers in human resources occupations (70.8%) and social and community services (70.2%; Catalyst, 2018b).

The National Association of Women Business Owners (NAWBO) offers more hopeful statistics when looking at small independently owned businesses and women as entrepreneurs. They reported that there are now 11.6 million women-owned businesses in the United States and that these businesses employ nearly 9 million people and generate almost $1.7 trillion in revenue (NAWBO, 2018). Almost 40% of new entrepreneurs in the United States are women, yet other areas of the world like Latin America and the Caribbean have a higher ratio of female entrepreneurs to male entrepreneurs than North American countries. Of the technology startups in the United States in 2017, only 17% had a woman founder.

The reasons for this underrepresentation are numerous and will be explored in more detail in chapter 7 of this book. Reasons range from outright gender bias in hiring and promotions, to women being less likely to engage in self-promoting behaviors and less aggressive in salary negotiations, to work–family conflicts (Rhode, 2017). These issues are present across all employment sectors.

Government

The Center for American Women in Politics (CAWP) at Rutgers University provides current data and information about women's political participation in the United States, along with education, training, and scholarship. What follows is a snapshot from CAWP of women's representation in 2019. The midterm elections in November of 2018 saw a wave of women being elected to public office. Despite this "pink wave," after the election women only hold 25, or 25.0%, of the 100 seats in the Senate and 102, or 23.4%, of the 435 seats in the House of Representatives. Of these women, four senators and 43 representatives identify as women of color. Congresswoman Nancy Pelosi (D-CA), the first woman Speaker of the House, holds the highest position in the House and is second in the line of presidential succession. In state governance, 86 women hold statewide elective executive offices across the country, or 27.6% of the 312 available positions. These include 9 governors, 15 lieutenant governors, and 62 other elected officers. Among these women, 46 are Democrats, 38 are Republicans, and 2 are nonpartisan. Women constitute

28.6% of the 7,383 state legislators in the United States. Among the 100 largest cities in the United States, 23 had women mayors, including 7 African American women, 1 Latina, and 2 Asian American women (CAWP, 2019).

Despite former presidential candidate Mitt Romney's claim that he had "binders full of women" to choose from, as the numbers show, women are still underrepresented in political leadership. Deborah Rhode (2017) archly remarked that the goal is "to get women out of binders and into office" (p. 35). She notes that almost half of the states in the United States have yet to elect a woman governor or senator and that there has never been a female secretary of defense or secretary of treasury, two of the most powerful cabinet positions. Other countries have better representation of women in top leadership positions such as President Halimah Yacob of Singapore and President Sahle-Work Zewde of Ethiopia. It is especially important to have women in leadership in governmental sectors where policy is made, as their decisions are amplified to improve access and equity for all women. Rhode states:

> The problem is not performance. Researchers consistently find that when women run for office, they are just as effective in terms of fundraising and electability. They also receive the same amount of media coverage. Americans rate female candidates no worse than males, and in opinion surveys, women are rated equal to or better than men on seven of eight useful traits for politics. (p. 38)

What might account for women's underrepresentation, especially given that women constitute more than half of the voting public? Possible reasons include that women are less likely to be approached or to receive encouragement and training about running for office; they may be less confident and feel less competitive than male candidates; and women may still shoulder the bulk of family responsibilities that detract from the time it takes to campaign and govern. There also remain systemic issues such as sexism, double standards, and gender discrimination that affect women seeking elected roles both nationally and in local communities such as school boards and neighborhood associations. Organizations such as Elect Her and Emily's List work to give women the skills, resources, and confidence they need to enter and win elections.

Nonprofits and Higher Education

In the nonprofit sector, women hold only 20% of the leadership positions, yet constitute 75% of staffing positions (Rhode, 2017). Other sources report that, even when obtaining a nonprofit leadership position, women still make only 65% to 75% of what male nonprofit CEOs earn (GuideStar, 2017).

Reasons for this gap include spillover from corporate gender inequities, lack of diversity in nonprofits' boards and among hiring authorities, and salary compression (where there is little difference in pay between entry level and top positions) from women who have worked their way up through the ranks of a nonprofit (Alexander, 2017).

Women in academia face similar challenges. In 2016, 30.1% of university presidents were women (Pew, 2018). At top-ranked universities, women hold about 16% of provost and president positions (Rhode, 2017). Although a majority of college graduate and postgraduate students are women, only 25% of full professors are women (Rhode, 2017). This issue came to light recently when Donna Strickland was announced to be one of three women ever to be recipients of the Nobel Prize in Physics. Reporters were surprised to learn of her university rank as associate professor and questioned why she had not been named as full professor given her eminence. Strickland acknowledged that she had never applied for the title of full professor, but the situation raises important questions for the academy about the promotion pipeline for women faculty (Crowe, 2018). Faculty and upper-level administrators represent but a few of the women working on college campuses. Women disproportionately hold many of the service-oriented positions on campus such as housekeeping, food service, and even student affairs administration.

Women of color face additional pressures in campus roles. Edwards, Beverly, and Alexander-Snow (2011) report that faculty of color experience "questions about their place within the academy, cultural affronts to their personhoods, alienation, severe marginalization, and thus, pressure to prove continually that they deserve their positions" (p. 16). To support students of color, faculty and staff of color often take on disproportionate service roles including mentoring, organizational advising, and committee service, all while experiencing frequent microaggressions and inequity (Yamanaka, 2018). Overall, reasons for the gender gap in higher education include unconscious bias in hiring and promotion, a disproportionate service load falling on women educators, pipeline issues especially in STEM fields, and lack of mentoring.

Science and Health

Women account for about one third of all those employed in science-related fields according to a UNESCO Institute of Statistics fact sheet (UNESCO, 2017). And despite higher rates of female graduates for both undergraduate and graduate degrees in the United States, women still earn only one third of the PhDs in science-related fields. The STEM fields also happen to be fields where women are generally underrepresented. The U.S. Bureau of Labor

Statistics states that 3.2 million nurses (91%) are female and 330,000 (9%) are male (2018). In 2017, more women than men enrolled in U.S. medical schools for the first time, although overall women represent about 40% of doctors (Association of American Medical Colleges, 2017).

Ways to counteract the underrepresentation of women in STEM fields include getting girls interested in math and science. A host of gender-inclusive toys and television programs are being developed with this aim in mind. Goldieblox (2019), engineering kits designed with girls in mind, describes itself as a "disruptive children's media company challenging gender stereotypes with the world's first girl engineer character . . . offering tools that empower girls to build their confidence, dreams and ultimately, their futures" (para. 1). Savvy observers will notice that these engineering kits are still produced mainly in the colors pink and purple.

The AAUW offers suggestions for how colleges and universities can make STEM programs more inviting and accessible to women, including ensuring students have access to female faculty and mentors, updating course curricula to include inclusive readings and examples, and intentionally and actively recruiting women into STEM majors (2015).

Military

A 2017 Pew Report on women in the U. S. military reveals that the active duty force remains male dominated, but that women have made substantial inroads in recent decades. Pew reports that 15% of active-duty military personnel are women, up from 11% in 1990. In 2015, 17% of active-duty officers were female as compared to 12% in 1990, and 15% of enlisted personnel were female in 2015, up from 11% in 1990. The share of women in the ranks varies significantly by service branch. Women constitute nearly one in five active-duty personnel in the Air Force (19%) but only 8% of all Marines. Women make up 18% of the Navy and 14% of the Army. At the time I am writing this, the Supreme Court has effectively reversed a 2016 decision by the Obama administration to open the military to transgender service members. Other nations, especially those with mandatory military service, have more gender equity in their forces.

It has only been since 2016 that all positions in the military, including combat, are open to women. That said, some units such as the Special Forces require people to pass extraordinary physical tests. Women have served in intelligence gathering, as combat pilots, field artillery officers, special operations civil affairs officers, and even in the ultra-secretive Delta Force. In 2015, three women graduated from the Army Ranger School, the Army's premier leadership course. Two women have received the nation's third-highest honor, the Silver Star, since World War II.

Women in the military are far more likely than civilians to experience sexual violence and may be less likely to report assaults given the male-dominated military justice system. The Battered Women's Justice Project (2019) states that nearly 25% of women veterans who seek health care services from the Department of Veterans Affairs report experiencing at least one sexual assault while in the military compared to slightly more than 1% of male veterans. Women who enter the military at younger ages, those of enlisted rank, and those who experienced sexual assault prior to entering the military appear to be at increased risk of sexual assault while in the military. Survivors often experience mental health issues such as post-traumatic stress disorder, other anxiety disorders, depression, and substance abuse, all of which can lead to unemployment, homelessness, disruption of interpersonal relationships, further victimization, physical problems, and suicide.

Athletics

A recent article about gender equity in sports described how gender discrimination has existed since the inception of the very concept of "sports" (Pavlovich, 2017). In 1896, the founder of the modern Olympics, Baron Pierre de Coubertin, was quoted as saying "No matter how toughened a sportswoman may be, her organism is not cut out to sustain certain shocks" (Pavlovich, 2017, para. 3). Even today, the statistics are daunting. About 40% of professional athletes in the U.S. are women, yet they receive less than 8% of all sports media coverage. Hope Solo, long time goalkeeper for the U.S. Olympic team, notes how, despite the U.S. women's soccer team having won four World Cup championships and four Olympic championships, female professional soccer players still get paid significantly less than those on the men's professional team, which has a much more dismal record of wins.

The Women's Sports Foundation (2019) details how this discrepancy starts in collegiate athletics where male athletes get $179 million more in athletic scholarships each year than females. Additionally, collegiate institutions spend just 24% of their athletic operating budgets on women's sports, as well as just 16% of recruiting budgets and 33% of scholarship budgets on women athletes. Coaches in women's sports at the college level receive only 63% of the salaries of coaches of men's teams (Pavlovich, 2017). Title IX of the Education Amendments of 1972 attempts to level the playing field. Before Title IX, women were 2% of the college students participating in sports, and recent data indicate that 43% of the college students participating in sports are now women (www.ncwge.org). We will look more deeply at recent challenges to Title IX in chapter 7.

Other Fields

The previously mentioned fields are just a few in which women struggle for representation and equality. It is no surprise that men outnumber women in fields that have historically been more physical in nature such as the use and maintenance of heavy machinery, carpentry, electrical work, and construction, but other fields are perhaps more surprising. Only 16% of architects are women (Catalyst, 2018a). According to the American Bar Association, just 35% of lawyers were women in 2015, though nearly half of all law students are women. The United States Bureau of Labor Statistics (2018) reports that less than 20% of head chefs are women, though women make up the majority of food service professionals. Only 6% of commercial pilots are women. Of the top 600 highest earning comedians, less than 100 are women, and the same holds true in comedy writing (Feeny, 2013).

The research organization and think tank Catalyst describes how many of the occupations where women are underrepresented such as law, medicine, and aviation are those that pay very well. Further, 50 years of census data reveal that when women enter male-dominated fields, the overall pay rate declines (Miller, 2016). There is little to no data about transgender and other individuals who identify as nonbinary, but the assumption is they face similar issues in the workplace. Women working in a male-dominated field also are subject to more workplace sexual harassment (67%) than those working in female-dominated professions (47%) (Pew, 2018).

Elizabeth, who identifies as a white, cisgender, heterosexual, lower-middle-class, Catholic female, discusses how gendered stereotypes are affecting her search for sponsorships as a professional athlete.

Narratives and Counternarratives: Elizabeth's Story

Even after the passage of Title IX, there is still a stigma associated with women participating in sports. I spent my entire life fighting that stigma, fighting the sexism, and fighting for recognition as a female in the very "manly" sport of throwing discus. I tried to educate people that female throwers could be feminine and beautiful. Growing up around track and field events, I got picked on a bit, and I am sure being a successful thrower kept me from a few dates. None of that seemed to matter though, as I had one goal in mind and that was to become a professional discus thrower.

After about 14 years of discus throwing, my collegiate career was coming to an end, and that meant I would have to transition into my professional career, which entailed getting sponsors to pay for what either my parents or school had paid for most of my life. Track and field aren't like basketball or football. There is no draft or combine where a team picks you and then signs you for a multimillion-dollar contract and then you start training. In track, you have to train hard and perform well and hope someone notices and wants you to wear their brand. Some sponsorships are big, most are not. Often track athletes, especially in lower-profile events like women's discus, have to get multiple sponsorships just to make ends meet.

One day I was addressing the concern of sponsorships and how I would make ends meet with a former teammate who had been on the professional circuit a bit. She told me, "You're lucky that you are a pretty girl in a manly event, sponsors love girls that look good in their gear. Just wear some makeup and maybe even some fake eyelashes and you'll get sponsor deals for sure." At first, I took it as a compliment—who doesn't like being called pretty? But then reality set in. My looks shouldn't have anything to do with my sponsorship, my skill and performance should. Also, why should I have to change the way I compete just to get sponsors? I did not want to be a sellout, but I also need to be able to pay my rent. I have spent my entire life fighting the idea that throwers have to be manly and that I could still be feminine looking and a successful thrower. Now that I have been accepted by the sport, I feel wrong profiting from being a more feminine-looking athlete. I am facing a moral dilemma about whether to take money based on my looks instead of my talents, or to not be a sponsored professional athlete.

What Results From Nonrepresentation?

Are you disillusioned yet? I know the last section was hard to read, yet it is important to understand the status of women's representation across sectors and industries. Yes, some of these discrepancies are the product of women's choices (more on that in chapter 7), yet it is imperative to consider the pervasive, cultural, and systemic forces that constrain women's advancement. The following sections look at the implications of inequality in the workforce.

Gender Wage Gap

Even when women are represented in various fields, data consistently show a gender wage gap. This gap is typically reported as referring to the median annual pay of all women who are full-time, year-round workers compared to the pay of a similar cohort of men. As shown in Exercise 6.1, depending on the research you read or the radio, podcasts, and news sources you subscribe to, you may have heard a wide variety of opinions on whether or not the wage gap really exists. Some estimates of the gender pay gap are taken from

Exercise 6.1.
Take a Closer Look at the Gender Pay Gap

Find someone interested in exploring the gender pay gap with you. One of you might peruse the websites and resources that claim the gender pay gap persists today. These are worthy places to start:

- www.aauw.org/research/the-simple-truth-about-the -gender-pay-gap/
- www.pewresearch.org/fact-tank/2016/07/01/racial -gender-wage-gaps-persist-in-u-s-despite-some-progress/

Another person might search the web for legitimate news sources that argue the gender pay gap does not exist. Here are two:

- www.forbes.com/sites/karinagness/2016/04/12/ dont-buy-into-the-gender-pay-gap-myth/#3d820664766a
- http://time.com/3222543/wage-pay-gap-myth-feminism/

After sharing your information from your various sources, you both might investigate sources that attempt to explain the complexity of the debate. Here are a few:

- http://freakonomics.com/podcast/the-true-story-of-the-gender -pay-gap-a-new-freakonomics-radio-podcast/
- www.theatlantic.com/business/archive/2016/07/ paygap-discrimination/492965/
- http://harvardmagazine.com/2016/05/reassessing-the-gender -wage-gap

Think about how easy it was to find information that supports your original point of view. How hard was it to discern the data and methodologies used by these sources to ground their claims (assuming they actually were referring to data trends)? Try listing the various factors that affect how people come to their claim that the wage gap does or does not exist. Hopefully, even if your opinion did not change from your original stance, you have a much more complex understanding of the reasons why people argue various sides of this debate. What action might you take to share this information with others?

hourly or weekly pay rates or look at specific employment fields. Others take part-time work into account. Chen (2011) considers pay equity to be a fundamental human right.

The AAUW (2017) notes that

> the gender pay gap is the result of many factors, including occupational segregation, bias against working mothers, and direct pay discrimination. Additionally, such things as racial bias, disability, access to education, and age come into play. Consequently, different groups of women experience very different gaps in pay. (para. 6)

Estimates of just how big the gap is in 2019 vary from sources reporting no wage differences by sex, to women earning just 77% of what men earn across industries. Recent census data show women earning approximately 81% of what men earn; the median income for women is $41,554, while for men it is $51,640 (United States Census Bureau, 2019).

There are a variety of factors that influence how researchers measure the wage gap. Regardless of how it is measured, scholars tend to agree on a few trends across different data sets.

1. The wage gap has been narrowing in the last four decades, so that women now earn closer to what men earn. Horrific stories abound about wage discrimination in the 1950s and 1960s where women were paid less based on the assumption that they did not have to support a household like men do. A recent *Washington Post* op-ed noted that one reason the pay gap has recently narrowed is not necessarily because women are being paid more, but that earnings for men are falling due to a reduction in manufacturing jobs and the decline of organized labor (Stein, 2018). Overall median household income has steadily risen over the past 10 years, but researchers credit this to more people from each household being active in the labor market. So, the wage gap is shrinking, but has yet to be eliminated in most occupational fields.

2. The wage gap is bigger for most women of color. Women who identify as Latina earn only 53% of what men earn across occupations. American Indian or Alaskan Natives earn just 58%, and Black or African American women earn 61% of what men earn. White women earn closer to 77% of men, and Asian Pacific Islander women earn 85% of what men earn (AAUW, 2017). These gaps persist even when taking higher education and advanced degrees into account (Pew, 2016).

3. The wage gap has less to do with differences between occupations (e.g., women occupying lower-paying jobs like teaching, nursing, and social

work) and much more to do with differences within occupations (Miller, 2014). The prime example of this is women doctors and surgeons who earn just 71% of what their male counterparts earn. This within-occupation gap could be due to employers who tend to reward those who work longer hours and who spend more time on call or at the office, which may be harder for people who need flexibility in work hours and locations to accommodate childcare and other household responsibilities. It could be that the biggest way to shrink the wage gap is to offer temporal flexibility, or allowing workers to do their own work on their own time, and technology may be helping make that happen.

4. There are a wide variety of causes of the wage gap (Women Are Getting Even, 2019). These include sex discrimination in hiring, pay negotiation, and fair pay. Numerous experiments reveal gender discrimination in hiring. In a 2012 study, employers were given two identical resumes, one with a stereotypically female name attached and the other with a stereotypically male name. The resume of the supposed male was rated as more competent and hirable than when the same resume had a female name attached, and the recommended starting salary for the male was $4,000 higher (Rhode, 2014). Others note that sexual harassment and workplace bias contribute to wage discrimination as women leave or lose jobs, or even the ability to work. Motherhood does seem to affect promotion pipelines and wages lost from off-ramping and on-ramping due to parental leave and sexist assumptions about the commitment of working mothers. Other factors include cultural norms and expectations, work–family balance, age, and experience. One recent study found that, for those born in the United States, the region where you are born has a persistent effect on your wages and lifelong earnings, even when taking race into account (Rhode, 2014). Researchers found that sexist attitudes are most prevalent in the southeast and least prevalent on the west coast, with a variety of attitudes in the Midwest.

You may have read about actress Jennifer Lawrence learning through a series of Sony e-mail hacks just how much less she received on the 2013 movie *American Hustle* than her male counterparts. She had the following reaction:

When the Sony hack happened and I found out how much less I was being paid than the lucky people with dicks, I didn't get mad at Sony. I got mad at myself. I failed as a negotiator because I gave up early. I didn't want to keep fighting over millions of dollars that, frankly, due to two franchises, I don't need. (I told you it wasn't relatable, don't hate me.) But if I'm honest with myself, I would be lying if I didn't say there was an element of wanting to be liked that influenced my decision to close the deal without a real fight. I didn't want to seem "difficult" or "spoiled." At the time, that seemed like a fine idea, until I saw the payroll on the Internet and realized every man I was working with definitely didn't worry about being "difficult" or "spoiled.". . . . But this is an element of my personality that I've been working against for years, and based on the statistics, I don't think I'm the only woman with this issue. Are we socially conditioned to behave this way? (Lam, 2015, para. 2)

In chapter 7 we will explore the tension between women overcoming social conditioning by learning to be more effective negotiators and overcoming resistance in male-dominated spaces, and the need to address blatant systemic sexism and racism that account for many of these discrepancies.

Explicit Sexism

We would like to think that outright discrimination is a thing of the past when it comes to gender in the workplace. To some extent, there has been improvement around the blatant, hostile sexism of the 1950s and 1960s when women who transgressed the typical division of labor by trying to enter the workforce were faced with outright hostility, exclusion, and verbal, emotional, and physical harassment. Despite women's necessary presence in the labor force during World War II, when GIs returned home it was viewed as unpatriotic for women to hold on to jobs that could go to returning veterans. In fact, women who sought work were thought to have questionable morals or to be destitute (Guy & Fenley, 2014). In the early 1960s, only one in six women worked outside the home, and those who worked were typically of lower socioeconomic status. Stories of groundbreaking women who were among the first or only to integrate particular career fields are much loved in Hollywood. Check out, among many others, *The Crown, Frida, Hidden Figures, A League of Their Own, Mad Men, The Marvelous Mrs. Maisel, On the Basis of Sex,* and *Whale Rider.*

Gendered stereotypes persist. As Eagly and Carli (2007) explain,

The inequalities that individual men and women commonly experience are transformed into widely shared beliefs, not merely in men's greater status and power but also in their greater know-how and ability. Once people have associated men with high status and women with low status, men more readily exercise influence over women in new encounters, even outside of workplaces, and women more readily accept this influence. (p. 88)

Even today, explicit, hostile sexism exists in workplaces, especially when women's representation does not exceed token levels. Rhode (2014) notes

"Despite recent progress, women, particularly racial and ethnic minorities, often lack the presumption of competence enjoyed by white men and need to work harder to achieve the same results" (p. 28). Commonplace examples of overt sexism include

- comments on outfits or appearance;
- losing promotions and other opportunities when pregnant, or being asked in interviews if and when one plans to have a family;
- double standards such as women being called bitchy for being assertive, while men exhibiting the same behavior are rewarded for showing initiative;
- being assigned stereotypical tasks (e.g., taking minutes at meetings or being asked to plan the office party);
- constantly being interrupted or mansplained; and
- unwelcome sexual advances, requests for sexual favors, or other verbal or physical assaults.

The Double Bind, Stereotype Threat, and Internalized Oppression

Partly as a result of underrepresentation and inequality, women in leadership may face conflicting expectations about how they should function in the workplace. The dominant stereotypical narrative is that women should be helpful, warm, and friendly, often called "communal" qualities. Women are collaborators who do not promote or display individual accomplishments. This "story most often told" is in direct contrast with the stereotypes of effective leaders. Effective leaders are expected to be "direct and assertive, exhibit confidence and competence, and exert influence over others," often called agentic qualities (Eagly & Carli, 2007, p. 102). While not the only way to approach leadership, this set of characteristics is often referred to as agency, or the abilities to get things done.

The *double bind* occurs when the expectations that women be communal and collaborative clash with the expectations that leaders be agentic. When women encounter people in the workplace, they likely encounter differing sets of expectations about the appropriate balance between communal and agentic attributes. The result of these differing expectations may show up as resistance to women in leadership. Eagly and Carli (2007) describe these processes:

> Because of the double bind, people may resist a woman's influence, particularly in masculine settings. Sometimes they resist because they think she lacks communion, so they don't like her. Sometimes they resist because they think she lacks competence, so they don't respect her. (p. 102)

The resistance ascribed to women with other marginalized identities (e.g., women of color, or of certain faith traditions or sexual orientations) is often even worse. These women often face a triple bind—where stereotypical views of their multiple targeted identities can lead to further marginalization. For more on intersectionality, visit chapter 3.

A real-world example may help elucidate the double bind. Whatever you think about the politics of Hillary Clinton, she is a notable exemplar of the tension between being communal and agentic. When she first ran for president in 2008 many of her speeches and campaigning focused on her knowledge and prior experience in government—her work on gender equity and universal health care in the 1990s, her achievements as first lady and then as a U.S. senator for New York. She emphasized her agency or ability to get things done. When reporters asked how she might be a nontraditional first lady in 1992, Clinton said, "I suppose I could have stayed home and baked cookies and had teas, but what I decided to do was to fulfill my profession, which I entered before my husband was in public life" (Chozik, 2016). There was a strong backlash in the press and from many community groups that Clinton did not appear as warm and caring as people expected. There were some half-hearted attempts by her press team to humanize her to the electorate—having her share family cookie recipes in *Family Circle* magazine to try to make her seem more feminine and approachable. In the eyes of the world, she was failing at successfully navigating the double bind. By her second attempt to run for president in 2016, although she had added to her list of accomplishments by serving as secretary of state from 2009 to 2013 under President Obama, she focused far less on touting her achievements in the second campaign. She frequently talked about her fondness for her family and her love for her grandchildren. She threaded the needle of the double bind by trying to appear both competent and caring. Despite strong challenges by other Democrats, Clinton successfully secured her party's nomination for president of the United States in July 2016, becoming the first female candidate to be nominated for president by a major political party. Nevertheless, she continued to experience sexism, as when people pushed back at the idea of having a woman serve as commander in chief of the U.S. military (Palmieri, 2018).

In addition to the double bind, women may also experience *internalized oppression*, where one begins to believe at some level the sexist assumptions that pervade the culture around them. The effects of gender-based stereotypes continue to permeate perceptions of women's ability to lead throughout organizations. Internalized oppression may show up when someone asks for a volunteer to take notes at a meeting and you raise your hand since you are always asked to be the recorder in any group situation. It may show up in your speech when you say "I may be wrong but . . . " and undercut your own argument before you even make it. Rhode (2014) terms this phenomenon a *psychological glass ceiling* where women internalize negative gender stereotypes about women and are thus hesitant to do anything that makes them seem too pushy, assertive, or difficult.

Internalized oppression can operate in insidious ways, especially if you hold identities from multiple historically marginalized groups. *Stereotype threat* is the apprehension about confirming an unfavorable stereotype about a group to which you belong (Hoyt & Murphy, 2016). For me, this shows up especially strongly when it comes to my regulation of my emotions at work. I recall an incident with a male supervisor where I was so angry at the injustice of a particular situation that I burst into tears. The supervisor's conditioned response to my display of emotion was to try and comfort and appease me, saying things like "Don't feel bad about this, it is not your fault." My reaction was immediate. I told him, "I am not sad or feeling badly or taking any blame for this. These are tears of anger." I left feeling so mad at myself for exhibiting a gender stereotype that women are emotional and need placating, when in fact I was pissed!

As Carli and Eagly (2007) wisely note, "The challenge for female leaders is further complicated by the fact that gender stereotypes are not merely descriptive, but prescriptive as well" (p. 128). This situation is also an example of *benevolent sexism*, where a person thinks they are operating from a place of caring and understanding, but they are actually perpetuating sexist attitudes, beliefs, and behaviors (Glick & Fiske, 1996, 2001). Benevolent sexism refers to a more understated type of prejudice in which women are stereotyped as affectionate, delicate, and sensitive. Those who hold benevolent sexist beliefs conceptualize women as weak individuals who need to be protected and provided for (Glick & Fiske, 1996). Although these traits and attitudes seem to encompass behaviors that favor women, research has shown that benevolent sexism is just as oppressive as hostile or explicit sexism (Glick & Fiske, 2001).

Implicit Bias

Implicit bias refers to the way people unconsciously and often unwillingly exhibit bias toward others. These hidden biases are rooted in various aspects of our life but should not be mistaken for conscious or explicit bias (as in the discussion of explicit sexism earlier in this chapter) and preferential treatment that is generally prohibited in many laws and cultures. Studies on implicit bias have found that institutions such as education, the judicial system, and health care are influenced by these unconscious biases and attitudes (Adams et al., 2013).

Implicit bias exists because we are surrounded by pervasive gendered assumptions from the moment we enter the world, and some would say even before then. Because of the ways our brains operate, these biases shape our perception such that we look for information to confirm our previously held beliefs and discount information that contradicts those assumptions, a process called confirmation bias (Kahneman, 2011). If women are in turn offered fewer opportunities because of implicit bias, a cycle of self-fulfilling prophecy may be established (Rhode, 2014) with the result being that women are prevented from "developing the social capital and sponsorship necessary for success in many workplace contexts" (p. 30).

One of the most commonly used inventories for testing implicit bias is the Implicit Association Test or IAT (Greenwald, McGhee, & Schwartz, 1998), which claims to reveal the strength of unconscious associations people make in their minds. These associations could be relatively benign (e.g., associating candy with happiness, or snakes with fear) or may have significant implications (like associating women as passive, or older people with incompetence). If you have never taken any of these assessments, as listed in Box 6.1, you might visit https://implicit.harvard.edu/implicit/ to take a free test. Taking the IAT typically involves the test taker being shown a series of words or images (e.g., images of men or women) and measuring the time lapse between seeing an image and clicking on positive or negative words (e.g., *leader, caring, assertive*, etc.) associated with that image. The program measures the delay in reflex response time, which indicates the amount of cognitive processing involved in trying to overcome implicit thinking. The longer the response time, the more significant implicit bias you may be working to avoid. Test takers receive feedback at the end of the test about whether their implicit biases are slight, moderate, or strong.

The IAT was embraced by many different groups as a way to potentially measure unconscious bias. Companies such as Facebook, Google, and Starbucks regularly use the IAT and train employees in uncovering implicit biases. The test has also been used with juries, police officers, teachers, and universities, yet there are emerging critiques of the science behind the test (Kaufman, 2011; Lopez, 2017). A thorough review of the test psychometrics is beyond the scope of this chapter, but users should take a moment to review the limitations of these kinds of measures. Critiques center around how individual results may vary if you take the test multiple times (e.g., in full disclosure, I scored as slightly biased against women in the Gender-Career test the first time I took it, and no significant bias the second time), and that results are best viewed in the aggregate after multiple times taking the same test in many varied contexts. The test creators agree that factors such as mood, environment, and social desirability (e.g., a desire not to be seen as sexist) may influence the results. Another major critique is that there seems to be little correlation between IAT results and actual behaviors (Kaufman, 2011).

Box 6.1.
Available Implicit Association Tests

Age

Arab-Muslim

Asian

Disability

Gender-Career

Gender-Science

Native

Presidents

Race

Religion

Weight

Sexuality

Skin-tone

Weapon

Source: https://implicit.harvard.edu/implicit/

The AAUW commissioned the creation of an IAT tool to measure implicit associations about women and leadership. Findings revealed that even women who identified as feminist had a slight tendency to more quickly associate leadership with men than with women (2016c). Those who self-identified as nonfeminists and men showed greater bias, leading AAUW to conclude "Our implicit biases can hurt others, but they can also work against our own identities, sincerely held beliefs, or even our careers" (2016c, para. 2). You can read more about the results in AAUW's (2016a) research report *Barriers and Bias: The Status of Women in Leadership* and by following their social media hashtag #leadHERship.

How to Counteract Implicit Bias

Regardless of your IAT scores, or your beliefs about whether implicit bias can actually be measured, it stands to reason that we are products of the world we inhabit. We receive messages about what is good or bad from friends and family, religion, education, media, and work, leading each of us to have implicit biases and assumptions. A 2016 AAUW article details ways we can counteract our implicit biases, starting with becoming aware they exist and working to change them. Individuals can guard against bias in the following ways:

- When assessing the behavior or performance of someone from an historically marginalized group, try to focus on concrete specific factors of what actually happened, rather than relying on your gut feelings.
- Notice when your responses, decisions, or behaviors might have been caused by bias or stereotypes, and make an intention to think positive thoughts when encountering those individuals or other members of stigmatized groups in the future.
- Imagine, in detail, people who violate expected stereotypes in a positive way and practice thinking about these positive examples. Thinking about these people may help make these counterstereotypic examples pop up in your mind in the future.
- Make an effort to assess and think about members of stereotyped groups as individuals. Recall their individual traits and how they differ from stereotypic expectations. (AAUW, 2016c, paras. 4–8)

What Can We Do About Stereotypes, Prejudice, and Discrimination?

Beyond personal efforts to counteract implicit bias, stereotype threat, and the double bind, what can organizations and systems do to counteract the effects of stereotypes, prejudice, and discrimination on women in leadership? Employers and organizations can take specific steps to create more equitable and just workplaces. Laws and policies can be created that offer legal protections to those facing discrimination. Activism and social movements work to bring attention to issues that laws and policy have failed to address.

Employers and Organizations

Employers and organizations should work toward creating equitable workplace cultures. This involves gender equity in hiring and recruitment, pay and promotions, and workforce training on overcoming implicit and explicit biases. Symphonies and orchestras across the world have started conducting blind auditions where performers are heard but not seen, resulting in a dramatic increase in the number of women hired as professional musicians (Goldin & Rouse, 2000). A tech company called Salesforce, which employs

30,000 people and is valued at over $10 billion, researched gender pay inequity of their own employees. When they learned that more than 10% of female employees made significantly less than male counterparts in similar jobs, they gave pay raises to create equity even though it cost the company millions of dollars a year. Salesforce also learned that they were promoting women every 30 to 36 months into the same kind of jobs as they were promoting men every 18 to 24 months, and that when men had children, their earnings went up 6%, but when women had children, their earnings decreased 4% with each child, likely due to unconscious bias that mothers are less committed to the workplace. This commitment to creating gender equity led to Salesforce being ranked by *Fortune* magazine as the number one place to work among large companies (CBS News, 2018).

Chapter 7 will explore in more detail the kinds of organizational innovations that are shown to create a level playing field and include changes to recruitment, flexible work options, rethinking evaluations and rewards, and using data from institutional assessments to inform policies and decisions.

Laws and Policies

In 1963 the Equal Pay Act was passed; it stated that men and women who perform jobs of "equal skill, effort, and responsibility, and which are performed under similar working conditions" cannot be differently compensated (United States Equal Employment Opportunity Commission, 2019). Pay differentials are permitted when they are based on seniority, merit, quantity or quality of production, or a factor other than sex. In correcting a pay differential, the pay of the lower paid employee must be increased, rather than allowing employers to reduce the pay of those with higher salaries.

The following year, the Civil Rights Act of 1964 prohibited discrimination on the basis of race, origin, color, religion, or sex. Other legislation was initiated to offer protection to working women. Passed in 1978, the Pregnancy Discrimination Act protected pregnant employees, although it was not until the passage of the Family and Medical Leave Act in 1991 that parents were guaranteed the right to take time off regardless of gender. In 2009, one of President Obama's first pieces of legislation was the Lilly Ledbetter Fair Pay Act, which restores some protections against discrimination that had been stripped in a 2007 Supreme Court case and incentivizes employers to make their payrolls more equitable (Alter, 2015).

Progress is still slow. In 2014, the Paycheck Fairness Act, a bill that would have made it illegal for employers to retaliate against employees who discuss their wages failed in the Senate. The Equal Rights Amendment, passed by Congress in the 1970s, still has not been approved by enough states to become ratified. Sex discrimination cases remain notoriously difficult to win. One depressing statistic is that less than 20% of sex and race discrimination acts filed with the Equal Employment Opportunity Commission resulted in outcomes favorable to the complainant (Rhode, 2017).

Activism and Movements

There are also a number of grassroots movements seeking to elucidate sexism, inequity, and gender oppression in the workplace. The #MeToo movement began when activist Tarana Burke started using the phrase in 2006 to encourage women of color who were victims of sexual harassment to share their stories to develop empathy, empowerment, and community. After the Harvey Weinstein scandal in 2017, a number of high-profile celebrities embraced the cause and shared their own experiences with sexual harassment and assault on social media with the goal of raising awareness of the rampant nature of the problem. The movement was adapted by various groups to show the diverse nature of sexual harassment including across sectors and disciplines #metoomiltary, #astroSH (astronomony); across countries #moiaussi (Canada); #YoTambién (Spain); and my personal favorite, the French movement #balanceTonPorc, which translates to "expose your pig"; and across genders #himtoo, although the movement has been slower to include the experiences of transgender and nonbinary individuals.

The 16 Days of Activism Against Gender-Based Violence is an international campaign coordinated by the Center for Women's Global Leadership and used by activists around the world as an organizing strategy to call for the elimination of all forms of gender-based violence, including workplace violence (Sixteen Days Campaign, 2019). Started in 1991, 16 Days takes place every year between November 25 and December 10 and is run by over 6,000 organizations in 187 countries, making it one of the largest transnational equity initiatives. Part of this movement's goal is to connect feminist movements with unions and labor organizations who have long been advocating for workplace equity and inclusion. They also take a special interest in domestic labor such as housekeeping where women are especially vulnerable and often come from migrant backgrounds or lack legal status.

This chapter examines the effects of stereotypes, prejudice, and discrimination on women's leadership.

Rosemary's story shows how the intersections of gender and culture shape expectations and experience and what happens when one resists. Rosemary identifies as a Latina, cisgender, working-class, young, Christian female.

Narratives and Counter Narratives: Rosemary's Story

It was a daily routine at my household. My father would come home exhausted and impatient after a long day of menial labor. He demanded his daughters serve him food. My sisters and I would immediately respond in obedience just as my mother taught us. I stood near the stovetop, preparing dinner as always. My head hung low as my father raged, reminding me that my role as a daughter was to serve him with no hesitation. My uncle, who sat right next to him at the dinner table, drunkenly laughed and agreed. I felt hopelessly trapped as I silently continued to flip the tortillas. I could not understand why my mother allowed my father to blindly believe the idea of masculine dominance.

My father's Salvadorian culture engrained a strong belief of machismo in my household, and this limited me in several ways. It restricted me from having friends, doing extracurricular activities at school, and having a normal teenage girl's life. My mother constantly nagged about the unfair mistreatment she endured because of my father's strong and aggressive masculine pride. Despite it all, I was taught in my household that my role, along with my sisters, was to clean and cook for the men at home. My mother unknowingly fueled this belief as she lectured me saying "What will your husband say if you can't properly cook or clean?" I became angry at my mother. However, I did not realize until later that my mother was not in a position to defend herself or her daughters. She was trapped in the same position I was. My father's machismo and use of control restrained my mother from finishing her education and from working. What good is an education if you were meant to serve? My father tried to discourage my sisters and me from pursing an education but I never once believed in his absurd way of thinking. I did not want to accept this notion of masculine dominance for my own future.

Yet unexpectedly, my mother found the courage to leave my father after 25 years of marriage. It left my father broken, but it forced him to shift his narrow-minded perspective. The women he controlled for years had rejected his final demand. The separation required my father to raise three daughters on his own, which consequently restored our relationships. Most importantly, the fear instilled in me by my father faded as the power dynamics in my household were eradicated.

NAVIGATING
ORGANIZATIONS
AND SYSTEMS

Metaphors for Women in Leadership

Success isn't about how much money you make; it's about the difference you make in people's lives.

—Michelle Obama, Speech at the Democratic National Convention, 2012

M̲ost books addressing the barriers facing women in leadership devote much of their space to how women climb the corporate ladder. This chapter summarizes some of the pivotal research on women and career attainment and seeks to make a larger statement about the joys and challenges of leadership. Not every person's leadership journey is limited to the world of work and careers. Many of the obstacles described in this chapter also exist for women navigating community organizing and involvement, those raising families, and people with dedicated avocations. Additionally, much of the research on women and leadership in the career world focuses on people with multiple privileged identities who are in white-collar careers. Some of this information is included, but as a field we need to do better about drawing on the voices of women from diverse backgrounds to transform our understanding of effective leadership. Women who hold traditionally marginalized identities associated with race, culture, gender, ability, and sexual orientation face additional challenges navigating organizations and systems.

Metaphors for Women in Leadership

Metaphors are literary devices used to invite comparisons between two subjects in order to focus on their similarities and shared traits. They take complex concepts and relate them to more commonplace objects or ideas in order to make them more understandable. Metaphors describing women in leadership abound. Carli and Eagly (2016) describe the metaphor of the glass ceiling as "the overwhelmingly most popular general metaphor for women's lack of access to leadership" (p. 516). The concept was popularized after it was used in a *Wall Street Journal* article by Hymowitz and Schellhardt (1986) to describe the presence of an invisible obstruction that stymied women's career advancements into executive positions. Later the metaphor became synonymous with gender gaps in pay and promotions. In 1991, a bipartisan Glass Ceiling Commission was established to investigate possible discrimination against women that blocks their advancement to management positions (United States Glass Ceiling Commission, 1995).

The glass ceiling is far from the only metaphor used to describe the challenges women face in the world. See Table 7.1 for a host of descriptive phrases used to illustrate the obstacles to women's advancement. Though these metaphors originated to describe barriers women face in the world of work, they also may apply to many other life situations such as community and religious involvements and even family dynamics.

Depictions of women's early attempts to enter certain career fields described a *concrete wall,* or absolute barrier to entry. It was not that long ago that women were not allowed to be doctors or lawyers or to serve in the military. Women are still excluded from some professions, such as leadership positions in certain religions, and greatly underrepresented in others as described in chapter 6. Since women were denied access to higher education until the early 1900s, and into the 1960s and 1970s for some institutions, they had limited access to the schooling required for many well-paid and high-status occupations. Other types of occupations, like those that required physical labor, also excluded women, which resulted in them being omitted from much unionizing and pro-labor protections as well. Chapter 5 explored gender equity on college campuses and how lack of access to education limited women's leadership aspirations and advancement for centuries. The forces of socialization around gender and leadership are ingrained from childhood through college, and they manifest in the world of work as well.

If a woman avoids hitting a concrete wall and is able to enter a profession, she still may eventually encounter a *maternal wall* (Williams, 2004). The maternal wall refers to a type of bias that can occur as women get pregnant or seek parental leave. Studies reveal that performance reviews of female

TABLE 7.1
What's in a Metaphor?

Metaphor	Definition
Concrete Wall	Refers to when there is an absolute barrier to entry into particular career fields.
Glass Ceiling	Implies that women face obstacles once they have risen to very high levels of leadership.
Glass Escalator	Describes the phenomenon in female-dominated professions where women climb the ladder while their male peers glide past them on an invisible escalator, shooting straight to the top.
Glass Cliff	Refers to how women can rise to leadership, but when they are brought in to turn things around during dire times, they often bear the blame if things do not go well. While women may have managed to break through the glass ceiling, they are then pushed off the glass cliff.
Maternal Wall	Describes a type of bias that can occur as women get pregnant or seek parental leave. Maternity may cause others to make negative assumptions about competency, to assume emotionality and irrationality, or to assume a lack of commitment to job functions.
Sticky Floor	Implies that women are prevented from any advancement beyond entry-level positions.
Leaky Pipeline	Refers to the way that women disappear from some careers over time, such as certain STEM fields.
Leadership Labyrinth	Reflects the myriad obstacles, choice points, and on-ramps and off-ramps that women face throughout their careers.

managers plummet after pregnancy (Halpert, Wilson, & Hickman, 1993). This bias may result when maternity causes coworkers to make negative assumptions about competency, to assume emotionality and irrationality, or to assume a lack of commitment to job functions. Pregnant people and new mothers also may experience a heightened form of the double bind if they exhibit assertiveness or other traits viewed as counter to stereotypically maternal behaviors. Williams (2004) describes how benevolent stereotyping can also occur when colleagues assume that a mother does not want to travel to a conference or training, does not want important committee assignments, or would not want to be part of projects requiring nontraditional work hours. She states, "It is one thing for an employer to be sensitive to a woman's new responsibilities and quite another for a woman to feel that she must live up to her colleagues' expectation that she play television mom June Cleaver" (p. 19). It should be noted that fathers may also face a paternal wall in the workplace. Additionally, women do not actually have to have children to have maternity issues affect their career choices. People may choose to enter or avoid a particular position or career field in anticipation of one day having children. And women are routinely (and usually illegally) questioned about their plans for motherhood as part of job search and promotion processes.

Goudreau (2012) describes the phenomenon of the *glass escalator.* This phenomenon often occurs in woman-dominated professions such as teaching and nursing where women work hard to climb the leadership ladder. Meanwhile, their male peers in these same professions glide past them on an invisible escalator, advancing straight to the top. Statistical trends show men being promoted at faster rates than women even in female-dominated professions, so that men are often overrepresented in the leadership of these professions. Goudreau notes, "Because of stereotype matching, men more readily fulfill our notions of what a manager should look like. And when you're in a female-dominated profession, there are fewer people that have the ability to match it" (para. 7).

Even when women arrive at the top of the organizational ladder, there are still unforeseen obstacles. Ryan and Haslam (2005) describe the phenomenon of the *glass cliff* and show evidence that women are overrepresented in precarious leadership positions. In other words, women can rise to leadership, but when they are brought in to turn things around during dire times, they have to bear the blame if things do not go well. So, while women may have managed to break through the glass ceiling, they may then be pushed off the glass cliff. The phenomenon of the glass cliff may occur because women are only given entry to particular executive positions when more traditional male prospects find the positions unattractive. Proudford (2007) describes the importance of women in leadership having a significant network of allies to offer advice about what kinds of opportunities they should take on (to help avoid glass cliffs) and to support each other through perilous leadership waters.

Sociologist Catherine White Berheide coined the metaphor of the *sticky floor* to describe obstacles women face much earlier in their career paths, far before they hit the metaphorical glass ceiling. The sticky floor refers to discriminatory practices slowing women's advancement including "occupational segregation that places women in dead-end jobs, underpayment of workers in female-dominated occupations and the lack of flexibility and absence of job ladders in these professions" (Carli & Eagly, 2016, p. 517). Recently, popular-press books have used the metaphor of the sticky floor to describe women who opt out of leadership and who create their own barriers to success (*It's Not a Glass Ceiling, It's a Sticky Floor: Free Yourself From the Hidden Behaviors Sabotaging Your Career Success* [Shambaugh, 2007]). Later in this chapter we will interrogate the phenomenon of blaming women for their own lack of advancement. Hopefully your critical antenna goes up

Box 7.1.
What's Wrong With You? Building a Publishing Career by Blaming Women

- *Girl, Wash Your Face: Stop Believing the Lies About Who You Are So You Can Become Who You Were Meant to Be* (Hollis, 2018)
- *Girl, Stop Apologizing: A Shame-Free Plan for Embracing and Achieving Your Goals (Hollis, 2019)*
- *Lean In: Women, Work, and the Will to Lead* (Sandberg, 2013)
- *Nice Girls Don't Get the Corner Office: Unconscious Mistakes Women Make That Sabotage Their Careers* (Frankel, 2014)
- *Nice Girls Don't Get Rich: Avoidable Mistakes Women Make With Money* (Frankel, 2009)
- *Nice Girls Just Don't Get It* (Frankel & Frohlinger, 2018)

when you read a book title that suggests women are solely at fault for holding themselves back rather than acknowledging organizational and systemic barriers to success. Some of these well-intentioned books are listed in Box 7.1.

The *leaky pipeline* is another metaphor that describes the way that women disappear from some careers over time. It is frequently used to describe women's experiences in the fields of science, technology, engineering, and math (STEM, or if you add medicine, STEMM, or if you add arts, STEAM). As part of the STEM and Gender Advancement (SAGA) Project, UNESCO (2017) reports that women constitute less than 30% of scientific researchers worldwide. Dasgupta and Stout (2014) describe where "leaks" occur over three stages of the STEM pipeline. In childhood and adolescence, parents, teachers, and peers may subtly steer girls away from math and other STEM fields. In emerging adulthood, women may be underrepresented in STEM classes, have fewer women faculty and mentors in STEM fields, and feel an overall lack of belonging, which may result in underperformance and attrition. After they have entered their professional careers, more women leave the STEM pipeline due to workplace isolation, lack of supports for maternity leave and other family obligations, and inadequate mentorship along the way. By the time workers enter career maturity, there are markedly fewer women in leadership positions in STEM fields. Some scholars critique the leaky pipeline metaphor (Miller & Wai, 2014), stating that the metaphor "partially explains historical gender differences in the U.S., but no longer describes current gender differences in the bachelor's to PhD transition in STEM" (para. 1). Others state the pipeline only leaks in some career fields like biology, but ironically not in more male-dominated fields like physics or engineering (Cannady, Greenwald, & Harris, 2014). The leaky pipeline metaphor has also been used to describe limitations to women's advancement in nonprofit and government careers.

Let's return to the dominant metaphor for women and leadership, the glass ceiling. There are myriad creative takes on the glass ceiling metaphor describing how it functions in various contexts and career fields. Here are a few from a quick search:

- *Breaking Through the Brass Ceiling: Strategies of Success for Elite Military Women* (Iskra, 2008)
- *Breaking the Grass Ceiling: Women, Weed & Business* (Picillo & Devine, 2017)
- *Breaking Through the Stained-Glass Ceiling: Shattering Myths & Empowering Women for Leadership in the Church* (Jones, 2014)
- *Dancing on the Glass Ceiling: Women, Leadership, and Technology* (Olcott & Hardy, 2005)
- *Glass Ceilings and Dirt Floors: Women, Work, and the Global Economy* (Hinze, 2015)
- *The Class Ceiling: Why It Pays to Be Privileged* (Friedman & Laurison, 2018)

Carli and Eagly (2016) have long challenged the aptness of the glass ceiling metaphor. They feel it falls short for several reasons. The glass ceiling metaphor implies that women cannot advance to the highest level of leadership and are confined to lower levels. As there are a growing number of female chief executives, the glass ceiling metaphor erroneously suggests the presence of an absolute barrier at high levels in organizations. The image of the ceiling suggests that women face few challenges reaching that second-highest level, which mistakenly implies that women have equal access to entry-level and middle-management positions. The glass composition of the ceiling "creates an impression that the obstacles women face are invisible and undetectable until the last minute when women bump into it and are denied further advancement" (p. 516). Thus, the metaphor wrongly suggests that barriers to women are difficult to detect and unforeseen. The metaphor also implies that the status of women remains relatively unchanged over time until someone breaks through the ceiling, creating an opening for anyone following after. This assumes the barrier is homogenous and ignores the complexity and variety of obstacles women face on their leadership journeys. The metaphor also fails to recognize the diverse strategies women devise to become leaders and ignores the idea that thoughtful problem-solving can facilitate women's paths to leadership.

Instead of the glass ceiling, Eagly and Carli (2007) propose the metaphor of a *leadership labyrinth,* which allows for the varied challenges confronting women as they travel, often on indirect paths, in their leadership journey. If you are not familiar with labyrinths, see Exercise 7.1. Labyrinths are ancient symbols that suggest the idea of wholeness. Labyrinths combine the imagery of the circle and the spiral into a meandering but purposeful path that represents a journey to a person's own center and back out again into the world (Labyrinth Society, 2019). Labyrinths have long been used as meditation and prayer tools. This metaphor of the leadership labyrinth acknowledges that paths to the top exist and some women find them, though routes can be difficult to discover. Leadership educator Adrian Britton uses the analogy of a corn maze to describe the leadership labyrinth, as there are many twists and turns that can be hard to figure out while you are inside of them. As someone who once was lost in a corn maze for two hours, I find this to be an apt analogy for the struggles of leadership. Carli and Eagly (2016) offer the following:

> Some paths to leadership are more direct than others, and some paths lead nowhere or are dead ends. Finding a successful route to the center is thus not guaranteed and requires persistence and effort. Unlike the glass ceiling and the sticky floor, the image of a labyrinth provides a more subtle and complex metaphor. The labyrinth does not focus on obstacles women face either very early or very late. Instead, the labyrinth implies that women face challenges throughout their careers, from the moment they begin to chart a course to leadership until they reach their goals. The labyrinth metaphor suggests that advancement is difficult, but not impossible. Finding the center does require effort and careful navigation, but it can be achieved. (pp. 517–518)

Exercise 7.1.
Finger Labyrinth

Labyrinths are often used as a tool for meditation, contemplation, or prayer. One way to practice is to use your finger to trace the following design. Start at the opening at the bottom of the image and think of an intention for your reflection or meditation. You might choose any of the mantras from a typical loving kindness meditation (Smith, n.d.), including:

May I be happy just as I am.
May I be peaceful with whatever is happening.
May I be healthy and strong.
May I care for myself in this ever-changing world graciously and joyously.

(*Continues*)

Exercise 7.1. (*Continued*)

Hold your chosen intention as you move toward the center of the labyrinth. When your finger arrives at the center, shift your intention from your own happiness and well-being and expand your thoughts to encompass the interconnectedness of all life. Now move your finger back the way you came.

May all beings in the air, on land, and in the water be safe, happy, healthy, and free from suffering.

Source: Loving-Kindness mantra adapted from Smith (n.d.)

Women's Nonlinear Career Paths: On-Ramps and Off-Ramps

The metaphor of the leadership labyrinth implies that women, especially, may experience nonlinear career paths. Hewlett (2007) describes a trend termed the *opt out revolution* where large numbers of highly qualified women are choosing to leave mainstream careers. Reasons for opting out range from public policy issues such as a lack of childcare and flexible work options for women to personal choices, often unfairly blamed on women's lack of ambition, unwillingness to work long hours, or not thinking to ask for leave or flexible work arrangements when needed.

Some reports indicate that up to 43% of highly qualified women *off-ramp* or voluntarily leave their careers for a period of time (Hewlett & Luce, 2005; Light, 2013). These career interruptions may be due to *pull factors*, centered in family responsibilities such as childcare or elder care, or due to *push factors* resulting from the workplace. Push factors may include feeling underutilized or underappreciated, being underpaid or underpromoted, or the lack of a supportive climate for women. Hewlett (2007) notes that 93% of highly qualified women who chose to off-ramp and leave the workforce report that they want to return to their careers at some point. This desire may stem from a career as a source of identity, as a source of independent income, or from a sense of altruism and wanting to give back. The challenges of on-ramping after having been away from the workforce for an extended period can be intense. Many women returning to careers experience the stigma of having been away and may see losses in earning power. Returning workers may be perceived as less committed, may no longer get the best assignments, and may struggle to catch up with processes or technology that may have shifted while they were away. Any of these experiences may serve to create a crisis of confidence and lower a woman's ambition. Because of this stigma, many women work hard to juggle family life along with a focus on a full-time career.

In a *Harvard Business Review* article titled the "Myth of Having It All," Hewlett (2002) cites shocking statistics that at midlife, between one third and one half of all successful career women in the United States do not have children. She notes that "33% of such women (business executives, doctors, lawyers, academics, and the like) in the 41-to-55 age bracket are childless—and that figure rises to 42% in corporate America" (para. 1). Of men with similar status, only 19% are childless. Hewlett attributes the decline to several factors. One is the lack of equal-status partners. According to the U.S. Census Bureau (2019), at age 28 there are four college-educated, single men for every three college-educated, single women, and at age 38, there is one man for every three women. The time crunch is an obvious contributing factor in that career women are asked to work long hours, and jobs may involve significant travel. Many high-achieving women work more than 50 or 60 hours per week, leaving little time for other interests. Most women also work what is called the "second shift," referring to women being the primary provider of domestic and household labor. This discrepancy between who is responsible for groceries, housework, appointments, and other tasks persists despite men assuming more responsibilities at home than in prior decades. And we should not forget that single women take on all these roles. There are also biological reasons for childlessness. Many career women consider their 20s and early 30s as essential time to establish a reputation and leadership profile in their careers. These years also happen to be prime childbearing years. Women who postpone child-rearing may find themselves facing infertility and limited maternal options. I recall receiving a shocking voicemail from my mother letting me know that while I was working on my doctorate, my eggs were getting old. She had just watched a news show about infertility in working women and was truly trying to be helpful. I think.

Rather than off-ramp from careers for an extended period, some women take a more scenic route. Instead of off-ramping or stepping out, some women choose to step back (Hewlett, 2007). This might include taking part-time work, telecommuting, seeking flexible work arrangements, or turning down promotions. Research shows that 38% of women have deliberately chosen a position with fewer responsibilities and lower compensation to fulfill responsibilities at home, and 36% worked part-time for a period. This number is likely increasing with the advent of flexible work opportunities such as driving for a ride-sharing company or working online. There are benefits to staying connected to a workplace, including access to supportive colleagues and networks, the ability to find meaning and value in one's work, and the chance to contribute to a larger community. It can be extremely challenging to on-ramp after one has been away from the world of work for a significant amount of time. Women may be stigmatized for being away and labeled as out of touch with the industry; they may face very real financial penalties and have to take significant pay reductions or settle for lower-level work than before they off-ramped (Hewlett, 2007). Exercise 7.2 invites you to consider your own leadership labyrinth.

It should be noted that much of the research about off-ramps and on-ramps assumes a certain amount of privilege, both in income level and in partnerships. The fact remains that many women do not have the option to not work. Women with hourly and low-paying jobs seldom have the luxury to decide if they want to keep working. Many already work multiple jobs just to keep up with expenses. These commitments are compounded by the fact that many low-wage positions do not come with any paid parental leave or even paid vacation days. The lower the wage, the less likely a worker is to have any flexibility about scheduling, time off, and flexible work. The sad irony is that the more someone needs adaptable work environments, such as single mothers, the less likely they are to get it.

Barriers to Advancement: Personal

Are women getting in their own way and limiting their access to leadership? This chapter will now review and critique one of the most financially successful books about women and leadership in recent decades, Sheryl Sandberg's 2013 book *Lean In: Women, Work, and the Will to Lead*. Sandberg, who is the chief operating officer of Facebook and a billionaire, wrote a manifesto of sorts about what women need to do to be more successful in male-dominated

Exercise 7.2.
Draw Your Personal Leadership Labyrinth

Every semester, students in my women and leadership classes are invited to draw their own leadership labyrinths. We usually start this exercise by inviting students to imagine their future lives. Participants are asked to imagine themselves 10 years in the future, and to develop images in their mind for each of the following questions. This activity has worked for people of all ages, genders, and backgrounds. Even if you are an adult learner or returning student, your story is still being written.

Ten Years From Now:

- Where do you live? In what kind of house, condo, apartment, or yurt? Do you rent or own? Where is it located?
- Do you work outside the home? What kind of job do you have? Is it 9 to 5? Flexible hours? How much money do you make? Do you have health insurance? Are you paying off student loans or other debt?
- Are you partnered? Who is this person? What kind of work do they do?
- What do you do for fun? For renewal?
- Who cleans the house? Does the laundry? Takes care of the yard if you have one? Does the shopping? The cooking and cleaning? Who pays the bills?
- Do you have pets? Who feeds/grooms/exercises them?
- Do you have children? How many? When did you have them? Did you take time off of work? Were you paid during that time? Did your partner take time off? If so, who does carpool? Are they in school or daycare? Are you in the PTA?
- Are you in touch with your relatives/family? Your partner's family? How often do you see them? Do they assist you with childcare? Do they need assistance?
- Now imagine something unexpected happens—your workplace closes for a month and you receive no paycheck, you become injured on the job, have a child with special needs, and so on. What are your coping strategies?

After this reflective exercise, participants are asked to depict the next 10 years of their lives by drawing their own version of a labyrinth. These have taken many forms including spirals, mazes, decision trees, actual

(*Continues*)

Exercise 7.2. (*Continued*)

> trees with branches, maps, and metro stops. As they develop their laby-
> rinths, participants are asked to label choice points or places where they
> will have decisions to make (about school versus work; having children;
> promotions; etc.) and to depict how the on- and off-ramps might impact
> their career trajectory. Next, participants are asked to label possible bar-
> riers, including personal, organizational, and systemic forces that might
> affect their journey. Finally, we post our labyrinths as if in an art gallery
> and experience each other's imagined journeys.

workplaces. As of 2018, the book has sold 4.2 million copies worldwide
and still sells roughly 12,500 copies a month and has resulted in Sandberg
appearing on the covers of *Time* and *Fortune* magazines and appearing on
TV shows like *60 Minutes* and *Nightline* (Newman, 2018). Sandberg created
LeanIn.org and her book and TED Talk have resulted in the creation of hun-
dreds of *Lean In* circles, including some on college campuses, where groups
of women meet regularly to discuss and apply the principles of her book.

   Lean In ideology has been subject to numerous worthy critiques, the
most compelling of which is that the book situates women's lack of advancement in individual inadequacy rather than in structural and systemic barriers (Brooks, 2014; Cobble, Gordon, & Henry, 2014; hooks, 2013; Oliver,
2018; Slaughter, 2012). Although Sandberg does pay lip service to the fact
that women are subject to discrimination, including subtle and blatant sexism and sexual harassment in the workplace, she states that there are a
host of barriers women create for themselves when they internalize certain stereotypes and gender roles. The aim of her book is to help women
stop getting in their own way and to overcome internal barriers critical to
gaining power. Here is Sandberg's (2013) description of how women hold
themselves back:

> In addition to external barriers erected by society, women are hindered by
> barriers that exist within ourselves. We hold ourselves back in ways both
> big and small, by lacking self-confidence, by not raising our hands, and by
> pulling back when we should be leaning in. We internalize the negative
> messages we get throughout our lives—the messages that say it is wrong
> to be outspoken, aggressive, more powerful than men. We lower our own
> expectations of what we can achieve. We continue to do the majority of the
> housework and childcare. We compromise our career goals to make room
> for partners and children who may not even exist yet. Compared to our
> male colleagues, fewer of us aspire to senior positions. (p. 8)

She goes on to offer advice to women about choices they can make to increase their access to leadership and power. These include ways to increase self-confidence (chapter 2: "Sit at the Table"; chapter 6: "Seek and Speak Your Truth"); to get partners to do more at home (chapter 8: "Make Your Partner a Real Partner"); to keep one's foot on the gas pedal at work (chapter 7: "Don't Leave Before You Leave"); and to not hold women accountable to unattainable standards (chapter 9: "The Myth of Doing It All"). Her stories are compelling, and her advice goes down very easily and may even inspire readers to make important changes in their approach to leadership.

However, there are several ways that her argument falls short. Most glaring is the lack of awareness about the role of economic, educational, race, ability, and class privilege in thinking about these issues. The vast majority of American women do not have choices to "reduce commitments" or "simplify their lives" and still get by (Cobble et al., 2014). Slaughter (2012) agrees, stating:

> Millions of other working women face much more difficult life circumstances. Some are single mothers; many struggle to find any job; others support husbands who cannot find jobs. Many cope with a work life in which good day care is either unavailable or very expensive; school schedules do not match work schedules; and schools themselves are failing to educate their children. Many of these women are worrying not about having it all, but rather about holding on to what they do have. (para. 23)

Cobble and colleagues address the problem clearly—that *Lean In* "reinforces the belief that feminism is a cause of and for privileged women—successful women got there by 'leaning in'" while the rest of us have only ourselves to blame" (para. 21). In her essay "Dig Deep: Beyond *Lean In*", activist scholar bell hooks (2013) suggests that the prescriptions in the book could even undermine feminism itself and labels this ideology as *faux feminism, trickle-down feminism*, or *corporate feminism*. hooks (2013) clarifies:

> Sandberg's definition of feminism begins and ends with the notion that it's all about gender equality within the existing social system. From this perspective, the structures of imperialist white supremacist capitalist patriarchy need not be challenged. And she makes it seem that privileged white men will eagerly choose to extend the benefits of corporate capitalism to white women who have the courage to "lean in." It almost seems as if Sandberg sees women's lack of perseverance as more the problem than systemic inequality. Sandberg effectively uses her race and class power and privilege to promote a narrow definition of feminism that obscures and undermines visionary feminist concerns. (para. 5)

Slaughter's controversial 2012 article in the *Atlantic*, "Why Women Still Can't Have It All," takes on Sandberg and the problematic partial-truths and clichés we tell ourselves. One of these is that women are not committed enough to our own success. Sandberg calls this an ambition gap, but Slaughter shows how women are limited by a system designed to force impossible choices. She questions why school schedules cannot match work schedules now that we are no longer an agrarian society. Another cliché is that women can have it all, just not at the same time. Slaughter questions whether there is any best sequence of how to schedule career and family timelines and instead calls for more flexible workplaces that support family leave whenever people choose it. Whereas Sandberg exhorts us to find and marry the right person, Slaughter details a system that makes little time for out-of-work relationships. Years earlier, Audre Lorde (1984) titled these gendered expectations the *mythical norm* and showed how these social forces actually feed oppressive actions.

Finally, *Lean In* also fails to address the effects of intersectional identities. For example, Sandberg suggests that women should become more assertive and bargain for advancement without considering how applicable this advice might be to different groups of women who may experience multiple interlocking forms of oppression. In a 2018 *Fast Company* article, Oliver notes that Sandberg talks about getting a seat at the table, but for many women of color the table is broken. Oliver cites data and asks,

> With only 3% of the C-suite held by women of color compared to 18% by white women—and a significant departure of women of color leaving corporate America, if systems are not created to hire and advance women of color now, what will our companies look like in the future? (para. 17)

Women of color are developing their own prescriptions for career success. Minda Hart's (2019) book *The Memo* and her #SecureTheSeat podcasts and website take a deeper look into the career struggles women of color face. She quotes Shirley Chisolm, the first African American woman elected to Congress in 1968, who apocryphally said, far before Sandberg, "If they don't give you a seat at the table, bring a folding chair" (p. xiii).

Lean In offers easy prescriptions for change. Cobble and colleagues (2014) compare these platitudes with magazine articles about how to organize your closet or your schedule. The result for most women is that even the best organization possible still leaves women overworked, underpaid, and underrespected. Although Sandberg acknowledges these limitations in her writing by stating

> I know some people believe that by focusing on what women can change themselves—pressing them to lean in—it seems like I am letting our institutions off the hook. Or even worse—they accuse me of blaming the

victim. Far from blaming the victim, I believe that female leaders are key to the solution. (pp. 10–11)

Oliver (2018) reminds us that the

> *Lean In* narrative puts the responsibility back on women instead of focusing on key systemic workplace issues that hold women back. . . . The pay gap, maternity and sick leave, healthcare, and professional development are organizational issues that cannot be solved with women just working harder and longer. (para. 11)

Pierce (2015) notes, "*Lean In* reminds me a lot of respectability politics, in which you show the oppressor you're hardworking and well-behaved, instead of actually challenging the system that makes you oppressed in the first place" (para. 7).

Barriers to Advancement: Organizational

Hopefully the previous section has convinced you that it is not just women's choices that suppress women's attainment of leadership roles and positions. The Center for Creative Leadership (CCL) notes that "relic policies, practices, and perceptions continue to undermine the advancement of women and contribute to a persistent glass ceiling in the workplace" (CCL, 2018, p. 22). Indeed, many workplaces demand that employees work long hours, travel frequently, or relocate periodically, all of which may be harder for women and anyone with care-taking responsibilities. Hewlett (2007) describes how many women choose to off-ramp or leave positions because they do not feel valued at work. She states, "The data show that feeling underutilized or underappreciated are more significant problems than overwork. Not being consulted or not getting a sought-after (and deserved) plum assignment is much harder than dealing with additional responsibility" (p. 415). CCL (2018) points out the persistence of unconscious bias against women where an assertive man may be labeled as strong, but a female counterpart might be branded as bossy. If women do not feel valued or that they fit within the organizational culture, they may find other ways to spend their time that are more satisfying and personally fulfilling.

Another often less talked about reason that women face challenges at work is the presence of other unsupportive women. Sadly, the high school mean girls might show up in the workplace as well. This phenomenon, called the queen bee syndrome, refers to situations where women who have already achieved status or power in an organization may be less likely to sponsor or promote other women (Drexler, 2013). Side note that this syndrome has nothing to do with the singer Beyoncé Knowles Carter. I once taught a class where students were confused about why Queen Bey would keep others down. I had to clarify that from what I have read about her, Queen Bey does not seem to suffer from queen bee syndrome.

There are a host of reasons why someone might become a queen bee, including that the patriarchal culture of work may encourage those who managed to rise to the top to become obsessed with maintaining their authority, even at the expense of other women. A survey by the Workplace Bullying Institute (2010) found that female bullies directed their hostilities toward other women 80% of the time, while men were equal opportunity offenders. Drexler (2013) describes how the queen bee phenomenon is alive and well today. She states:

> This generation of queen bees is no less determined to secure their hard-won place as alpha females. Far from nurturing the growth of younger female talent, they push aside possible competitors by chipping away at their self-confidence or undermining their professional standing. It is a trend thick with irony: the very same women who have complained for decades about unequal treatment now perpetuate many of the same problems by turning on their own. (para. 6)

If the climate or culture of an organization is replete with verbal abuse, job sabotage, misuse of authority, or outright verbal or sexual harassment, it is no wonder women may have trouble navigating the leadership labyrinth.

Strategies for Gender Equity: Personal

Beyond the platitudes of leaning in and finding an awesome partner, what can women do to create a more equitable experience in the world of work? A report from the AAUW on *Barriers and Bias: The Status of Women and Leadership* (2016a) makes suggestions, displayed in Box 7.2, for what women can do to close the leadership gap.

Slaughter (2012) makes an additional suggestion that people abandon the narrative of the meteoric leadership rise that glorifies people making partner or entering the executive suite before the age of 40. She writes:

> Assuming the priceless gifts of good health and good fortune, a professional woman can thus expect her working life to stretch some 50 years, from her early or mid-20s to her mid-70s. It is reasonable to assume that she will build her credentials and establish herself, at least in her first career, between 22 and 35; she will have children, if she wants them, sometime between 25 and 45; she'll want maximum flexibility and control over her time in the 10 years that her children are 8 to 18; and she should plan to

Box 7.2.
Strategies for Individuals to Close the Leadership Gap

Become a student of leadership. There are thousands of academic and popular books, journals, and webinars for women seeking leadership roles in business, politics, education, and a host of other fields. We recommend that women immerse themselves in the leadership literature most relevant to their own career paths.

Seek evidence-based leadership training. Focused, interactive training can be empowering when implemented well. For example, AAUW's Elect Her program trains college women to run for office on campus and beyond. AAUW also holds an annual National Conference for College Women Student Leaders (NCCWSL), which brings together nearly 1,000 women to hone their leadership skills, learn about public policy issues facing women today, participate in a career and graduate school fair, and network (www.nccwsl.org).

Ask for more. Learn and practice negotiation skills to ensure that salaries and benefits start fair and stay fair. AAUW Start Smart and AAUW Work Smart salary negotiation workshops teach women effective techniques to negotiate their salary and benefits at different stages of their careers.

Find a sponsor or become one. Investing in the next generation of leaders takes time and effort. Be on the lookout for opportunities to learn from people in leadership positions, and as you advance in your field, make it your responsibility to invest in future leaders.

Explore and address your biases. We all have implicit biases that are in conflict with our conscious beliefs. Find out about your biases and learn some practical tips for avoiding the mental shortcuts that can lead to unfounded judgments. Information about the gender and leadership IAT is included in chapter 6.

Understand stereotype threat. Simply knowing about stereotype threat can help diminish its effect on you. Role models can be helpful in countering stereotypes. Encouraging a growth mindset in yourself—that is, the belief that your mind is always learning and growing—can serve as a defense against the notion of fixed capabilities, which is at the core of stereotype threat (Hoyt, Burnette, & Innella, 2012).

(*Continues*)

Box 7.2. (*Continued*)

Set leadership goals. When women don't meet all the qualifications for a position, they are less likely than men to pursue it. Even if you don't want to pursue leadership roles at this stage of your life, look ahead to opportunities that are on the horizon.

Plan for potential career interruptions. Work–family balance can be difficult for anyone to achieve. Although women are still more likely than men to handle the housework and caregiving, men are increasingly taking on these roles. Taking time out of the workforce can be the right decision for both men and women.

Seek out employers that promote women in leadership. Before you join a company, take a look around: Do you see women and people of color in leadership roles? Blazing a trail is a possibility, but it can be challenging.

Look for volunteer opportunities that include leadership skill development. This report focuses on positional leadership, but there are many types of leadership. Volunteer leaders have been involved in building schools, libraries, and hospitals; they have fought for civil rights and advocated for children and the poor. Volunteering can be a wonderful way to develop your leadership skills while helping to make a difference in the world.

Note. Adapted from AAUW (2016a).

> take positions of maximum authority and demands on her time after her children are out of the house. (p. x)

Instead of thinking of employees as nearing retirement in their 60s, what if that age and stage was recast as a time of peak leadership performance? Consider rethinking the story you are writing about the speed of success. Finally, it behooves all people to find advocates and allies across genders. Chapter 9 of this book will give strategies for identifying and developing relationships across aspects of difference. Having coalitions and support systems along your journey is essential.

Strategies for Gender Equity: Organizational

In a recent report on *Talent Reimagined: Seven Emerging Trends for Transformative Leaders*, the CCL (2018) cites the importance of creating a work environment that advances women leaders as one of the best ways companies can address skills gaps and foster innovative workplaces. The report addresses the stagnation of women in senior organizational roles and cites recent data that show recruiting women as both board members and employees results in increased financial performance, thus making a strong business case for creating more equitable and welcoming workplaces (CCL, 2018). The CCL (2018) report goes on to note that having larger percentages of women in an organization also predicts greater job satisfaction, higher levels of employee engagement, and decreased rates of burnout—for all workers, regardless of gender, age, ethnicity, or leadership level. It concludes that "in short, having more women in the workplace is associated with positive outcomes for both women and men" (p. 21).

Businesses and organizations can take active steps to create more equitable workplaces. CCL (2018) recommends that workplaces reinvent mentoring and executive development programs, revamp diversity training, and recast human resource policies to promote greater awareness, flexibility, and work–life balance for all employees, not just women. CCL suggests six key strategies to help women "kick some glass" (p. 21). These are the following:

Address the leadership challenges and needed competencies for women. In order to ensure that women leaders have the experiences and resources they need, CCL recommends organizations provide access to on-the-job learning, as well as coaching, mentoring, and other leadership workshops and programs. Developing internal talent can help businesses avoid high turnover costs and strengthen the leadership pipeline for women.

Leverage the power of choosing. As women work to navigate the leadership labyrinth, they need to be intentional about their careers and development as leaders. Female leaders in organizations should be encouraged to exert greater influence over the choices they make, take the lead in shaping conversations about their careers, and take greater ownership over their career choices.

Create the right networks. Rather than submitting to queen bees and others who might seek to limit influence, organizations should establish a culture where all people are afforded access to the networks that open doors for them by providing sponsors and advocates who will challenge and support them. Developing meaningful relationships can be assets in getting access to information, earning promotions, and gaining opportunities, which matters because "effective leaders rely on networks to influence others and to get results" (CCL, 2018, p. 22).

Rethink systems and challenge assumptions. Organizations must actively examine themselves to unearth ways that unconscious bias in the organization affects opportunities and motivation for women. Areas that might need to be rethought or retooled to be more equitable include scheduling practices, opportunities for networking and mentoring, social norms, and talent management processes.

Attract and retain a diverse workforce. Implementing gender-neutral and inclusive hiring processes, parental leave policies, flexible work arrangements, and succession planning are essential to attract strong woman candidates. They stress the values that women, people of color, and individuals with differing abilities contribute to ensure diverse perspectives that can help propel a company forward.

Consider a women-only leadership development experience. Organizations might consider offering female-only programs or initiatives where women can form relationships, share experiences, and offer ideas for future organizational possibilities. These spaces should be inclusive of women of all identities.

In alignment with the CCL recommendations, Slaughter (2012) offers one further important addition for how to make organizations more equitable across genders. She suggests that companies change the culture of face time and allow for flexible scheduling. Many industries foster the cult of the billable hour, and even those that do not may actively reward those who come in early and stay late, and those who are willing to work over weekends and forgo vacations. Given all the technology in the world, employers can now offer workers much more flexibility about how communication happens. Workplaces that embrace video-conferencing for meetings and allowing employees to phone or Skype into conversations are much more likely to be woman and family friendly.

Even if individuals and organizations work hard to address the equity gap in leadership, there are still important policy changes that need to be made. Box 7.3 outlines AAUW's (2016a) suggestions for policymakers. This chapter concludes with Slaughter's (2012) call to action.

> The best hope for improving the lot of all women . . . is to close the leadership gap: to elect a woman president and 50 women senators; to ensure that women are equally represented in the ranks of corporate executives and judicial leaders. Only when women wield power in sufficient numbers will we create a society that genuinely works for all women. That will be a society that works for everyone. (para. 23)

Box 7.3.
Strategies for Policymakers to Close the Leadership Gap

Tackle persistent sex discrimination. The gender imbalance in leadership can be solved only by creating an equitable workplace. Enforcement agencies like the U.S. Equal Employment Opportunity Commission (EEOC) and the U.S. Department of Justice need adequate resources to enforce existing civil rights laws so that employers can get the technical assistance they need and employees can get meaningful access to the protections they deserve.

Strengthen pay equity laws. Passage of the Paycheck Fairness Act would create incentives for employers to follow the law, empower women to negotiate for equal pay, and enforce the laws we already have. State and local policymakers can follow the lead of states like California and Massachusetts and strengthen their state's equal pay provisions.

Increase salary transparency. The federal government is helping to fight the pay gap by making sure federal contractors do not retaliate against employees who share salary information. In addition, the U.S. Department of Labor and the EEOC must finalize and implement new regulations to collect wage data by gender and race from employers. These data will provide better insight into the wage gap and discriminatory pay practices that hold women back across industries and occupations.

Strengthen leave policies. While some employers choose to provide these protections as a benefit to some or all employees, many U.S. workers do not have guaranteed paid annual leave, paid time off for illness or family care, or paid parental leave. Without these policies, caregiving responsibilities can hinder women's career trajectories and leadership opportunities. The Family and Medical Insurance Leave Act would establish paid medical and parental leave for all workers, and the Healthy Families Act would allow workers to earn paid sick days to cover temporary and minor illnesses and caregiving. State and local policymakers can also pass laws that set these standards for all workers.

Update laws to protect pregnant workers. Pregnancy should not prevent a woman from pursuing her career. The Pregnant Workers Fairness Act would require employers to make reasonable accommodations to protect

(Continues)

Box 7.3. (*Continued*)

the health of pregnant workers and ensure that they are not forced out of their jobs or denied leadership opportunities.

Support educational programs for women seeking high-wage jobs. Jobs that have been traditionally held by men tend to be in high-wage, high-growth fields. Educational programs that provide bias-free counseling and promote gender equity can encourage effective workplace culture change.

Fully enforce Title IX. Title IX prohibits sex discrimination in education, including discriminatory policies in admissions, recruitment, counseling, and athletics and in addressing the persistent sexual harassment and violence in our schools. These factors all limit women's ability to complete their education and pursue leadership opportunities. The U.S. Department of Education needs adequate funding to provide technical assistance and to fully enforce the law. The High School Data Transparency Act would help schools, parents, students, and community members ensure the promise of Title IX by making information about gender and sports in high schools publicly available.

Note. Adapted from the AAUW (2016a).

Sage's narrative in the next section describes just a few of the many challenges faced by women of color in the workplace. The challenges range from stereotyping to microaggressions to racial battle fatigue.

Sage identifies as an African American, biracial, cisgender, heterosexual woman who grew up working class, is middle-aged, and identifies as spiritual.

Narratives and Counternarratives: Sage's Story

Working in education, I have found myself engaging with many well-intentioned white liberal/progressive women over the years. These interactions may seem inconsequential at first glance, but after further reflection have been extremely problematic for my wellness and my longevity in my career as an educator. These experiences, often filled with racial microaggressions, could have been pivotal learning moments for my colleagues. However, I often refused to engage them so as to avoid being seen as the "angry Black woman" and because I suffered from my own racial battle fatigue in which I was exhausted from giving others learning at my own expense. My traditional strategies for coping with this exhaustion include: lamenting to friends who get it, talking to other women of color who have had similar experiences, escaping with family and friends, and venting about how I was yet again victim to another incident of sexism and racism. However, as my career has progressed, the intersections of my race and gender as a Black woman have created a series of experiences that have culminated in me labeling academia as a hostile working environment. Although I do not have a job as physically demanding as my father who is a welder for a steel company, I have battled my fair share of verbal assaults and insinuations that have questioned my integrity, professionalism, and ability as a leader.

Several years ago, I held a position as a director in one of the divisions on campus. I was one of a few women of color in this position but had to navigate a supervisor who was uninformed about how to create an inclusive workplace culture. Here are just a few of the more problematic incidents I faced in the workplace. Early in my job I was told I was hired to specifically focus on the students of color who had been known for causing "trouble" in the community. I was repeatedly asked to recruit more students of color for campus events to make sure that we have students of color represented to ensure we *looked* inclusive. I was approached at the office holiday party and told "I can't wait until you have some kids so we can have some brown babies run around at this event." At first glance these experiences seemed like simple microaggressions, but as I continue to consider my overall experience as a leader for my department, I realized that my judgment was often questioned. Whenever I pushed back or spoke up, I was labeled as too emotional, or told that I was unable to see the Big Picture. Interestingly, I was later praised for implementing cultural change in the department and our department received two major awards as a result of our work in creating cultural change and leadership programs.

8

BEWARE OF PRECARIOUS PEDESTALS

Degendering Leadership

Imagine living in a world where there is no domination, where females and males are not alike or even always equal, but where a vision of mutuality is the ethos shaping our interaction.

—bell hooks, *Feminism Is for Everybody: Passionate Politics*, 2000a

If you do a web search for the terms *women* and *leadership* you will get hits for resources like "twenty reasons women make great leaders," "why the world needs more women in leadership," and even "why women are better leaders than men." These ideas are dangerously seductive. Since we exist in a world that overtly privileges masculine traits and behaviors as described throughout this book, it is tempting to fantasize about the opposite (see Exercise 8.1). If women ruled the world, there would be more collaboration, more interdependence, empathy, and understanding. Yet we must heed feminist-poet-activist Audre Lorde's admonition that "the master's tools will never dismantle the master's house" (Moraga & Anzaldúa, 2015, p. 95). That is to say if we perpetrate the same injustice and oppression that we experience onto others we have done nothing but perpetuate a continuation of racist, patriarchal thought. Instead we must find new ways of being, or as Lorde suggests "divide and conquer, in our world, must become define and empower"(p. 96). Instead of continuing a binary and exclusionary approach to leadership, how might we degender leadership and create more equitable and liberatory ways of learning and leading?

This chapter reviews traditional leader prototypes and explores research about whether there really are gender-based differences in leadership. It explores the nature and sources of power and related concepts such as influence and empowerment. Next, this chapter examines attempts to establish

Exercise 8.1.
What If Women Did Rule the World?

While it perhaps is not prudent to indulge this either/or thinking in the real world (i.e., only men or only women should rule the world), I heartily endorse engaging with it in your fantasy life. There are several recent books that postulate a world run by women. Naomi Alderman's (2019) *The Power* depicts a dystopian world where women develop a new organ of the body, the skein, which enables them to generate electric shocks that can manipulate, harm, and kill. This abruptly shifts the balance of gender power and the nature of reality itself. The book begs the question: What would happen if women were physically more powerful than men? Would other types of power follow, and would women recreate the oppressive system with which they are most familiar?

If you prefer nonfiction, Egyptologist Kara Cooney (2018) explores what Egypt gained from its liberal reliance on women in leadership roles, and what today's world can learn from its example in her book *When Women Ruled the World: Six Queens of Egypt.* If you are more egalitarian in your fantasy life, check out Ursula K. Le Guin's (1987) sci-fi classic *The Left Hand of Darkness* about the planet of Winter, an alien world without sexual prejudice, where the inhabitants can change their gender whenever they choose. Although this book was later critiqued for centering the male experience, it was ahead of its time in depicting gender fluidity.

a great woman theory of leadership and warns about the dangers of placing women on "precarious pedestals" where they are valued for gendered traits. It details how even positive stereotypes can create fertile ground for exclusion by suggesting that women must lead in particular ways. The chapter then examines the additional challenges women of color and those with multiple historically marginalized identities face as they navigate leadership. The theory of culturally relevant leadership learning is presented.

Traditional Leader Prototypes

You read in chapter 6 about the IAT and how it claims to surface implicit or unconscious assumptions about groups of people. This test is based on implicit personality theory and attribution theory, which describe how people form inferences about the abilities of others based on social, behavioral, and environmental cues (Dugan, 2017; Hall & Lord, 1995). These theories describe how people develop schemas and prototypes about what collections of attributes and qualities characterize particular kinds of people (Dinh & Lord, 2012). Each of us has a set of beliefs about what a prototypical leader might look like and what kinds of traits, values, and behaviors they might hold. Think back to Box 2.1, which detailed fundamental beliefs about leadership and whether leaders must be charismatic or ethical or embody other specific traits. Researchers have studied leader prototypes and found a long list of characteristics people typically associate with leaders including, among others, charisma, intelligence, dedication, and even attractiveness. Dugan (2017) reviewed much of the research around leader prototypes and summarized that in the United States, leader prototypes are strongly related to gender, sex, race, and age and that "the leader prototype for most people is white, cisgender, male, and more youthful" (p. 76).

This may not come as a surprise to you. Leadership, especially when viewed from a historical perspective, is predominantly defined by those who held positional roles, who usually held many privileged identities. Women and people of color were often excluded from leadership roles, research, and practice (Komives & Dugan, 2010). Haber-Curran and Tillapaugh (2018) describe how, when gender is addressed in leadership, it is usually considered from a binary or man/woman perspective, leaving transgender and other gender nonconforming individuals completely out of the equation.

Let's briefly revisit the story most often told concerning the evolution of theorizing about leadership that was reviewed in chapter 2. Early conceptions of leadership such as the great man theory overtly privileged masculine traits and behaviors. In fact, as discussed in chapter 2, all the industrial theories of leadership were developed with male leaders in mind, indicating that early studies of leadership are rife with hegemonic masculinity. The seminal Ohio State and University of Michigan studies of leadership indicated that effective leadership behaviors involved both paying attention to relationships (called consideration, or concern for people) and to tasks (called initiating structure, or concern for production). Not surprisingly, women leaders scored higher on relationships and men on task and production scales (Bass, 1990). As society shifted from a production to a knowledge economy, more hierarchical approaches to leadership have given way to more collaborative, relational, and shared approaches. These participatory or democratic approaches to leadership are often referred to as women's ways of leading.

One of the most popular modern leadership theories is transformational leadership, where leaders and collaborators raise each other to higher levels of morality and motivation (Bass, 1990; Burns, 1978). More recent research reveals that women practice transformational leadership more than men

(Chandler, 2011). Research on the social change model of leadership (see chapter 3) reveals that women score significantly higher on the capacity for socially responsible leadership than men (Dugan, Komives, & Segar, 2009). It is important to note that the MSL, which measures social change outcomes, is one of the first leadership studies to include detailed data from trans* and non-binary participants, and results suggest these populations do experience important challenges in leadership development (Dugan, Kusel, & Simounet, 2012). One finding revealed that transgender males who transitioned to females (MtF) reported experiencing lower levels of leadership capacity, efficacy, and attainment of leadership roles than those who transitioned from female to male (FtM) or who identified as intersex. This is likely due to the loss of male privilege and shifting role expectations.

Associating industrial theories of leadership with men and postindustrial theories with women is problematic. As Kezar and Wheaton (2017) describe, "Clearly, there are many women who utilize and enact traditional hierarchical conceptualizations of leadership and some that blend the two approaches. Still others act in ways that defy any of the commonly described forms of leadership" (p. 20). Additionally, not all men practice leadership from a command-and-control or hierarchical perspective. Hopefully by now you are convinced that a binary approach to gender and leadership is limiting and understand that leaders hold multiple social identities that influence the way they conceptualize, practice, and evaluate. In fact, leaders with identities that have been traditionally marginalized or oppressed tend to approach leadership from more collaborative lenses (Kezar & Wheaton, 2017).

Are There Gender-Based Differences in Leadership?

If you are using concepts from this book to spice up your conversations with friends and family, here is a good topic: Are men biologically predispositioned to be natural leaders? In their seminal book *Through the Labyrinth: The Truth About How Women Become Leaders*, Alice Eagly and Linda Carli (2007) describe how people's stereotypes about women and leaders create resistance to women in leadership. Much of this resistance is grounded in a body of research called evolutionary psychology. Evolutionary psychology suggests that men and women evolved different personalities and approaches to leadership based on historical differences in roles and biology. For example, because men had to compete for access to fertile women, they are more likely to be aggressive, competitive, and to take risks. And because child rearing mostly fell to women, they evolved to be more nurturing and concerned with safety and security. Eagly and Carli vehemently disagree with this line of thinking. They cite the existence of matrilineal societies such as the Vanatinai in New Guinea as proof that division of labor is not genetically determined. The authors argue that patriarchy is not an inherent feature of human societies, but one that emerged as a result of social and economic development that led men to work away from the home and gave them freedom from childrearing and control over resources. It is these different roles occupied by men and woman that have powerful effects on behavior and personalities. As culture and societies change, so do the roles and psychology of men and women, and the need to be more inclusive in the analysis of leadership and gender. This sheds light on the "are leaders born or made" discussion from chapter 2.

So, do men and women differ in their approach to leadership? Eagly and Carli (2007) conclude that "research demonstrates small sex differences in some of the traits that are relevant to good leadership—for example, assertiveness, gregariousness, risk-taking, and moral integrity" and that "these findings imply female advantage at least as often as male advantage" (p. 134). This is vastly different from much of the rhetoric around women and leadership where differences by gender have been used as an excuse to limit or deny women's access to leadership. See Table 8.1 for a summary of Eagly and Carli's meta-analytical research on sex differences in leadership.

Taken in sum, it is evident that there are small differences across gender in leadership, and that these differences are often exaggerated in how people think of leadership and gender. Perhaps leaders are best served by adopting an androgynous approach where leaders exhibit a variety of attributes. As early studies of leadership suggest, leadership requires attention to both task-oriented and relationship-oriented processes. Eagly and Carli (2007) caution that because leadership is not directly tied to overtly feminine or masculine qualities, people whose gender expression (see chapter 2) is extremely masculine or feminine may actually be at a disadvantage in modern leadership.

Tillapaugh and Haber-Curran (2017) critique the entire field of leadership studies for continuing to frame research on gender and leadership from a binary (man/woman) perspective. This not only erases those who do not identify with traditional gender labels but also ignores important conversations about how gender functions as a lens in leadership. The authors note:

> Given the expanding discourse on gender as well as leadership in our society, educators need to have a better understanding of women, men, and transgender or gender nonconforming individuals and how they understand and practice their leadership rather than just examining leadership differences between genders. (p. 16)

TABLE 8.1.
Findings From Research About Gender Differences in Leadership

Attribute Related to Leadership	Summary of Scholarship
Aggressiveness	Studies show men exceed women in physical aggression expressed toward same-sex peers and in workplace aggression. Men are only slightly more verbally aggressive than women.
Dominance and Assertiveness	Men score only slightly to moderately higher than women on measures of dominance and assertiveness. Men and women may express assertiveness differently in that men promote self-interest while women may express assertiveness through group-oriented behaviors. Men express more interest in social hierarchies and social domination than women.
Neuroticism*	Women generally score higher than men on *neuroticism*, defined as exhibiting poor emotional adjustments and negative emotions.
Extraversion*	Mixed results. Women score higher on exhibiting warmth, positive emotions, and gregariousness, while men score higher on assertiveness and excitement seeking.
Openness to Experience*	Mixed results. Women score higher on valuing aesthetics, feelings, and actions, while men score higher on values, ideas, and fantasies.
Agreeableness*	Women generally score higher than men on *agreeableness*, defined as exhibiting qualities of caring, trusting, compliance, and gentleness.
Conscientious-ness*	Mixed results. Women score higher on dutifulness, achievement striving, and order, while men score higher on self-discipline, deliberation, and competence.
Emotional Intelligence and Empathy	Women generally score higher than men on emotional intelligence or the ability to "recognize and regulate emotions in ourselves and others" (Eagly & Carli, 2007, p. 2). Emotionally intelligent leadership promotes a focus on three facets: consciousness of self, consciousness of others, and consciousness of contexts (Shankman et al., 2015). Women also score higher on consciousness of others.
Risk-Taking	Men generally score higher than women, though the difference has been shrinking over time.
Morality and Ethics	Women generally score higher on moral orientation than men. This may be linked to women generally scoring higher on religiosity than men.

Note. Adapted from Eagly and Carli (2007).

* Traits marked with an asterisk represent the personality traits known in psychology as the Big Five and are often measured in personality assessments. Eagly and Carli note that, with the exception of extraversion and conscientiousness, these traits are only weakly predictive of leadership behavior.

Women and Power

What comes to your mind when you hear the word *power?* Many of the students in my leadership classes have a negative reaction to the word. It can conjure images of abuse, victimization, and disenfranchisement. Others may think back to the discussion in chapter 2 of different sources of power—power from position, from knowledge or expertise, from the ability to reward or punish, or from your relationships and who you know. Despite limited gender differences in leadership, some studies have shown that men and women have different approaches to power. While men are more likely to view power as something that is finite, women tend to have a more expansive view. Kezar and Wheaton (2017) describe another array of research detailing how women lead differently from men. They cite women's enhanced skills in listening, reaching out for input, and engaging in democratic decision-making. Since women are more likely to view leadership as a shared process, women in leadership may be more apt to focus on collaboration, networking, and partnering—all processes of sharing power.

Some scholars recommend more intersectional analysis of gender and leadership in relation to power. Tillapaugh, Mitchell, and Soria (2017) encourage students to notice ways that conversations about power are gendered, where power might look natural on a man, whereas a powerful woman might be seen as problematic or in need of special scrutiny or explanation. One of the places to look for examples of this is among the candidates running for the 2020 Democratic party nomination for president of the United States. Listen to how commentators analyze the candidates' expressions, positions, and style in gendered ways. How power is perceived by others may be moderated by one's social identities and other factors. It is also important to distinguish power from authority. Some view authority as conferred power, or the formal right to make decisions that comes from holding a position or office. Often authority can be articulated and designated (e.g., setting the scope or limits of one's authority), but people rarely talk about the limits of power. So perhaps power is more personally held, while authority is formally ascribed.

Empowerment, the practice of sharing power and enabling others to exercise their own authority and influence, is frequently cited as a benefit of women in leadership. Kezar and Wheaton (2017) describe how empowerment involves processes of "breaking down hierarchical structures that contain power within only certain groups that hold positional authority through the creation of teams and the delegation of authority" (p. 21). Empowerment is typically considered a good thing, but it also merits a critical analysis. See Exercise 8.2 for more on troubling the idea of empowerment. Can power ever really be given away? What types of exploitation may be carried out under the guise of empowerment? Many of us have been victims of what I have termed *false empowerment*, where people are invited to exercise agency and independent authority on a decision or program only to find that the decision was made elsewhere, or to be countered when you make a decision contrary to what those with positional power had in mind. Like any ideology, power reflects the larger milieu in which it operates. When empowerment is reduced to a management buzzword or a motivational poster on the wall it may actually be perpetuating powerlessness. Writing about empowerment in the field of nursing, Clifford (1992) notes:

> Of all the nonsense being spread about power today (and it seems we're positively fixed on it—with everything from "power breakfasts" to "power suits"), perhaps the most pernicious is that power is a state of being rather than energy, status rather than dynamism, a seat rather than a vehicle. (p. 1)

New York Times contributor Jia Tolentino (2017) laments how empowerment, especially for women, has become commodified. She describes being hit with an onslaught of products that claim to transmit and increase female power, and how women of different socioeconomic classes are largely left out of the conversation. She notes:

> Sneakily, empowerment had turned into a theory that applied to the needy while describing a process more realistically applicable to the rich. The word was built on a misaligned foundation; no amount of awareness can change the fact that it's the already-powerful who tend to experience empowerment at any meaningful rate. Today "empowerment" invokes power while signifying the lack of it. It functions like an explorer staking a claim on new territory with a white flag. (para. 4)

This is not to say that you should not seek to be empowered or to empower others. I am merely suggesting that we think more critically about who is served by the concept of empowerment and whether power can ever be given away.

The Great Women Theory of Leadership: The Problem With Positive Stereotypes and Precarious Pedestals

Kezar and Wheaton (2017) describe a set of characteristics that have been labeled "women's ways leadership" (p. 20). This type of leadership involves a focus on ethics and values and people who "emphasize mutual power and influence processes, attend to relationships and tasks, and encourage democratic

Exercise 8.2.
Troubling Power and Empowerment

If we agree that power is present in all relationships as put forward in chapter 2, in what ways do you feel like you have access to power? Which kinds of power? In what ways are you disenfranchised? How will you avoid the danger of concentrated power and its potential for abuse? How will you speak truth to power and similarly surround yourself with people capable of critically evaluating diverse sources of information? What do justice, equity, and empowerment look like in the organizations of which you are a member?

Keep pondering the distinctions between leadership and management, authority and power, empowerment and disempowerment, and so on. For more musings, NASPA Student Affairs Professional in Higher Education has a student leadership program knowledge community that routinely shares fun podcasts related to various leadership themes and ideas. Episode 34 focuses on power and authority. You can listen at this web address: https://soundcloud.com/user-606900324-709612745

and participatory forms of decision-making" (p. 20). As described previously, empirical research on gender differences often reveals very small actual differences between men and women's leadership styles, yet these differences are often exaggerated. Also, gendered views are often extremely resistant to change. In some ways, it feels empowering to say that women's leadership is the antidote to all the evils in the world, yet we know the truth is far more complex. We need all people, men, women, and those who identify beyond binary gender labels, to work in more inclusive and egalitarian ways.

One of the best deconstructions of the danger of labeling any set of characteristics as women's ways of leadership is Pittinsky, Bacon, and Welle's (2007) writing on *The Great Women Theory of Leadership? Perils of Positive Stereotypes and Precarious Pedestals.* They pose questions such as: Does a gendered perspective advance our understanding of leadership? What are the unintended results of holding gendered notions of leadership? How might expectations shape behavior? And do stereotypes about women diminish our expectation that men will engage in collaboration, cooperation, personal contacts, encouragement, and participation?

Pittinsky and colleagues describe four perils that occur when we elevate women's ways of leading as unique from broader conceptions of leadership.

First, if women are said to lead in certain ways, those who do not exhibit these gendered characteristics may be excluded from leadership or be told that they should lead in more gender-congruent ways. Take, for example, the agentic and assertive woman who has a commanding personality. Her direct approach may violate gendered expectations that women should be collaborative and relational. She may lose credibility or be labeled as controlling or bitchy whereas a man exhibiting similar behaviors is seen as strong and decisive. Second, although there is some evidence that women tend to lead in more participatory or democratic styles while men tend toward more autocratic or directive styles, most research on gender differences in leadership reveals very small differences across gender. A glaring limitation of these studies is that almost none invited participants to identify as genderfluid, leaving those voices out of the research entirely. The third peril of placing women's ways of leading on a pedestal addresses how people with different beliefs and expectations can view the same behavior differently. This can result in molding, where we start to describe our behavior and leadership in gendered terms, even when the data do not support the assertion. This process can reinforce stereotypes about gender and leadership. The strong agentic woman described here may find herself in situations where she is expected to be collaborative and less forceful, simply because of her gender. Finally, the fourth peril describes how gendered views of leadership become a polarizing force, reinforcing dichotomous views and limiting options for all leaders.

Leadership and Intersectional Identities

Eagly and Carli (2007) describe how people's stereotypes about women and leaders create resistance to women's leadership. They detail the tension between women leaders being expected to fulfill the feminine gender role by being warm, friendly, and nice, while also being expected to fulfill the masculine leadership role by displaying assertiveness and competence. This tension is just one of the many pressures facing women in leadership. Now consider the situation for women who hold several historically marginalized identities. The book *Women and Leadership: Transforming Visions and Diverse Voices* (Chin, Lott, Rice, & Sanchez-Hucles, 2007) describes the experiences of many women of color as they navigate leadership and deal with gendered racism. Some of these pressures are described in the following vocabulary list. Having the vocabulary to name thoughts, feelings, or experiences can go a long way toward preventing the internalization of these ideas.

Being the "First" or "Only"

When women break through glass ceilings or successfully navigate leadership labyrinths to gain positions of power in organizations, they may be the first or only representative with their particular set of identities (woman, transgender, woman of color, etc.). This experience of breakthrough offers unique pressures. Women may worry about how their job performance may be extrapolated to all who come after them and feel an extra pressure to succeed. Women may be lauded for their achievements, while simultaneously experiencing an onslaught of microaggressions. Sanchez-Hucles and Sanchez (2007) describe women of color being complimented on how articulate they are, or how different they may be from other people of color. The real and psychological burden of these comments cannot be ignored.

Burnout

Women in leadership, especially those with historically marginalized identities, are vulnerable to burnout. The isolation and constant challenges inherent in navigating traditional leadership environments can exact a large psychological and physical toll. Gorski and Chen (2015) found the following categories of symptoms experienced by activists facing burnout: (a) deterioration of psychological and emotional well-being, (b) deterioration of physical well-being, and (c) disillusionment and hopelessness. Often these symptoms lead to people withdrawing from triggering places and spaces either temporarily or permanently. Researcher William Smith (2010) coined the term *racial battle fatigue* while studying how racialized microaggressions affected Black students at predominantly white colleges and universities. Related to burnout, racial battle fatigue describes the psychophysiological symptoms, such as anxiety, frustration, shock, anger, and depression, that people of color may experience living in and navigating historically white spaces.

Code-Switching

Code-switching refers to the practice of going back and forth between cultures of one's identities and majority culture. Women with multiple social identities are often adept at adapting to fit in with mainstream culture (read white, masculine, cisgender, and heteronormative) in order to access power, information, and opportunity; however, they have to guard against not adapting so well that they lose their history, culture, and identity. This can be a tightrope to walk. It is important to understand the culture and rules of an organization or social setting, particularly the ones that are unspoken or unwritten, so that you can make conscious decisions about when to operate within versus outside of the culture.

One of the most complex examples of code-switching and stereotype threat I have seen depicted on television is in Issa Rae's HBO show *Insecure* (North & Matsoukas, 2016). Issa's friend Molly works at an elite law firm and has worked incredibly hard to fit in as an African American woman in a majority white male culture. An African American woman, Rasheeda, is hired as an intern at the firm and shows up as her full authentic self, including her use of language and behaviors from her urban background. Molly is faced with trying to help the intern assimilate to the firm culture, while also acknowledging her own anxieties about having to change herself to advance. *New York Times* critic Angelica Bastien (2016) describes the code-switching in this episode as follows:

> Given all that black women are forced to deal with—from police brutality to being told that our natural hair is unprofessional—it isn't surprising that we learn to create armor between ourselves and the rest of the world. This armor takes a variety of forms. But one particular to the black community is code-switching. We learn early and often that the way we are in spaces with other black people is not the way we should be in professional circles. So the clipped words, slang and biting humor we use with friends becomes smoothed out. We take on a style that our white peers find safe and non-threatening. It isn't lying, it's a means of survival. But what happens when a black coworker finds code-switching to be dishonest and the language we use to define ourselves fails? When Molly takes the intern aside and suggest that she "switch it up a little bit" Rasheeda takes offense. Molly's desire to get Rasheeda to act in a way that fits the aesthetics of a high-powered law firm isn't a wholly selfless act—she also wants to protect herself. When you work in worlds where black faces are rare (especially in positions of power) a mistake your coworker makes may reflect unfairly on you. In many ways, code-switching is related to the ways in which we create public and private selves.

Epistemic Privilege

Sanchez-Hucles and Sanchez (2007) describe how "being at the intersection of interlocking indices of oppression can allow a unique view as to how dimensions like race, class, gender, ability, and sexuality operate as loci of power in society" (p. 215). Moya (2001) terms this process *epistemic privilege*, or the advantage that oppressed people may have in understanding how the world works, and offers as an example how some women of color have used their marginalization to create critiques of organizations, processes, and systems, as well as to foster creative approaches to leadership. This concept is closely tied to that of *epistemic injustice*, which describes the unfairness about how knowledge is communicated and understood, including silencing, smothering, exploitation, and oppression (Fricker, 2007).

Hierarchies of Oppression

Hierarchies of oppression refers to the tendency to essentialize people to one salient identity rather than acknowledge their many intersectional identities, and to assess which of one's marginalized identities is most subject to oppression. This oppression can also occur among people as they compare whose identities are more oppressed by society. Most argue that, since all oppressions are linked, there should be no hierarchy of oppression. Lorde (1983) describes it this way:

> Within the lesbian community I am Black, and within the Black community I am a lesbian. Any attack against Black people is a lesbian and gay issue, because thousands of other Black women are part of the lesbian community. Any attack against lesbians and gay men is a Black issue because thousands of lesbians and gay men are Black. There is no hierarchy of oppression. . . . I know I cannot afford the luxury of fighting one form of oppression only. I cannot afford to believe that, freedom from intolerance is the right of only one particular group. And I cannot afford to choose between the fronts upon which I must battle these forces of discrimination, wherever they appear to destroy me, it will not be long before they appear to destroy you. (p. 9)

Miasma Condition

Sanchez-Hucles and Sanchez (2007) note that women leaders from historically marginalized backgrounds often face extra challenges and stressors in the workplace. Even when workplaces guard against overt racism and discrimination, they often espouse a "fiction of equality" where those from dominant identities assume an equal playing field. The reality is often far different when unconscious biases and micro-aggressions are unchecked. Livers and Caver (2003) call this reality a *miasma*, referring to the wariness, defensiveness, and alertness required of those from underrepresented backgrounds that taxes one's energy, time, productivity, and creativity. Sanchez-Hucles and Sanchez (2007) describe how miasma "promotes the double burden of contending with increased scrutiny by others while being vigilant in attending to possible landmines in the environment that could threaten one's status" (p. 219). They describe ways to defend against organizational miasma that include establishing a network of trusted associates to assess and validate concerns and perceptions about inequality, as well as organizations providing better support and mentoring in ways that value the differences of diverse leaders.

Reciprocal Empowerment

Sanchez-Hucles and Sanchez (2007) describe reciprocal empowerment as a leadership style of respect, reciprocity, equality, and personal authority that is characterized by concepts such as mutuality, compassion, collectivity, engagement, and consensus to enhance oneself and others. They note how women in leadership positions may be uncomfortable identifying as leaders because of connotations of individuality, dominance, and hierarchy in traditional approaches to leadership that may lead to others minimizing their contributions and effectiveness.

Stereotype Threat

In a 2005 Catalyst study of women's leadership, respondents cited stereotypes as the number one barrier to their advancement. Sanchez, Hucles, Sanchez-Hucles, and Mehta (2007) examine the intersection of leadership and ethnicity. They describe how ethnic stereotypes for women can lead to real status differences in the workplace; how racial stereotypes are often more pervasive than those based on gender; how women of color often contend with sexual stereotypes; and how token status "may lead to inaccurate assessment of work productivity and unrealistic expectations that can promote burnout, fatigue, and unwillingness to seek high level positions" (p. 238). Stereotype threat occurs when women internalize these negative perceptions into their own self-perception (Hoyt & Murphy, 2016).

Many women of color feel the need to work twice as hard as others and have to remain constantly vigilant about counteracting dominant stereotypes related to their marginalized identities. This stereotype threat can lead to high anxiety, be draining, and lead to burnout and dropping out. For example, an African heritage friend of mine shared how hard she works to never be late to meetings as she does not want to contribute to the inaccurate perception that Black people are never on time. Like everyone, she occasionally faces unavoidable circumstances that cause her to be late, but the toll of that experience weighs especially heavy on her as she feels she is letting down her entire community rather than just treating it as a one-off part of life.

Tokenism

Tokenism refers to the practice of making only a perfunctory or symbolic effort to be inclusive to members of minority groups, especially by recruiting a small number of people from underrepresented groups in order to give the appearance of racial or sexual equality within a workforce. The result of tokenism is often the appearance of diversity without actual inclusion.

Triple Jeopardy

Women of color in leadership roles may experience triple jeopardy because of the many stereotypes associated with gender, race, and ethnicity that their multiple identities may trigger in others (Sanchez-Hucles & Sanchez, 2007). Sanchez-Hucles and Davis (2010) describe the complexities that ensue when women of color come from a variety of cultural and ethnic backgrounds and must conform to "European American prototypes representing traditional ethnic, racial, and gender behavior" in addition to gendered leadership prototypes (p. 174).

As women of color navigate leadership and deal with gendered racism, they may face any of the aforementioned barriers to leadership. Additionally, they may feel socially isolated or invisible, may feel greater pressure to perform and make fewer mistakes, may be seen as less credible, may have their identities misperceived or constantly interrogated, may have trouble accessing mentors or supporters, and may experience more stress and burnout (Turner, 2001).

Sage identifies as an African American, biracial, cisgender, heterosexual woman who grew up working class, is middle-aged, and identifies as spiritual.

Narratives and Counternarratives: Sage's Story

Whenever I've worked somewhere for a while, and once my white colleagues see me beyond the stereotype of an angry Black woman, I enter an unasked-for circle of trust. I become the person for my white colleagues to work out their white privilege. I am often expected to help them deal with their white guilt and help them feel better. These moments often occur after a student of color questions their authority or expresses frustration for a policy that they oversee. If my colleagues are unable to reconcile the matter with the student, or if a misunderstanding ensues, these colleagues often need assistance in learning how to mitigate these situations. They often make claims of, "I hope I did not come across wrong," "My point was to be fair and consistent, you know, I cannot treat certain students differently," "Do you think I came across racist when I said . . ."

While I understand that, at times, difficult conversations with students need to be debriefed and I am often willing to assist those in need, this becomes problematic when this continues to occur repeatedly. As a Black woman, I find that my body is often expected to do extra emotional labor that is often an exhausting experience. This labor is in addition to my racial battle fatigue, in addition to defending against microaggressions; there is also the extra labor employed as a result of my identity. Further, because I am often the only person of color in the department, there seems to always be this higher standard expected of me, for which I am always noticed and I often contemplate how Black am I allowed to actually be. I know that I am expected to exude exceptional leadership skills in my position and part of those include empathy and teamwork, and I am often torn with how to demonstrate those skills while also managing my own wellness.

Degendering Leadership

Equating leadership with masculinity is dangerous. This chapter troubles the notion that women tend to lead in more participatory or democratic styles, whereas men tend toward autocratic or directive styles. It describes the dangers inherent in putting women's leadership on a "precarious pedestal" where it is seen as something distinct from other approaches to leadership. This tendency for people to describe leadership in gendered ways has led to a call to degender leadership (Katuna, 2019; Pittinsky et al., 2007). Leadership needs to be degendered because gendered approaches exclude those whose approaches to leadership do not match stereotypes. Gendered approaches also typically ignore transgender, nonbinary, and intersex leaders. Gendered approaches may also lead to stereotype threat where women internalize negative beliefs about their capability for leadership (Hoyt & Murphy, 2016).

When I was discussing this chapter with colleagues, leadership educators Trisha Teig and Amber Wiest posed a powerful question. They asked, "Is the goal to degender or to regender leadership?" This question suggests that if we recognize the centrality of multiple identities to the leadership process, then degendering leadership may function to deny or dissociate the effects of gender (or other identities) on leadership. Teig stated, "Since our bodies show up with us in leadership spaces, we cannot disassociate them from our work." She suggested that although we need to move away from stereotypical approaches to leadership, we also need to reexamine how our embodied selves shape how we lead and how that leadership is perceived. This thinking is in line with the emerging field of somatic leadership that draws on neuroscience, emotional intelligence, and mindfulness to prioritize the body in leadership learning (Hamill, 2013).

Regardless of whether you believe we need to degender or regender leadership, it is important to question the role gender plays in leadership. Does a gendered perspective advance our understanding of leadership? What results from holding gendered notions of leadership? How might expectations related to gender shape behavior? Two ways to bring a critical examination of gender to leadership are to focus on intersectionality and to embrace culturally relevant leadership.

Focus on Intersectionality

Because intersectionality reveals the connections among multiple social identities, it invites us not to reduce individuals to single categories or stereotypes.

Instead, we should acknowledge the multiple compounding effects of these interactions in how people understand and navigate their own leadership identity, behavior, and effectiveness. This requires doing our own self-work to understand our own privileged and oppressed identities and how they may show up in leadership. It means refusing to essentialize others and seeking to understand leadership from the lens of multiple social identities, communities, and contexts. It means guarding against burnout and the physical and psychological toll it takes to navigate unwelcoming or even hostile spaces. It means going beyond gendered conversations about women's ways of leading or feminine leadership styles to instead degender leadership. Jones (2016) captures the importance of this process as follows:

> Taking an intersectional view of leadership (i.e., incorporating attention to multiple social identities and larger structure of inequality) provides a powerful tool for intercultural engagement and promotes culturally relevant leadership practices grounded in an authentic sense of self. Understanding of social identities is crucial for developing skills and sensibilities for effectively engaging across differences and for an increasingly diverse and global world. (p. 33)

Embrace Culturally Relevant Leadership Learning

The culturally relevant leadership learning (CRLL) model (see Figure 8.1) was developed in response to the proliferation of leadership theories and approaches that do not take identity into account. As this chapter demonstrates, leadership must involve and address "the advantages and disadvantages difference creates" (Bertrand Jones, Guthrie, & Osteen, 2016, p. 10). At the center of this model are three dimensions of development that inform the leadership learning process—identity, capacity, and efficacy. Identity, described as "ongoing, lifelong engagements to understand ourselves within the context of our lives" (Bertrand Jones et al., 2016, p. 13), is foundational to leadership. Your identity, or who you are, is shaped by historical, political, and cultural forces, as well as your intersectional social identities, and your leadership identity (explored in chapter 3). How you conceptualize your identity may inform your leadership capacity, or the combination of knowledge, skills, and attitudes necessary to engage effectively in the leadership process (Dugan, 2017; Guthrie & Chunoo, 2018). Your leadership identity and capacity both inform and are informed by your leadership efficacy. Discussed in chapter 2, leadership efficacy refers to your own beliefs about your abilities to exercise your leadership knowledge and skills in a given situation (Dugan et al., 2013).

Campus climate has an important moderating effect on student growth, development, and learning. As such, the CRLL model involves addressing five domains of culture that affect leadership learning. The model seeks to

Figure 8.1. The CRLL model.

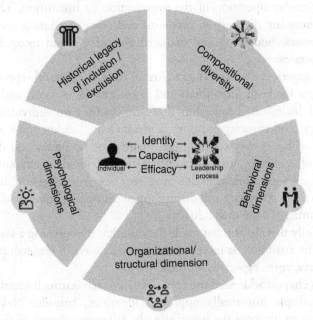

Note. Guthrie, Bertrand Jones, and Osteen (2016). Used with permission.

address the ways that leadership has historically excluded certain voices, such that "a hidden, or unintentional, curriculum operates as a subtext throughout leadership learning" (Bertrand Jones, et al., 2016, p. 16). CRLL requires that people address the historical legacy of inclusion or exclusion within any leadership environment or context. It focuses on compositional diversity, or the number and proportion of various populations present in a particular context or environment. It suggests an examination of the psychological dimension of any particular organization or space where leadership is exercised. For example, what are perceptions about discrimination, stereotyping, or conflict in a given space? What attitudes about difference exist? How do members of that culture or community react to issues related to diversity and inclusion (Bertrand Jones et al., 2016)?

The model also takes the behavioral and organizational/structural dimension into account. The behavioral dimension examines the interactions among members of an organization or community and the quality of interaction within culturally diverse groups. This might include the frequency and quality of conversations within and across difference, also termed *sociocultural conversations*, exposure to counternarratives and content representing diverse views and experiences, and cultivation of the habits of critical reflection

(Dugan & Velazquez, 2015). The organizational/structural dimension looks at the day-to-day operation of the organization or institution. This might include examining diversity in programs and curricula, hiring and recruitment processes, budgeting and financial allocations, and recognition and reward processes.

Taken together, the component parts of the CRLL model represent myriad strategies for both individuals and organizations to assess and enhance equity and inclusion. Leadership that only focuses on individual identities, efficacy, and capacity-building is insufficient. Leaders must also learn to grapple with larger systemic forces, maintained by power and dominant narratives of exclusion, and their effects on individual agency and action. Culturally relevant leadership learning requires going beyond individual learning to also interrogate and disrupt organizational, institutional, and systemic dynamics (Owen et al., 2017).

Hopefully this chapter has made the case that stereotyping a set of traits, behaviors, or attributes as indicative of women's ways of leadership is detrimental to everyone, especially women.

As this chapter addressed the complexities of navigating leadership while holding multiple historically oppressed identities, consider Nako's story about trying to navigate the two distinctly different cultures of the United States and Japan.

Nako identifies as a Japanese, cisgender, heterosexual, middle-class female.

Narratives and Counternarratives: Nako's Story

Growing up in Japan, I was taught that it was inappropriate to demonstrate my abilities, talents, and knowledge to others. I was also raised to avoid criticizing other people or specific incidents because it was more important for me to emphasize group harmony. Japanese society privileges the virtue of humility, especially among women. Being critical is related to the unfavorable propensity of showing off one's abilities and knowledge to others; the qualities of being critical and being humble contradict one another.

However, in the United States, I have observed that value is often assigned to the characteristic of being critical, especially among academics, of which I am one. During my academic career in the United Sates, I have developed the more critical aspects of my nature and learned to apply critical thinking to my analyses of various situations. One day, when I was traveling with my mother, we started to argue about a certain topic. In fact, I do not even remember the particular subject of the disagreement; however, I vividly remember that my mother started to cry silently because she felt that I had become too critical and had started to express my opinions too strongly. This incident was a kind of wake-up call for me. Although I currently reside in the United States, I am still, fundamentally, a member of Japanese society. I suddenly felt that, as a Japanese woman, I could not be quite as critical as I had become. I recognized that I must be able to exist within two distinct cultures and ideologies every day because even though I currently live in the United States, I am not American.

I am constantly reminded about my un-Americanness. One day, I told a white male colleague about something that had happened to me earlier that day: "Today, in my class, one student laughed at my English." The experience had been an uncomfortable one, as I had long entertained negative ideas about how my nonnative-English accent and imperfect English-language proficiency might affect my academic career in the United States. I had hoped that, by sharing this unpleasant experience with someone, I would be able to make sense of it in a more constructive way. He responded by telling me that, for him, "Everyone is the same, no matter who they are. I do not think about people's race or ethnicity or any other different identities." I regarded this as a typically color-blind statement, but also wondered if I was being too sensitive to his seemingly inoffensive statement. I knew that my familiarity with the literature concerning issues of social justice was prompting me to view his perspective in this negative way. As an Asian woman and nonnative-English speaker, was I being too sensitive to issues of social justice?

Straddling the divide between two different cultures—American and Japanese—has provided me with quite a few opportunities to reflect on my dual identity and life philosophy. Perhaps it might be more accurate to say that I have had the experience of living in accordance with two distinct ideologies. Because I currently live in the United States and work in academia, I often ask myself the following question: "If I were a white male native-English speaker, would my experience be different?"

9

REIMAGINING WOMEN
AND LEADERSHIP

Strategies, Allies, and Critical Hope

Most activism is brought about by us ordinary people.

—Patricia Hill Collins, "We Don't Need Another Dr. King," 2000

The future depends entirely on what each of us does every day; a movement is only people moving.

—Gloria Steinem, *Outrageous Acts and Everyday Rebellions*, 1987

hapter 8 concluded with recommendations about how to address systemic forces that affect how gender and leadership are constructed and practiced. This final chapter continues to move from a critical contemplation of gender and leadership to concrete strategies for action. We start by considering how all oppressions are interrelated and how positionality, identity, and power intersect to shape approaches to leadership for social change. As not all problems can be solved the same way, diverse levers for social change are described. We consider Harro's cycle of socialization and our own positionality in that cycle. The chapter concludes with common issues faced by agents of change: how to deal with those who do not buy into your cause; how to avoid burnout; and finally, how to maintain critical hope.

Feminist Leadership Across Social Change Movements

Previous chapters have addressed the concept of intersectionality. Versions of this idea have been part of Black feminist thought since the 1970s. Members of the Combahee River Collective referred to the matrix of domination and ideas of interlocking systems of oppression to describe how racial, sexual, heterosexual, and class oppression are, in fact, linked (Collins, 1990;

Moraga, & Anzaldúa, 2015). There is power in moving beyond either/or dichotomous thinking. One benefit of moving beyond categorizing people and instead thinking in intersectional ways is that we can move past the idea that categories of difference must be ranked. Chapter 8 addressed the phenomenon of hierarchies of oppression, where the tendency is to place people into only one identity category (e.g., Asian; woman; Jewish) rather than acknowledge their many intersectional identities, and to assess which of one's marginalized identities is most subject to oppression. By definition, *feminist leadership* should be both antisexist and antiracist.

Collins (1990) suggests that "replacing additive models of oppression with interlocking ones creates possibilities for new paradigms" where "the goal is not merely to survive or to fit in or to cope; rather, it becomes a place where we feel ownership and accountability" (p. 223). The point here is that as we become accepting of intersectional identities and see how all oppressions are linked, we understand how feminist leadership exists in almost all social change movements. I recently saw this point in action when a woman of color who was active in the #MeToo movement on campus was confronted by a male peer who led campus activism related to the Black Lives Matter movement. He asked the woman if her activism around sexual violence and sexual assault detracted students' energy and commitment to work on Black Lives Matter. Her answer was that any time she works on #MeToo issues, she is also communicating that Black Lives Matter because of the identities she holds. Rather than engage in an "oppression Olympics" the woman encouraged others to always center their marginalized identities so that change can happen on multiple fronts. Activists are finding many paths to center their activism in their identities. My campus has student groups called Undocublack (students of color who also hold undocumented status), FLIP (first-generation students from low-income backgrounds), BlackFemmes (a celebration of queer and trans Black people of all genders), Working Mothers Alliance, Jews for Palestinian Justice, and more.

So how do we unite with others to disrupt existing power structures around gender and leadership? Dugan (2017) reminds us that not everyone enters authoritarian structures on equal footing. Positionality, identity, knowledge, and power all intersect to shape our approaches to social change. Strategies people can use to interrogate existing structures include: engaging in critical self-reflection, using social and cultural capital to disrupt dominant narratives, moving through critique to reconstruction and being proactive, and teaching others how to engage in social change (Dugan, 2017).

Shea and Renn (2017) argue that feminist leaders should not shy away from thinking of power as inherently adversarial. Instead they recommend feminist leadership subvert power to create organizational and social change. Activists can do this by naming and challenging oppressive structural power inherent in their organizations. This is a way to counteract feelings of powerlessness. I saw this in practice on my campus when students sued the university to release the details of agreements between large donors, such as the Koch brothers, and the university. Shea and Renn suggest feminist leaders also share power in collaborative and collective ways. Power can be shared by inviting others to have input on decisions; educating each other about strategies and tactics for change; and sustaining each other through support, recognition, and promoting well-being.

Leadership Levers for Social Change: A Taxonomy of Action

Not all problems can be solved the same way. Different social issues require the use of distinct levers of change. Haber-Curran and Tillapaugh (2018) remind us that "engaging in socially just leadership requires a wide range of leadership capacities, behaviors, and approaches for people of all genders" (p. 85). They offer a detailed list of the knowledge, skills, and values necessary to be an effective agent of change. Among many others, these include an understanding of "the limitations of traditional, hierarchical, and authoritarian conceptualizations of leadership," acknowledging how these approaches may leave out individuals and can "further reinforce gendered privilege and oppression" (p. 87). They encourage students to value "inclusive feminism that seeks to end sexism, genderism, and cissexism" (p. 87) and to use strategies that involve "critical examination and inquiry at individual, group, and systemic levels" (p. 87).

Table 9.1 details a variety of different strategies for making change. Which of the levers are most suited to the issues you care about? One can see how direct service might be the most powerful when confronted with someone in immediate need, whereas advocacy or capacity building might be most useful when trying to shift an unjust policy.

The Cycle of Liberation

Remember Harro's (2013b) cycle of socialization reviewed in chapter 4? Harro realized that as people come to more deeply understand the nature of oppression and the roles they play in it, they are increasingly motivated to do something about injustice beyond personal changes. If we can name the many forces that socialize and oppress us, might we also be able to use that knowledge to counteract these forces and seek liberation? Harro designed

TABLE 9.1
Forms of Civic Engagement

Form of Engagement	Description
Direct Service	Giving personal time and energy to address immediate community needs. Examples include tutoring, serving food at a shelter, building or repairing homes, and neighborhood or park clean-ups.
Community Research	Exploring a community to learn about its assets and how it is being affected by current social problems. This form of civic engagement provides knowledge that other efforts can build upon.
Advocacy and Education	Using various modes of persuasion (e.g., petitions, marches, letter-writing) to convince government or corporate decision-makers to make choices that will benefit the community. Raising public awareness of social issues by giving speeches to community groups, distributing written materials to the general public, or providing educational activities in schools.
Capacity Building	Working with the diverse constituencies of a community, building on existing assets to solve problems and make it a better place. Creating a space for everyone in the community to have a say in what the community should be like and how to get there.
Political Involvement	Participating in processes of government, such as campaigning and voting. This includes keeping informed about issues in the local, national, and global communities in order to vote responsibly and engaging in discourse and debate about current social issues.
Socially Responsible Personal and Professional Behavior	Maintaining a sense of responsibility to the welfare of others when making personal or professional decisions. Using one's career or professional training to benefit the community. This category describes personal lifestyle choices that reflect commitment to one's values: recycling, driving a hybrid car, or bicycling to work; buying or not buying certain products because of unjust corporate policies or choosing to work for companies with socially just priorities.
Philanthropic Giving	Donating funding or needed items, organizing or participating in fundraising events.
Participation in Associations	Participating in community organizations that develop the social networks that provide a foundation for community-building efforts, including civic associations, sports leagues, church choirs, and school boards.

Note. Owen & Wagner (2010).

the cycle of liberation based on patterns of events common to every success-ful critical transformation or liberation effort. She cautions that the cycle, depicted in Figure 9.1, is not a "how to" since every change effort is differ-ent, but is instead a description of what has worked for others. Harro's model depicts seven stages of change, although people can enter and exit the model at any point, and most processes of transformation take many cycles through the model. Working to end oppression is sadly never completely done. Harro defines *liberation* as critical transformation, or being able to name and address the systemic structures and forces that contribute to oppression.

Waking Up

Harro (2013b) believes that most people enter the cycle of liberation as a result of experiencing a critical incident that causes them to look at them-selves and the world in new ways. For some, exploring the ideas in this book might create dissonance and invite you to consider concepts of gender and leadership from different perspectives than you had before. Maybe you have never thought of yourself as capable of leadership but now feel more effica-cious because you have practiced some of the leadership efficacy building strategies covered in chapter 3. Others may experience injustice on a daily basis and thus are already "woke."

Getting Ready

The next phase of the liberation cycle involves consciously dismantling and rebuilding aspects of ourselves based on our new views and perspectives. Harro (2013a) states, "Once we know something, we can't not know it any-more" (p. 620). This is reminiscent of Buddhist philosopher Thich Nhat Hanh's (1992) words, "Once there is seeing, there must be acting. Otherwise, what's the use of seeing?" (p. 91). Important processes at this stage include introspection, education, and consciousness raising. While these processes serve to empower the self, they must be accompanied by processes of dis-mantling our stereotypes, ignorance, discriminatory or privileged attitudes, and behaviors that limit ourselves and others such as collusion and oppres-sive language and actions. Part of this process is building a set of tools to use throughout the process, as well as seeking inspiration and connections in our journeys. What tools are in your tool belt for combatting gender injustice? For creating more equitable systems of leadership?

Reaching Out

The next phase in Harro's (2013b) cycle involves practicing the skills and tools we gained in the getting ready phase. This may include speaking out and naming injustices when we disagree instead of staying silent. Perhaps this book caused you to think in new ways about topics such as feminism, the pay gap, rights for transgender people, or the need to name benevolent sexism when you see it. How are you articulating your beliefs among your family, friends, and coworkers? This stage involves risk as others might push back and question your ideas. It also can foster new connections as others notice and support your commitments.

Building Community

Social change never happens in isolation. It requires sustained dialogue with others. As we discussed in previous chapters, building community involves dialoguing with people who are like us (who share the same social identities, or similar commitments to a cause) and with people who are different from us. The latter part is much harder and may require questioning assumptions, rules, roles, and structures. Why is spending time in sustained dialogue with people who disagree with us essential to social change? Harro (2013a) says, "We will never be able to focus on the real challenge—changing the system—until the barriers and boundaries that divide us are minimized" (p. 622). Consider how different this approach is from the labeling and name-calling we witness on social media. It is a radical act to spend time exploring our differences and deeply listening to those with whom we might initially disagree. Harro describes the outcomes of this process as enhancing our energy, resources, inspiration, understanding, compassion, empathy, humanness, and motivation. Who are you dialoguing with who is similar to or different from you?

Coalescing

This step involves joining with allies to move into action by interrupting and confronting oppressive systems. This can include any of the actions described in Figure 9.1 such as educating, fundraising, lobbying, conducting action research, working on policy, activism, and allyship. Consider how many of us rush to this stage without first doing the work of the prior three stages. Action and activism done with preparation, thoughtful intention, and diverse coalitions can be much more powerful than activism alone. For wonderful examples of activist journeys, read the two narratives at the end of this chapter and note how the two women featured discuss their journeys through the cycle of liberation.

Creating Change

For Harro (2013b), creating change refers to the process of critically transforming institutions and creating new culture. This stage asks participants to demonstrate leadership, question assumptions, take risks, share power,

Figure 9.1. Harro's cycle of liberation.

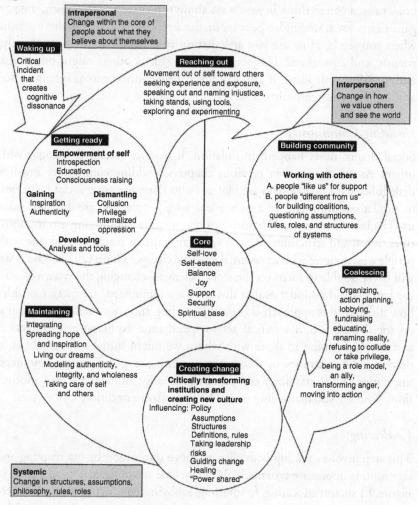

Note. Harro (2013b). Used with permission.

influence policy, and guide change. There are myriad resources on how to create change. For practical strategies, I recommend the book *Do Good Well* (Vasan & Przybylo, 2012), which was written by young women activists and offers a host of information on everything from how to use the media to achieve your goals to how to measure and evaluate your change efforts.

Maintaining

Harro (2013b) reminds us that making change happen is not the last step in the cycle of liberation. It can be even harder to nurture and maintain new

Exercise 9.1.
Mapping Your Own Journey

Place a check mark next to the change processes and skills presented in Harro's (2013b) cycle of liberation that you feel are already in your leadership toolkit. Place a star next to those to which you aspire. Place a question mark next to any concepts you are unfamiliar with or want to learn more about.

Consider the core of the model. Reflect on your own practices of self-love, self-esteem, balance, joy, support, security, and spirituality. How are you cultivating these in your own life? In your work with others? If you feel comfortable, you might share your results with others working on similar change efforts as you are. Groups and organizations could do a collective map of their approach to liberation. Remember that your journey is uniquely yours. It is an old saying that comparison is the thief of joy. How you navigate the cycles of socialization and liberation is unique to you.

structures, rules, roles, and assumptions. This step involves more than just organizational work. It also requires modeling authenticity, integrity, and wholeness. It includes spreading hope and inspiration, as well as accepting accountability. Finally, it involves taking care of others and yourself. How do you practice self-care in your journey toward change?

Whether you are thinking about how to navigate the leadership laby-rinth, or considering which of the stages of the cycle of liberation are most useful to you (see Exercise 9.1), it is important to reflect on your own jour-ney with gender and leadership, and your own positionality in the cycle of liberation.

Ally Development: You've Got to Have Friends

Change work is always better when you have friends and allies for the journey. A *social justice ally* is defined as someone who will interrupt oppression when it is aimed at a target person or group; someone who recognizes privilege and will question and resist institutionalized oppres-sion as much as possible (Reason, Broido, Davis, & Evans, 2005). Allies are most effective when they realize that oppression hurts all people, not just the target of oppressive acts (Davis & Harrison, 2013). I learned this the hard way when one of my friends called me out for not being more vocal on social media about police brutality against people of color. She had noticed that I was always vocal when a gender issue was involved but was mostly silent when it was an issue related to race. Although I consider myself a social justice ally in other spaces, I was worried that using my voice on police brutality issues might take away attention from others more directly affected by the issue. My friend challenged my thinking about my own visibility and lack of risk-taking in calling out injustice wherever it may occur. I am grateful for her willingness to engage with me about this and I have shifted my actions as a result. I am also able to bring my gender identity to the cause and ask why more attention is paid to brutality against men of color than the equally horrifying violence against women of color.

There are several models of how people become social justice allies (Alimo, 2012; Broido, 2000; Edwards, 2006; Ortiz & Rhoads, 2000; Reason et al., 2005). Similar to the cycle of liberation, people generally move through stages of unawareness of social injustices, to increasing awareness and education about social justice, followed by integration and commitment to social action (Linder, 2015). Edwards's (2006) model describes three kinds of allies for social justice. Allies centered in self-interest generally feel motivated by a connection to one person, rather than to a group or issue, and seek to protect that individual. Altruistic allies may be guilt motivated in their allyship as their awareness of unearned privilege grows. These altruistic allies may evolve from working for people in the target group to working with targeted individuals. Allies for social justice feel connected to a larger issue, such as sexism, rather than to an individual, and understand their own role in perpetuating oppression.

Allies may not always be obvious or look like you. It is important to consider the role of men and people who are gender-nonconforming in feminism and liberation work. Johnson (2005), says this best: "The simple truth is that injustice can't be solved unless people who are heterosexual or male or Anglo or white or economically comfortable feel obligated to make the problem of privilege their problem and do something about it" (p. 10). In her address to the United Nations, Emma Watson (2014) wisely asked, "How can we effect change in the world when half of us do not feel invited or welcome to participate in the conversation?" (para. 18). The movement toward gender equity must be an inclusive one. Marine and colleagues (2017) describe how college-aged feminists are more likely to believe that feminists can be any gender, and that gender identity and expression are malleable. These beliefs invite men and transgender and genderqueer friends as more than allies in the feminist movement, but as essential to the work of social change.

Check out Leigh's narrative about how her brothers helped shape her self-confidence for leadership. Calliope describes how her dad's unwavering support molded her as a feminist.

Leigh identifies as a white, cisgender, heterosexual, middle-class woman.

Narratives and Counternarratives: Leigh's Story

It is the men in my life who have always supported me, protected me, cared for me, and made me feel like I could accomplish anything I set my mind to. Growing up in a large family is probably my greatest gift. Not many people can say that they have four older brothers and an older sister, but I am one of the lucky few. I can recall one day coming home from school and being upset because the boys at recess said that girls weren't allowed to play kickball anymore. All of my brothers said those boys were crazy and were probably just scared because they knew how good I was. That same day, they played kickball with me in the backyard for hours. During our game, they gave advice on how to kick the ball super hard and high so I could show the boys at school that I was even better than them. I was told to not listen to those boys and to play kickball anyway because they weren't allowed to keep me from doing anything I wanted to do.

My older brothers were constantly pushing me to be better in a positive way. They helped coach me through all sports whether it was soccer, basketball, swimming, or even dance and gymnastics. They taught me how to be competitive and a good team player. They encouraged me to be tough and strong, but also to be honest and not afraid to share my feelings. They constantly helped me with my homework and stressed the importance of school. I learned how to be respectful, polite, but also bold and charismatic. They preached self-confidence to me and said I didn't need to cake my face with makeup, wear certain clothes, or do anything to get a guy's attention because they should like me for me. But most of all, they always let me know that I could do anything I set my mind to and no one could tell me I had less worth because of my gender. They set very high standards and examples of the man I would want to be with. A lot of people don't get to have those examples in their life, so I feel extremely fortunate. I truly believe that their wisdom and support has helped me avoid many of the issues challenging women today, as well as prepared me to face inequality in the future.

Calliope identifies as a white, cisgender, heterosexual, middle class, Greek Orthodox woman.

Narratives and Counternarratives: Calliope's Story

The support from my dad is not sparkly, loud, or flashy. It is constant though. Quiet and constant. Powerful and constant. It is a standard. I cannot think of a specific moment when I knew my dad supported me as a girl, and later as a woman. There is no memory that makes me smile or brings tears to my eyes. When I think of the support from my dad, it is simply a given. Something I have taken for granted for as long as I can remember. My dad has established his support and respect for my mom, two sisters, and me in small, ordinary, and even boring ways. He quietly built our confidence and encouraged self-love all while shooting baskets or juggling the soccer ball in the front yard.

My dad's love and support is evident in his admiration for our mom. The way he speaks to her with love and respect. The way he laughs with her and at her when they are goofing around. The way he remains calm and has conversations when he is upset. The way he treats her like an equal, a partner, and the love of his life.

It is evident when he calls and asks if he should pick up pads or tampons on his way home. The way he doesn't avoid eye contact or talk in hushed tones when talking about periods or sex, the way other men do. The way he never makes us feel ashamed for a bodily function that we never asked for, yet are constantly made to feel embarrassed about.

It is evident when we have lively discussions at dinner about powerful women in history or the media. The way he does not have a distaste when using the words *woman* and *powerful* in the same sentence. The way he celebrates our female idols, educates himself on their accomplishments, and sends us birthday memes when it is Gal Gadot's birthday.

It was evident when he took me in his arms when the "love of my life" broke up with me when I was 15. When he did not avoid my tears, and tell me to wait for my mom to get home and deal with "girl stuff." When he held me, and let me cry, and told me I was the most amazing girl. When he told me I only deserve the best.

It was evident when my sister came home crying because the boys wouldn't let her play basketball anymore because she was better than them. When he told her to never let any boy dim her brightness. When he went outside to practice with her so she would become even better. When he told her to take a three pointer, flip the boys the finger, and walk off the court (which was later vetoed by my mom).

These are not huge life events. These are not memories that will go down in history. But they are aspects of an upbringing that fostered self-love, confidence, and power. They are part of a quiet lull that created three strong women.

Dealing With Nonfeminist Others

No matter how many times you are exhorted to talk across differences and to listen deeply to those who hold differing views from yours, there will be people who do not understand your commitments to gender equity and feminist leadership. This may be merely frustrating if they are a distant acquaintance or someone you don't see very often, but can be deeply hurtful if they are a family member or a close friend. Other than avoidance, what are some strategies for dealing with nonfeminist others in your life?

Talk to Them

It is important not to meet resistance with resistance. Consider inviting resistors into dialogue. Caprino (2017) offers powerful questions that might open up someone's thinking about gender inequality. You might work through these questions if your resistor is willing, and if you have the energy and emotional well-being to engage in this way. Invite your resistor to engage in an open-ended, nonjudgmental, nonhierarchical way. You might have to model what vulnerability looks like. For more guidelines about how to open agenda-free dialogues, check out Nash, Bradley, and Chickering's (2008) book *How to Talk About Hot Topics on Campus: From Polarization to Moral Conversation.* Caprino (2017) suggests the following logical sequence of open-ended questions to help reveal the limits of sexist thinking.

1. Do you believe that women and men deserve equal rights and equal opportunities? If not, why not, specifically?
2. Do you oppose the idea that every human being on the planet deserves equal rights and equal access to all opportunities? If you oppose it, what are you concerned will happen if equality is achieved? What are the downsides, in your way of thinking?
3. Do you believe that only certain groups of people should be allowed to have access to certain opportunities and rights? If so, which groups should be favored and granted this access, and who should decide that?
4. Do you believe that it would be inherently fair to grant women access to only partial rights while men have full array of other rights and opportunities?
5. Think back on what has shaped all your beliefs about these issues. Where did they come from specifically? Childhood, early adulthood? Your personal experiences with gender, or what you read and watch in the media? Who in your "tribe," family or peers influences your beliefs today?

6. What makes you mad and agitated to read in the media, about gender and equality?
7. Do you believe that a world that prevents certain people from accessing full rights and opportunities would lead to a fair, healthy, prosperous world for all?
8. In the end, do your beliefs actually feel right for you? Do they feel aligned with who you really are—healthy, whole, integrity-filled, compassionate, and fair? (para. 11)

Set Boundaries

If dialogue gets you nowhere yet you have to or want to stay in relations with a resistor, consider setting your own boundaries. The family of one of my friends is very divided when it comes to politics. For years, every holiday meal was tarnished by yelling, name-calling, and divisive political talk. My friend's mother couldn't take it anymore, so the family agreed to a "no politics at the dining room table" policy. To further encourage this, her mother set aside a small room in the house to be the political engagement zone, affectionately called the PEZ. Whenever political issues arose, she would invite the instigators to "take it to the PEZ." Another friend's family has the opposite approach. They set aside one room in the house as a "safe zone" where no political dialogue can happen. People can retreat to the safe zone when they grow weary of engaging about hot topics.

Know Your Limits and Use Your Support System

If someone wants to have a rational discussion about different views of gender and leadership, that's one thing, but know your boundaries for when conversations move into name-calling, blatant sexism, or resorting to violent words or actions to resolve differences. As difficult as it sounds, there may come a point when you can no longer engage with toxic people. If you do have to engage, aim for very brief interactions about innocuous topics. I have certain family members with whom I only talk about the weather. Take advantage of your allies and support system as safe spaces to vent and to encourage positivity.

Avoiding Activist Burnout

One common symptom among people who care deeply and work tirelessly to promote equity and justice is that they often face activist burnout. Because people's passion and identities are often so connected to their activism work, they are especially susceptible to burnout or a loss of energy and interest in activist activities. This is certainly true for many students I know who care deeply about gender justice and degendering leadership. Gorski and Chen (2015) describe a culture of selflessness, even martyrdom, among activists that causes them to work beyond role boundaries and expectations, which can lead to exhaustion. Politics and power struggles within activist movements and organizations can also lead to activist burnout. Gorski and Chen interviewed a wide variety of social justice activists and found three over-arching symptoms of activist burnout: the deterioration of psychological and emotional well-being; the deterioration of physical well-being; and feelings of disillusionment and hopelessness. The symptoms often lead to people withdrawing from activist organizations and commitments.

What can be done about it? First and foremost, we must challenge the culture of martyrdom among activists. Many participants in the Gorksi and Chen (2015) study felt it was taboo to discuss feelings of burnout among other activists, as if even acknowledging the strain of activism indicated that one was less committed to the cause. Second, we must center self-care practices as a key component of activism (Chen & Gorski, 2015). You've heard the talk on airplanes about first putting the oxygen mask on yourself, before you proceed to help others. There is wisdom here for everyone who works to make transformational change. Prioritizing physical and mental health is essential if activist movements, such as seeking gender equity, are to be sustained.

Maintaining Critical Hope

People who learn to sustain hope in the face of struggle have discovered the importance of critical hope to leadership. This does not refer to naïve hope, or people who negate the difficulties of sustaining the work necessary to overcome injustice. Remember the nine learning tasks of leadership presented in Table 2.1? Of these, learning to sustain hope in the face of struggle is perhaps one of the most essential skills of leadership. Preskill and Brookfield (2009) explain why:

> Hope will not make change happen, but without hope change is impossible. Without a sense that ordinary people working together are potentially limitless, the journey toward justice cannot even begin. . . . Hope is not a sufficient condition to bring about humane, positive change, but it is a necessary precondition for doing so. Leaders learning hope and, in turn, learning to bring hopefulness to others create a climate of possibility, an atmosphere that anything can happen. (pp. 175–176)

Love (2013) put forward the idea of a liberatory consciousness. She states that anyone who is committed to changing systems and institutions to create great equity and social justice must develop a liberatory consciousness. This kind of thinking enables people to live their lives in oppressive systems and institutions with intentionality and awareness, rather than submit to the forces of socialization. A liberatory consciousness enables people to maintain an awareness of the dynamics of oppression without giving in to despair and hopelessness. It allows us to maintain an awareness of roles played by those in the system without blaming them for the roles they play, while also intentionally challenging systems of oppression.

Hopefully this book has invited you to think in new ways about how we are socialized about gender and leadership, how the concepts show up on college campuses, and the implications of this socialization for the world of work and family. It is not enough to simply become familiar with the theories and terminology. I invite you to move from inquiry, or learning about a topic, to action, or taking steps to create more equitable and just spaces around you. This is the journey toward liberation. We can wait for others to call out injustice wherever they see it, or to advocate for more gender inclusive leadership and organizations, or we can roll up our sleeves and get to work. *After all, we are the leaders we've been waiting for.*

This book concludes with narratives from two college women who exercised leadership in their communities, formed coalitions, organized others, built authentic relationships, and continue to work toward social justice. Like all of the narratives included in this book, these women's words invite us to consider our own deep commitments and inspire us to continue leading for social change.

Shauna identifies as a Black, first-generation, Caribbean American, working-class woman.

Narratives and Counternarratives: Shauna's Story

At 16 years old, I attended my first protest. Bundled up in my North Face jacket, hat, and scarf I stood out in the cold with my friends and community members to protest a local university that was intent on building new dorms on land that had been promised to the community for affordable housing. As I stood outside, among the crowd of people, I felt an immense sense of pride and responsibility for taking care of the neighborhood that had been transformed by this same work decades before.

Just a year earlier, I had been hired as a youth tour guide for a nonprofit organization called MYTOWN. MYTOWN hired high school students to learn about the history of Boston and give historical walking tours of Boston's South End neighborhood. The tours, however, were not about Paul Revere or John Hancock; rather, they featured the stories of underrepresented people who had contributed to a more complete picture of Boston's story. The tours focused on Black, Latinx, Asian, and multicultural history. The tours highlighted the work of everyday community members to protest the Southwest Corridor highway that would destroy working-class family neighborhoods. We shared the story of unionizing efforts of the Brotherhood of Sleeping Car Porters and residents of Roxbury who in response to neglect from the city attempted to create their own city, Mandela, hoping to embody self-determination. The history I was learning and then teaching to both my peers and adults, was something that I'd never heard about in school despite being enrolled in one of Boston's top public high schools. Learning about a Boston that included people who looked like me, shared my immigrant story, and lived in neighborhoods that I lived in, made me feel a deep connection to my city and made me want to impact change. I wanted to fight for Boston, my community, and young people.

The deep connection that I had for Boston followed me into adulthood. I returned to my city after college and began working as a youth worker for some of the same organizations that I had grown up in as a youth. When the funding for summer youth jobs was being cut, I immediately rallied with other youth workers in the city to organize. We knew that having sustainable youth opportunities was critical to not only combat youth violence but also give youth the tools they needed to be successful. Quickly, this group knew that we couldn't stop there and organized a group of both youth and adults that would fight for issues that tied the two together. Founding the United Youth and Youth Workers of Boston, we held demonstrations, community meetings, and meetings with city officials to address access to youth jobs, city and private funding for programs, CORI reform, and youth violence. My appreciation for the city had grown into a deep commitment to relationship building and social justice. I was transformed, and today I continue to weave my experiences into my work helping to empower youth, change communities, and build solidarity.

Kalia identifies as Black, working-class, cis-woman from the south and a first-generation college and master's graduate.

Narratives and Counternarratives: Kalia's Story

I started organizing as a junior at a predominantly white high school in Richmond, Virginia. A couple of friends and I decided to start an African American Student Union at the school and received a lot of pushback from our classmates. For me, this was the first time that I realized that being Black was not the "norm" and loving my Blackness was an act of resistance. Moving into college, I began my journey as a first-generation college student from a working-class Black family. While managing all of the obstacles to my education (financial, emotional, and environmental), I began to get involved in the Virginia Student Power Network (VSPN), an organization that mobilizes around higher education issues and college debt. My engagement with VSPN allowed me the opportunities to lobby at the General Assembly, organize and participate in direct actions throughout the state, and speak at Capitol Hill with Senator Tim Kaine.

Around this time, Michael Brown was murdered in Ferguson, Missouri, by Darren Wilson. Wilson was not indicted for the murder, and we saw the birth of the Black Lives Matter movement as we know it. Being a student activist at the time, I began to get more involved in racial justice organizing. I joined a Black feminist racial justice organization in DC and started working on my campus to demand a radically inclusive learning community. With many Black students on my campus, we generated a list of demands and an escalation strategy to encourage our administration to support their Black students. It was in these very moments that I learned the importance of community youth organizing. Audre Lorde (2015) once said, "Without community, there is no liberation" (p. 95). I believe that through my experiences with organizing and activism, my understanding of my identity as a Black woman has greatly expanded.

Adaptive Leadership. The activity of mobilizing people to tackle tough challenges and to thrive (Heifetz, 1994). Heifetz suggests there are two types of challenges in the world—*technical problems,* where the solutions already exist in the world, and *adaptive challenges,* where answers are not known and thus require experiments, new learning, and adjusted behaviors.

Agency. A sense of possessing power—or "having the energy, intelligence, resources, and opportunity to act on the world" (Brookfield, 2005, p. 47).

Agent Identities. Those aspects of the self that align with groups socialized to allow benefit from unearned privilege.

Ally. A social justice ally is someone who will interrupt oppression when it is aimed at a target person or group; someone who recognizes privilege and will question and resist institutionalized oppression as much as possible (Reason et al., 2005). Allies are most effective when they realize that oppression hurts all people, not just the target of oppressive acts (Davis & Harrison, 2013).

Authentic Leadership. Leadership that involves leading with purpose, meaning, and values, and developing authentic enduring relationships (George, 2003).

Bechdel Test. Refers to a set of questions developed in 1985 by Alison Bechdel and allows people to rate sexism in a movie on three criteria: Do they have at least two women in the movie? Do these women talk to each other? Do they talk about something besides a man? Check out https://bechdeltest.com for a list of movies that do and do not pass this test.

Benevolent Sexism. A more understated type of prejudice in which women are stereotyped as affectionate, delicate, and sensitive. Those who hold benevolent sexist beliefs conceptualize women as weak individuals who need to be protected and provided for (Glick & Fiske, 1996). Although these traits and attitudes seem to encompass behaviors that favor women, research has shown that benevolent sexism is just as oppressive as hostile sexism (Glick & Fiske, 2001).

Burnout. Women in leadership, especially those with historically marginalized identities, are vulnerable to burnout. The isolation and constant challenges inherent in navigating traditional leadership environments can exact a large psychological and physical toll.

Chilly Classroom. Refers to how teachers can, often unintentionally, lessen the self-esteem and vocational aspirations of women by who they call on and affirm in their classroom.

Cisgender. A person whose gender identity and biological sex assigned at birth align (e.g., man and male-assigned). A simple way to think about it is: if a person is not transgender, they are cisgender.

Code-Switching. Refers to the practice of going back and forth between cultures of one's identities and majority culture.

Colorism/Shadism. Refers to the phenomenon where people with darker skin tones are subject to more prejudice and discrimination. This is illustrated by the "paper bag test" in the late 1800s and early 1900s where people with skin darker than a paper bag were not allowed to work in many establishments.

Community Engagement. "The collaboration between institutions of higher education and their larger communities for the mutually beneficial exchange of knowledge and resources in a context of partnership and reciprocity" (Carnegie Foundation for the Advancement of Teaching, 2015, para. 14).

Concrete Wall. Depictions of women's early attempts to enter certain career fields described a *concrete wall,* or absolute barrier to entry. It wasn't that long ago that women were not allowed to be doctors or lawyers or to serve in the military. Women are still excluded from some professions.

Confirmation Bias. Because of the ways our brains operate, biases can shape our perception such that we look for information to confirm our previously held beliefs and discount information that contradicts those assumptions.

Counternarratives. Refers to telling and listening to stories from those who have been historically marginalized. These narratives challenge dominant discourses that serve to target some and protect others from oppression (Davis & Harrison, 2013).

Critical Hope. "The process of learning to sustain hope in the face of struggle. Hope will not make change happen, but without hope change is impossible" (Preskill & Brookfield, 2009).

Critical Reflection. The process of analyzing, reconsidering, and questioning one's experiences within a broad context of issues and content knowledge (Jacoby, 2015, p. 26). There are often political dimensions to critical reflection so that experiences and issues are examined in light of social and political forces, hegemonic ideology, and link explicitly to further social action.

Critical Theory. A social theory oriented toward critiquing and changing society as a whole, in contrast to traditional theory oriented only to understanding or explaining it. It is about changing things, not just explaining them.

Culturally Relevant Leadership Learning Model (CRLL). A model of inclusive leadership that explores how capacity, identity, and efficacy of student leaders interact with dimensions of campus climate (Bertrand Jones et al., 2016).

Cycle of Socialization. A model developed by Bobbi Harro (2013b) that describes how the forces of socialization are pervasive, consistent, circular, self-perpetuating, and often invisible or unconscious and unnamed.

Democratic Dialogue/Dialogue Across Difference. Refers to the process of engaging with peers about differences (e.g., topics that elicit a wide range of perspectives) and across differences (e.g., with people with different backgrounds and beliefs).

Discrimination. A biased decision based on prejudice against an individual group characterized by race, class, sexual orientation, age, disability, and so on (Adams et al., 2007).

Double Bind. This occurs when the expectations that women be communal and collaborative clash with the expectations that leaders be agentic. When women encounter people in the workplace, they likely encounter differing sets of expectations about the appropriate balance between communal and agentic attributes. The result of these differing expectations may show up as resistance to women in leadership.

Effortless Perfection. Refers to the pressure people, especially women, feel to be smart, accomplished, fit, beautiful, and popular, all without exerting or displaying visible effort. The effortlessly perfect woman succeeds in all areas (personal, social, academic, career, health, and beauty) and acts as if everything comes easy to them.

Empowerment. The practice of sharing power and enabling others to exercise their own authority and influence. Be careful not to confuse true power sharing with *false empowerment* where people are seemingly included in decisions when in fact those decisions are being made unilaterally.

Emotionally Intelligent Leadership. An approach to leadership that builds on Daniel Goleman's (1995) idea of emotional intelligence as the ability to "recognize and regulate emotions in ourselves and others" (p. 2). Emotionally intelligent leadership promotes a focus on three facets: consciousness of self, consciousness of others, and consciousness of contexts (Shankman et al., 2015).

Epistemic Privilege. The advantage that oppressed people may have in understanding how the world works. Moya (2001) offers as an example how some women of color have used their marginalization to create critiques of organizations, processes, and systems, as well as to foster creative approaches to leadership.

Feminism. The struggle to end sexist oppression. Its aim is not to benefit any specific group of women, any particular race and class of women. It does not privilege women over men. It has the power to transform all of our lives (hooks, 2000a).

Gender Identity. A person's internal, deeply held sense of their gender. For transgender people, their own internal gender identity does not match the sex they were assigned at birth. Most people have a gender identity of man or woman, or boy or girl. For some people, their gender identity does not fit neatly into one of those two choices (see nonbinary and/or genderqueer). Unlike gender expression, gender identity is not visible to others.

Gender Expression. The external display of one's gender, through a combination of dress, demeanor, social behavior, and other factors, generally measured on scales of masculinity and femininity. Also referred to as "gender presentation" (woman-ness, man-ness, femme, butch, androgynous, gender neutral).

Gender Nonconforming. A term used to describe some people whose gender expression is different from conventional expectations of masculinity and femininity. Please note that not all gender nonconforming people identify as transgender; nor are all transgender people gender nonconforming. Many people have gender expressions that are not entirely conventional—that fact alone does not make them transgender. Many transgender men and women have gender expressions that are conventionally masculine or feminine. Simply being transgender does not make someone gender nonconforming. The term is not a synonym for transgender or transsexual and should only be used if someone self-identifies as gender nonconforming.

Gender Roles. Culturally based stereotypes that influence and create expectations for appropriate behavior for people based on biological sex. Gender roles are socially constructed and influenced by the media, family, environment, and society.

Gender Wage Gap. Even when women are represented in various fields, data consistently show a gender wage gap. This gap is typically reported as referring to the median annual pay of all women who are full-time, year-round workers compared to the pay of a similar cohort of men. Recent census data show women earning approximately 81% of what men earn; the median income for women is $41,554, while for men it is $51,640 (U.S Census Bureau, 2019).

Glass Ceiling. A concept popularized after it was used in a *Wall Street Journal* article by Hymowitz and Schellhardt (1986) to describe the presence of an invisible obstruction that stymied women's career advancements into executive positions. It implies that women face obstacles once they have risen to very high levels of leadership.

Glass Cliff. Ryan and Haslam (2005) describe the phenomenon of the glass cliff where women are overrepresented in precarious leadership positions. In other words, women can rise to leadership, but when they're brought in to turn things around during dire times, they have to bear the blame if things don't go well.

Glass Escalator. Describes the phenomenon in female-dominated professions where women climb the ladder while their male peers glide past them on an invisible escalator, shooting straight to the top. Statistical trends show men being promoted at faster rates than female peers even in female-dominated professions (Goudreau, 2012).

Hegemony. A form of social control whereby dominated or subordinate classes of people consent to their own domination, as opposed to being simply forced or coerced into accepting inferior positions, which results in the empowerment of certain cultural beliefs, values, and practices to the submersion and partial exclusion of others (Adams et al., 2007).

Hierarchies of Oppression. Refers to the tendency to essentialize people to one salient identity rather than acknowledge their many intersectional identities, and to assess which of one's marginalized identities is most subject to oppression. This oppression can also occur among people as they compare whose identities are more oppressed by society.

Ideology. The broadly accepted set of values, beliefs, myths, and explanations that appear to be true and desirable to a majority of the population. The function of ideology is to "maintain an unjust social and political order . . . by convincing people that existing social arrangements are naturally ordained and obviously work for the good of all people" (Brookfield, 2005, p. 41).

Implicit Bias. Implicit bias refers to the way people unconsciously and often unwillingly exhibit bias toward others. The Implicit Association Test, or IAT, (Greenwald et al., 1998) claims to reveal the strength of unconscious associations people make in their minds.

Impostor Syndrome. Refers to a specific form of self-doubt where people fear being found out as less than worthy, or a fraud.

Industrial Theories of Leadership. Scholars tend to describe older (pre-1990s) approaches to leadership as industrial theories, in that they focus on efficiency and effectiveness most suited to a manufacturing society.

Inheritors. Refers to the generation coming after your own, who will inherit the legacy of equity and gender justice created by those preceding them.

Instigators. Those currently working for gender equality such as someone who is part of a gender-specific organization or group, who can speak to the struggle to achieve gender justice in an increasingly divided world.

Institutional Betrayal. When schools and administrators fail to take appropriate action, students can experience a phenomenon called institutional betrayal (Linder & Myers, 2018). Institutional betrayal can include failing to prevent abuse, normalizing abusive contexts, creating difficult processes for reporting, failing to adequately respond to instances of harm, supporting cover-ups and misinformation, and punishing victims and whistleblowers (Smith & Freyd, 2014).

Internalized Oppression. Adams and colleagues (2013) define internalized oppression as the internalizing, or believing, on the part of the target group, the lies and misinformation that the agent group disseminates. They note that internalized oppression is always an involuntary reaction to the experience of oppression.

Intersectionality. Refers to the effects of interlocking systems of power, privilege, and oppression and how these forces shape lives and multiple social identities (Crenshaw 1989, 1991). Intersectionality includes three core concepts as defined by Collins and Bilge (2016): the *interlocking matrix of oppression,* or the intersections of various social inequalities; *standpoint theory,* or the idea that knowledge is subjective and stems from your unique social position; and *resisting oppression and objectification,* which are the goals.

Leadership. "A relational and ethical process of people together attempting to accomplish positive change" (Komives et al., 2013, p. 95).

Leadership Capacity. Refers to the knowledge, attitudes, and skills constituting one's ability to lead or engage in leadership successfully.

Leadership Development. The process of expanding people's abilities to engage effectively in leadership roles and processes (Day, 2001). It also involves the complex interplay among leadership capacity, motivation, identity, efficacy, and enactment (Dugan, 2017) and aspects of human and interpersonal development such as values and identity development (Guthrie & Jenkins, 2018).

Leadership Enactment. Refers to the manifestation of leadership behaviors; the process when people actually engage in leadership.

Leadership Identity Development (LID) Model. A framework for understanding how individuals develop the identity of being collaborative, relational leaders interdependently engaging in leadership as a group process. The model includes six stages (awareness, exploration/engagement, leader identified, leadership differentiated, generativity, and integration/synthesis) that address the process by which people become comfortable with nonhierarchical leadership and move from thinking of leadership as only positional to considering that leadership can happen anywhere (Komives et al., 2005, 2006, 2009).

Leadership Labyrinth. Reflects the myriad obstacles, choice points, and on-ramps and off-ramps that women face throughout their careers, and the idea that women travel many indirect paths in their leadership journey (Carli & Eagly, 2016).

Leadership Motivation. Refers to the desires that influence the likelihood of engaging in leadership.

Leadership Self-Efficacy. Refers to "individuals' belief in the likelihood they will be successful when engaging in leadership" (Dugan & Correia, 2014, p. 25). Leadership self-efficacy can be developed through enactive mastery, vicarious experiences, verbal persuasion, and healthy psychological and affective states (Bandura, 1997).

Leaky Pipeline. Refers to the way that women disappear from some careers over time (e.g., certain STEM fields).

Liberatory Consciousness. A liberatory consciousness enables people to maintain an awareness of the dynamics of oppression without giving in to despair and hopelessness. It allows us to maintain an awareness of roles played by those in a system without blaming them for the roles they play, while also intentionally challenging systems of oppression (Love, 2013).

Maternal Wall. Describes a type of bias that can occur as women get pregnant or seek parental leave. Maternity may cause others to make negative assumptions about competency, to assume emotionality and irrationality, or to assume a lack of commitment to job functions (Williams, 2004).

Miasma Condition. Defined by Livers and Caver (2003) referring to the wariness, defensiveness, and alertness required of those from underrepresented backgrounds in majority workplaces, which taxes their energy, time, productivity, and creativity.

Microaggressions. The everyday verbal, nonverbal, and environmental slights, snubs, or insults, whether intentional or unintentional, that communicate hostile, derogatory, or negative messages to target persons based solely upon their marginalized group membership. These messages may invalidate the group identity or experiential reality of target persons, demean them on a personal or group level, communicate they are lesser human beings, suggest they do not belong with the majority group, threaten and intimidate, or relegate them to inferior status and treatment (Wing Sue, 2010).

Myth of Meritocracy. The erroneous belief that people may hold, especially those from agent groups, that suggests that all people exist on a level playing field. These beliefs ignore how policies and practices differentially affect those with target identities. Simultaneously, people with agent identities may feel helpless to change who they are, rather than realizing it is systemic oppression that needs to be challenged.

Mythical Norm. The mythical norm describes the idealized characteristics of society that hold power and bring about oppression. Coined by Audre Lorde (1984), the term describes how America's "mythical norm" includes those in society who are "white, thin, male, young, heterosexual, Christian, and financially secure" (p. 116). Those who find themselves outside of this norm tend to attribute any oppression they face to only one of their differences. By singling out one difference, the oppressed ignore other causes and "distortions around difference" (p. 116) that also encourage oppression. The mythical norm within a society greatly impacts how oppression is viewed and therefore how oppression is communicated rhetorically. Women's movements are an example of this, showing women who focus their rhetorical and social efforts on their oppression as only women and not as members of a race, age, and class as well.

Nonbinary and/or Genderqueer. Terms used by some people who experience their gender identity and/or gender expression as falling outside the categories of man and woman. They may define their gender as falling somewhere in between man and woman, or they may define it as wholly different from these terms. The term is not a synonym for transgender or transsexual and should only be used if someone self-identifies as nonbinary and/or genderqueer.

On-Ramps and Off-Ramps. Refers to career interruptions where women leave the workplace (off-ramp) for an extended period and then have to work hard to reenter the world of work (on-ramp). These exits may be due to *pull factors*, centered in family responsibilities such as childcare or elder care, or due to *push factors* resulting from the workplace. Push factors may include feeling underutilized or underappreciated, being underpaid or underpromoted, or lacking a supportive climate for women.

Ophelia Complex. The process where, at adolescence, girls lessen their own interests and abilities in order to fit into prescribed ideas about what it means to be female.

Ornamental Intersectionality. Refers to the use of the word *intersectionality* casually, or the misapplication of the term, without understanding its roots in critical theory.

Paradoxes. Statements or propositions that appear contradictory at face value, but when investigated further may prove to be well founded or true.

Postindustrial Theories of Leadership. A term used to describe theories of leadership designed for use in the knowledge economy (post-1990s).

Power, Types of. *Legitimate power* refers to the power that comes from holding a title or position; the higher the status of the position, the more perceived power. *Reward power* is the ability to give positive or remove negative consequences, while *coercive power* is the ability to deliver negative consequences or remove positive ones. A person has *information power* if they have access to knowledge not available elsewhere or deemed important for a decision or task. *Expert power* comes from having unique knowledge, competencies, or skills. *Referent power* is derived from relationships, who a person knows, and their ability to draw on relationships as a source of support.

Predecessors. Refers to those who came before us in the fight for gender equity, such as a grandparent or a second-wave feminist, who have seen profound changes in the world during their lifetimes.

Prejudice. Exerting bias and bigotry based on uniform stereotypes (Adams et al., 2013).

Privilege. Refers to "the unearned rights, benefits, and immunities granted to some solely based on particular aspects of their identity" (Davis and Harrison, 2013, p. 35).

Queen Bee. Refers to a girl who "through a combination of charisma, force, money, looks, will, and social intelligence, reigns supreme over other girls and weakens their friendships with others, thereby strengthening her own power and influence" (Wiseman, 2009, p. 87). Queen bees are often surrounded by *sidekicks, pleasers/wannabes, bystanders, targets,* and *champions.*

Racial Battle Fatigue. Term coined by William A. Smith (2003) describing the tendency for students of color to constantly worry, have trouble concentrating, become fatigued, and develop headaches when navigating personal and professional spaces that have historically favored white people.

Reciprocal Empowerment. Sanchez-Hucles and Sanchez (2007) describe reciprocal empowerment as a leadership style of respect, reciprocity, equality, and personal authority that is characterized by concepts such as mutuality, compassion, collectivity, engagement, and consensus to enhance oneself and others.

Relational Leadership Model. The five components of relational leadership are being purposeful, being inclusive of people and diverse points of view, empowering those involved, being ethical, and recognizing that each of these elements is accomplished by being process-oriented. This model involves self-awareness about ways of knowing, being, and doing.

Self-Authorship. This is "the internal capacity to define one's beliefs, identity, and social relations" (Baxter Magolda, 2014, p. 27). The theory of self-authorship seeks answers to three core questions: How do I know? Who am I? How do I want to construct relationships with others?

Servant Leadership. Servant leadership begins with the natural feeling that one wants to serve. That is, the effective leader is a servant first (Greenleaf, 1977). The goals of servant leadership are to enrich the lives of individuals, build better organizations, and ultimately create a more just and caring world.

Sex. The classification of a person as male or female. At birth, infants are assigned a sex, usually based on the appearance of their external anatomy, and that is what is written on the birth certificate. A person's sex, however, is actually a combination of bodily characteristics including: chromosomes, hormones, internal and external reproductive organs, and secondary sex characteristics.

Sexual Orientation. Describes a person's enduring physical, romantic, and/or emotional attraction to another person (e.g., heterosexual, homosexual, gay, lesbian, bisexual, pansexual, asexual). Gender identity and sexual orientation are not the same.

Social Change Model. An approach to leadership as a purposeful, collaborative, values-based process that results in positive social change (Higher Education Research Institute, 1996). The model views leadership as a process rather than as a position and explicitly promotes the values of equity, social justice, self-knowledge, personal empowerment, collaboration, citizenship, and service. The model includes eight "Cs" essential to leadership: consciousness of self, congruences, commitment, collaboration, common purpose, controversy with civility, citizenship, and change. These values are clustered in three dimensions: individual, group, and community values.

Social Construction. Refers to the process whereby society and culture interact to create a host of meanings and associations about what is meant by certain words.

Social Location. Refers to the position one holds in society based on a variety of personal and social identities.

Social Pressure. The desire to fit in with a group of people, which can motivate girls and young women to act in destructive ways such as changing their attitudes, behaviors, or values to conform to group expectations.

Stereotype Threat. The apprehension about confirming an unfavorable stereotype about a group to which you belong.

Sticky Floor. Describes obstacles women face much earlier in their career paths, far before they hit the metaphorical glass ceiling. The sticky floor refers to discriminatory practices slowing women's advancement including "occupational segregation that places women in dead-end jobs, underpayment of workers in female-dominated occupations and the lack of flexibility and absence of job ladders in these professions" (Carli & Eagly, 2016, p. 517).

Structural Diversity. Also called *compositional diversity.* Refers to the number and proportional representation of various groups of people present in a given organization, system, or community. Scholars differentiate between structural diversity and the creation of inclusive and equitable climates.

Target Identities. Those aspects of the self that are often subject to socialized forces of oppression.

Tokenism. The practice of making only a perfunctory or symbolic effort to be inclusive to members of minority groups, especially by recruiting a small number of people from underrepresented groups in order to give the appearance of racial or sexual equality within a workforce. The result of tokenism is often the appearance of diversity without actual inclusion.

Transgender. An umbrella term for people whose gender identity and/or gender expression differs from what is typically associated with the sex they were assigned at birth. People under the transgender umbrella may describe themselves using one or more of a wide variety of terms, including transgender. Use the descriptive term preferred by the person. Many transgender people are prescribed hormones by their doctors to bring their bodies into alignment with their gender identity. Some undergo surgery as well. But not all transgender people can or will take those steps, and a transgender identity is not dependent upon physical appearance or medical procedures.

Trans*. Used as shorthand to mean transgender or transsexual—or sometimes to be inclusive of a wide variety of identities under the transgender umbrella. Because its meaning is not precise or widely understood, be careful when using it with audiences who may not understand what it means. Avoid unless used in a direct quote or in cases where you can clearly explain the term's meaning in the context of your story.

Transnational Feminism. Focuses on intersections across nationality (including race and ethnicity), sex, gender, and class within the context of modern-day imperialism and colonialism.

Triple Jeopardy. Women of color in leadership roles may experience triple jeopardy because of the many stereotypes associated with gender, race, and ethnicity that their multiple identities may trigger in others (Sanchez-Hucles & Sanchez, 2007).

Values. Standards that guide the behavior of individuals who hold them and serve as their basis for judging the behaviors of others. Values are also culturally influenced, and because of the values-laden nature of culture and processes of socialization, values may differ across gender, race, and ethnicity. Values determine short- and long-term goals and life satisfaction.

Womanist. Writer Alice Walker coined the idea of a Womanist movement to address the needs of women of color in her 1979 short story "Coming Apart." Walker (1984) suggests that feminism cannot be considered apart from culture and thus Black feminists need their own approach, independent of white feminism.

Womxn. Some have started using the spelling womxn where the x allows space for individuals who identify as genderfluid, genderqueer, gender nonconforming, or nonbinary to be included.

Abes, E. S., & Hernandez, E. (2016). Critical and post-structural perspectives on self-authorship. In E. S. Abes (Ed.), *Critical perspectives on student development theory* (New Directions for Student Services, No. 154, pp. 97–108). San Francisco, CA: Jossey-Bass.

Adams, F., & Horton, M. (1975). *Unearthing seeds of fire: The idea of Highlander.* Winston-Salem, NC: J.F. Blair.

Adams, M., Blumenfeld, W. J., Castaneda, R., Hackman, H. W., Peters, M. L., & Zuniga, X. (Eds.). (2013). *Readings for diversity and social justice* (3rd ed.). New York, NY: Routledge.

Alderman, N. (2019). *The power.* Boston, MA: Little, Brown & Company.

Alexander, L. B. (2017). *Why women are still underrepresented in nonprofit leadership and what we can do about it.* Retrieved from https://www.nonprofithr.com/women-underrepresented-nonprofit-leadership/

Alimo, C. J. (2012). From dialogue to action: The impact of cross-race intergroup dialogue on the development of white college students as racial justice allies. *Equity & Excellence in Education, 45,* 36–59.

Alter, C. (2015, April 14). Here's the history of the battle for equal pay for American women. *Time.* Retrieved from https://time.com/3774661/equal-pay-history/

American Association of University Women. (2014). *Close the confidence gap.* Retrieved from https://www.aauw.org/2014/05/19/close-the-confidence-gap/

American Association of University Women. (2015). *Solving the equation: The variables for women's success in computing and engineering.* Retrieved from https://www.aauw.org/research/solving-the-equation/

American Association of University Women. (2016a). *Barriers and bias: The status of women in leadership.* Washington DC: AAUW.

American Association of University Women. (2016b). *Ending campus sexual assault toolkit.* Retrieved from https://www.aauw.org/resource/campus-sexual-assault-tool-kit/

American Association of University Women. (2016c). *How to fight your own implicit biases.* Retrieved from https://www.aauw.org/2016/03/30/fight-your-biases/

American Association of University Women. (2017). *The simple truth about the gender pay gap.* Retrieved from https://www.aauw.org/research/the-simple-truth-about-the-gender-pay-gap/

American Association of University Women. (2018). *Women's student debt crisis in the United States.* Retrieved from https://www.aauw.org/research/deeper-in-debt/

American Student Government Association. (2019). *About.* Retrieved from https://asgahome.com/about-asga/

Anzaldúa, G. E. (1987). *Borderlands/La Frontera: The new Mestiza*. San Francisco, CA: Aunt Lute Books.

Arnett, J. J., & Tanner, J. L. (2006). *Emerging adults in America: Coming of age in the 21st century*. Washington DC: American Psychological Association.

Association of American Medical Colleges. (2017). *More women than men enrolled in U.S. medical schools in 2017*. Retrieved from https://news.aamc.org/press-releases/article/applicant-enrollment-2017/

Astin, H. S., & Leland, C. (1991). *Women of influence, women of vision: A cross-generational study of leaders and social change*. San Francisco, CA: Jossey-Bass.

Bandura, A. (1997). *Self-efficacy: The exercise of control*. New York, NY: W. H. Freeman.

Bass, B. M. (1990). *Bass and Stogdill's handbook of leadership: A survey of theory and research*. New York, NY: Free Press.

Bastedo, M. N. (2011). Curriculum in higher education. In P. G. Altbach, P. J. Gumport, & R. O. Berdahl (Eds.), *American higher education in the twenty-first century: Social, political, and economic challenges* (3rd ed, pp. 462-485). Baltimore, MD: Johns Hopkins University Press.

Bastien, A. (2016, October 23). *Insecure* season 1, episode 3 recap: Code-switching. *New York Times*. Retrieved from https://www.nytimes.com/2016/10/23/arts/television/insecure-season-1-episode-3-recap.html

Battered Women's Justice Project. (2019). *Military and veterans*. Retrieved from https://www.bwjp.org/our-work/projects/military-and-veterans-advocacy-program.html

Baxter Magolda, M. B. (2001). *Making their own way: Narratives for transforming higher education to promote self-development*. Sterling, VA: Stylus.

Baxter Magolda, M. B. (2004). Self-authorship as the common goal of 21st-century education. In M. Baxter Magolda, & P. M. King (Eds.), *Learning partnerships: Theory and modes of practice to educate for self-authorship*. Sterling, VA: Stylus.

Baxter Magolda, M. B. (2014). Self-authorship. In C. Hanson (Ed.), *In search of self: Exploring student identity development* (New Directions for Higher Education, No. 166, pp. 25–33). San Francisco, CA: Jossey-Bass.

Bechdel, A. (1986). *Dykes to watch out for* (Illustrated ed.). Ithaca, NY: Firebrand Books.

Benson, P., & Saito, R. (2000). The scientific foundations of youth development. In Public/Private Ventures (Eds.), *Youth development: Issues, challenges, and directions* (pp. 125–147). Philadelphia, PA.: Public/Private Ventures.

Bertrand Jones, T., Guthrie, K. L., & Osteen, L. (2016). Critical domains of culturally relevant leadership learning: A call to transform leadership programs. In K. L. Guthrie, T. Bertrand Jones, & L. Osteen (Eds.), *Developing culturally relevant leadership learning* (New Directions for Student Leadership, No. 152, pp. 9–21). San Francisco, CA: Jossey-Bass.

Bilodeau, B. L. (2009). *Genderism: Transgender students, binary systems, and higher education*. Saarbrücken, Germany: Verlag.

Broido, E. M. (2000). The development of social justice allies during college: A phenomenological investigation. *Journal of College Student Development, 41*, 3–18.

Brookfield, S. D. (1995). *Becoming a critically reflective teacher.* San Francisco, CA: Jossey-Bass.

Brookfield, S. D. (2005). *The power of critical theory: Liberating adult learning and teaching.* San Francisco, CA: Jossey-Bass.

Brooks, R. (2014, February 25). Recline, don't 'lean in': Why I hate Sheryl Sandberg. *Washington Post.* Retrieved from https://www.washingtonpost.com/blogs/she-the-people/wp/2014/02/25/recline-dont-lean-in-why-i-hate-sheryl sandberg/

Brown, B. (2010). *The gifts of imperfection: Let go of who you think you're supposed to be and embrace who you are.* Center City, MN: Hazelden.

Brown, B. (2012). *Daring greatly: How the courage to be vulnerable transforms the way we live, love, parent, and lead.* New York, NY: Gotham.

Brown, B. (2015). *Rising strong: The reckoning. The rumble. The revolution.* New York, NY: Spiegel & Grau.

Brown, B. (2017). *Braving the wilderness: The quest for true belonging and the courage to stand alone.* New York, NY: Random House.

Brown, B. (2018). *Dare to lead: Brave work. Tough conversations. Whole hearts.* New York, NY: Random House.

Brown University. (2018). *Brown LGBTQ Center's statement of values and support.* Retrieved from https://www.brown.edu/campus-life/support/lgbtq/

Burns, J. M. (1978). *Leadership.* New York, NY: Harper & Row.

Butler, J. (1990). *Gender trouble: Feminism and the subversion of identity.* London: Routledge.

Campbell, C. M., Smith, M., Dugan, J. P., & Komives, S. R. (2012). Mentors and college student leadership outcomes: The importance of position and process. *Review of Higher Education: Journal of the Association for the Study of Higher Education, 35*(4), 595–625.

Cannady, M. A., Greenwald, E., & Harris, K. N. (2014). Problematizing the STEM pipeline metaphor: Is the STEM pipeline metaphor serving our students and the STEM workforce? *Science Education, 98,* 443–460.

Caprino, K. (2017, March 18). What is feminism, and why do so many women and men hate it? *Forbes.* Retrieved from https://www.forbes.com/sites/kathy-caprino/2017/03/08/what-is-feminism-and-why-do-so-many-women-and-men-hate-it/

Carli, L. L., & Eagly, A. H. (2007). Overcoming resistance to women leaders: The importance of leadership style. In B. Kellerman & D. L. Rhode (Eds.), *Women and leadership: The state of play and strategies for change* (pp. 127–148). San Francisco, CA: Jossey-Bass.

Carli, L. L., & Eagly, A. H. (2016). Women face a labyrinth: An examination of metaphors for women leaders. *Gender in Management, 31*(8), 514–527. https://doi.org/10.1108/GM-02-2015-0007

Carnegie Foundation for the Advancement of Teaching. (2015, May). *Community engagement elective classification.* Retrieved from http://carnegieclassifications.iu.edu/

Cash, T. F., & Smolak, L. (Eds.). (2011). *Body image: A handbook of science, practice, and prevention* (2nd ed.). New York, NY: Guilford Press.

Catalyst. (2018a). *Quick take: Women in male-dominated industries and occupations.* Retrieved from https://www.catalyst.org/knowledge/women-male-dominated-industries-and-occupations

Catalyst. (2018b). *Quick take: Women in management.* Retrieved from https://www.catalyst.org/knowledge/women-management

CBS News. (2018, April 15). *Leading by example to close the gender pay gap.* Retrieved from https://www.cbsnews.com/news/salesforce-ceo-marc-benioff-leading-by-example-to-close-the-gender-pay-gap/

Center for American Women and Politics (CAWP). (2019). *Current numbers: Women in office.* Retrieved from https://www.cawp.rutgers.edu/current-numbers

Center for Creative Leadership. (2018). *Talent reimagined: Seven emerging trends for transformative leaders.* Greensboro, NC: Center for Creative Leadership.

Chandler, D. (2011). What women bring to the exercise of leadership. *Journal of Strategic Leadership, 3*(2), 1–12.

Chen, C. W. (2011). *Compliance and compromise: The jurisprudence of gender pay equity.* Leiden, Belgium: Martinus Nijhoff.

Chen, C. W., & Gorski, P. C. (2015). Burnout in social justice and human rights activists: Symptoms, causes, and implications. *Journal of Human Rights Practice, 7*(3), 366–390.

Chin, J. L., Lott, B., Rice, J., & Sanchez-Hucles, J. (Eds.). (2007). *Women and leadership: Transforming visions and diverse voices.* Malden, MA: Blackwell.

Chozik, A. (2016, November 5). Hillary Clinton and the return of the (unbaked) cookies. *New York Times.* Retrieved from https://www.nytimes.com/2016/11/06/us/politics/hillary-clinton-cookies.html

Clery Center. (2019). *Jeanne Clery disclosure of campus security policy and campus crime statistics.* Retrieved from https://clerycenter.org/

Clifford, P. G. (1992). The myth of empowerment. *Nursing Administration Quarterly, 16*(3), 1–5.

Cobble, D. S., Gordon, L., & Henry, A. (2014, September 26). What 'Lean In' leaves out. *The Chronicle of Higher Education,* B4.

Cokley, K., McClain, S., Enciso, A., & Martinez, M. (2013). An examination of the impact of minority status stress and impostor feelings on the mental health of diverse ethnic minority college students. *Journal of Multicultural Counseling and Development, 41*(2), 82–95.

Collins, P. H. (1990). *Black feminist thought: Knowledge, consciousness, and the politics of empowerment.* Boston, MA: Unwin Hyman.

Collins, P. H. (2000). We don't need another Dr. King. In J. Birnbaum & C. Taylor (Eds.), *Civil rights since 1787: A reader on the Black struggle* (pp. 908–909). New York, NY: NYU Press.

Collins, P. H. (2003). Some group matters: Intersectionality, situated standpoints, and Black feminist thought. In T. L. Lott & J. P. Pittman (Eds.), *A companion to African-American philosophy* (pp. 205–229). Malden, MA: Blackwell.

Collins, P. H. & Bilge, S. (2016). *Intersectionality.* Malden, MA: Polity Press.

Combahee River Collective. (1977). A Black feminist statement. In G. Anzaldúa & C. Moraga (Eds.), *This bridge called my back: Writings by radical women of color* (2nd ed.). Latham, MD: Kitchen Table/Women of Color Press.

Cooney, K. (2018). *When women ruled the world: Six queens of Egypt.* Washington DC: National Geographic.

Couric, K. (March 29, 2011). Amy Poehler tells Katie Couric "I just love bossy women!" *Glamour* Online. Retrieved from https://www.glamour.com/story/amy-poehler-tells-katie-couric-i-just-love-bossy-women

Crenshaw, K. (1989). Demarginalizing the intersection of race and sex: A Black feminist critique of antidiscrimination doctrine, feminist theory and antiracist politics. *University of Chicago Legal Forum, 1989*(1), 139–167.

Crenshaw, K. (1991). Mapping the margins: Intersectionality, identity politics, and violence against women of color. *Stanford Law Review, 43,* 1241–1299.

Crenshaw, K. (September 24, 2015). Why intersectionality can't wait. *Washington Post.* Retrieved from https://www.washingtonpost.com/news/in-theory/wp/2015/09/24/why-intersectionality-cant-wait/

Crenshaw, K., Gotanda, N., Peller, G., & Thomas, K. (Eds.). (1995). *Critical race theory: The key writings that formed the movement.* New York, NY: New Press.

Cronin, T. E., & Genovese, M. A. (2012). *Leadership matters: Unleashing the power of paradox.* Boulder, CO: Paradigm.

Croom, N., Beatty, C., Acker, L., & Butler, M. (2017). Exploring undergraduate Black womyn's motivations for engaging in "sister circle" organizations. *NASPA Journal About Women in Higher Education, 10*(2), 216–228.

Crowe C. (October 2, 2018). "I never applied": Nobel winner explains associate-professor status, but critics still see steeper slope for women. *The Chronicle of Higher Education.* Retrieved from https://www.chronicle.com/article/I-Never-Applied-Nobel/244699

Davis, T., & Harrison, L. (2013). *Advancing social justice: Tools, pedagogies, and strategies to transform your campus.* San Francisco, CA: Jossey-Bass.

Dasgupta, N., & Stout, J. G. (2014). Girls and women in science, technology, engineering, and mathematics: STEMing the tide and broadening participation in STEM careers. *Policy Insights from the Behavioral and Brain Sciences, 1,* 21–29.

Day, D. V. (2001). Leadership development: A review in context. *Leadership Quarterly, 11*(4), 581–613.

Dinh, J. E., & Lord, R. G. (2012). Implications of dispositional and process views of traits for individual difference research in leadership. *Leadership Quarterly, 23,* 651–669.

Drexler, P. (2013, March 6). The tyranny of the queen bee. *Wall Street Journal.* Retrieved from https://www.wsj.com/articles/SB10001424127887323884304578328271526080496

Dugan, J. P. (2017). *Leadership theory: Cultivating critical perspectives.* San Francisco, CA: Jossey-Bass.

Dugan, J. P., & Correia, B. (2014*). MSL insight report supplement: Leadership program delivery.* College Park, MD: National Clearinghouse for Leadership Programs.

Dugan, J. P., Kodama, C., Correia, B., & Associates. (2013). *Multi-institutional study of leadership insight report: Leadership program delivery.* College Park, MD: National Clearinghouse for Leadership Programs.

Dugan, J. P., & Komives, S. R. (2010). Influences on college students' capacities for socially responsible leadership. *Journal of College Student Development, 51,* 525–549.

Dugan, J. P., Komives, S. R., & Segar, T. C. (2009). College student capacity for socially responsible leadership: Understanding norms and influences of race, gender, and sexual orientation. *NASPA Journal, 45*(4), 475–500.

Dugan, J. P., Kusel, M. L., & Simounet, D. M. (2012). Transgender college students: An exploratory study of perceptions, engagement, and educational outcomes. *Journal of College Student Development, 53*(5), 719–736.

Dugan, J. P., Torrez, M. A., & Turman, N, T. (2014). *Leadership in intramural sports and club sports: Examining influences to enhance educational impact.* Corvallis, OR: NIRSA.

Dugan, J. P., & Velazquez, D. (2015). Teaching contemporary leadership: Advancing students' capacities to engage about and across difference. In S. K. Watt (Ed.*), Designing transformative multicultural initiatives: Theoretical foundations, practical applications, and facilitator considerations* (pp. 105–118). Sterling, VA: Stylus.

Duke University Women's Initiative. (2003). *Steering committee final report.* Retrieved from http://universitywomen.stanford.edu/reports/WomensInitiativeReport.pdf

Eagly, A. H., & Carli, L. L. (2007). *Through the labyrinth: The truth about how women become leaders.* Boston, MA: Harvard Business School Press.

Edwards, K. E. (2006). Aspiring social justice ally development: A conceptual model. *NASPA Journal, 43,* 1235–1256.

Edwards, N. N., Beverly, M. G., & Alexander-Snow, M. (2011). Troubling success: Interviews with Black female faculty members. *Florida Journal of Educational Administration & Policy, 5*(1), 14–27.

Fagell, P. (2018, October 30). Seven ways parents can teach girls to build one another up, instead of tearing one another down. *Washington Post.* Retrieved from https://www.washingtonpost.com/lifestyle/on-parenting/7-ways-parents-can-teach-girls-to-build-each-other-up-instead-of-tearing-each-other-down/2018/10/29/92550976-c016-11e8-9005-5104e9616c21_story.html

Feeny, N. (2013, July 11). Why aren't there more women on the top-earning comedians list? *Forbes.com.* Retrieved from https://www.forbes.com/sites/nolanfeeney/2013/07/11/why-arent-there-more-women-on-the-top-earning-comedians-list/

Field, A. T. (December 3, 2018). Fraternities and sororities sue Harvard over its policy against single-sex groups. *The Chronicle of Higher Education.* Retrieved from https://www.chronicle.com/article/FraternitiesSororities/245251

Foreman, A. (2016). *The ascent of woman.* BBC video series. Retrieved from http://www.ascentofwoman.com/

Frankel, L. P. (2009). *Nice girls don't get rich: Avoidable mistakes women make with money*. New York, NY: Business Plus.

Frankel, L. P. (2014). *Nice girls don't get the corner office: Unconscious mistakes women make that sabotage their careers*. New York, NY: Business Plus.

Frankel, L. P., & Frohlinger, C. (2018). *Nice girls just don't get it: 99 ways to win the respect you deserve, the success you've earned, and the life you want*. New York, NY: Harmony.

Friedman, S., & Laurison, D. (2018). *The class ceiling: Why it pays to be privileged*. Bristol, UK: Policy Press.

Freedman, R. (1988). *Bodylove: Learning to like our looks and ourselves*. New York, NY: Harper & Row.

French, J. R. P., Jr., & Raven, B. H. (1968). The bases of social power. In D. Cartwright & A. F. Zander (Eds.), *Group dynamics* (3rd ed., pp. 259–269). New York, NY: Harper & Row.

Fricker, M. (2007). *Epistemic injustice: Power and the ethics of knowing*. Oxford, UK: Oxford University Press.

Friedan, B. (1963). *The feminine mystique*. New York, NY: W.W. Norton.

Gay, R. (2014). *Bad feminist*. New York, NY: Harper Collins.

Gay & Lesbian Alliance Against Defamation (GLAAD). (2019). *An allies' guide to terminology*. Retrieved from http://www.glaad.org/sites/default/files/allys-guide-to-terminology_1.pdf

Gender Spectrum. (2019). *Understanding gender*. Retrieved from https://www.genderspectrum.org/resources/parenting-and-family-2/

George, B. (2003). *Authentic leadership: Rediscovering the secrets to creating lasting value*. Hoboken, NJ: Wiley.

Girl Scout Research Institute. (2008). *Change it up! What girls say about redefining leadership*. New York, NY: Girl Scouts of the USA. Retrieved from https://www.girlscouts.org/content/dam/girlscouts-gsusa/forms-and-documents/about-girl-scouts/research/change_it_up_executive_summary_english.pdf

Girls Inc. (2014). *Girls Inc. Girls' Bill of Rights*. Retrieved from https://girlsinc.org/app/uploads/2017/04/girls_bill_of_rights_2014.pdf

Glick, P., & Fiske, S. T. (1996). The ambivalent sexism inventory: Differentiating hostile and benevolent sexism. *Journal of Personality and Social Psychology, 70*(3), 491–512.

Glick, P., & Fiske, S. T. (2001). An ambivalent alliance: Hostile and benevolent sexism as complementary justifications for gender inequality. *American Psychologist, 56*(2), 109–118.

Goldiblox (2019). *About*. Retrieved from https://www.goldieblox.com/about/

Goldin, C., & Rouse, C. (2000). Orchestrating impartiality: The impact of "blind" auditions on female musicians. *American Economic Review, 90*(4), 715–741.

Goleman, D. (1995). *Emotional intelligence: Why it can matter more than IQ*. New York, NY: Bantam Books.

Gorski, P. C., & Chen, C. W. (2015). Frayed all over: The causes and consequences of activist burnout among social justice education activists. *Educational Studies, 51*(5), 385–405.

Goudreau, J. (2012, July 24). A new obstacle for professional women: The glass escalator. *Forbes.* Retrieved from https://www.forbes.com/sites/jennagoudreau/2012/05/21/a-new-obstacle-for-professional-women-the-glass-escalator/

Grady, C. (2018, July 20). The waves of feminism, and why people keep fighting over them, explained. *Vox.* Retrieved from https://www.vox.com/2018/3/20/16955588/feminism-waves-explained-first-second-third-fourth

Greenleaf, R. K. (1977). *Servant leadership: A journey into the nature of legitimate power and greatness.* New York, NY: Paulist Press.

Greenwald, A. G., McGhee, D. E., & Schwartz, J. L. (1998). Measuring individual differences in implicit cognition: The Implicit Association Test. *Journal of Personality and Social Psychology, 74*(6), 1464–1180.

GuideStar (2017). *GuideStar 2017 nonprofit compensation report.* Retrieved from https://trust.guidestar.org/highlights-of-the-2017-guidestar-nonprofit-compensation-report

Guthrie, K. L., Bertrand Jones, T., & Osteen, L. (Eds.). (2016). *Developing culturally relevant leadership learning* (New Directions for Student Leadership, No. 152). San Francisco, CA: Jossey-Bass.

Guthrie, K. L., & Chunoo, V. S. (Eds.). (2018). *Changing the narrative: Socially just leadership education.* Charlotte, NC: Information Age Press.

Guthrie, K. L., & Jenkins, D. M. (2018). *The role of leadership educators: Transforming learning.* Charlotte, NC: Information Age.

Guy, M. E., & Fenley, V. (2013). Inch by inch: Gender equity since the Civil Rights Act of 1964. *Review of Public Personnel Administration, 34*, 40–58.

Haber, P. (2011). Iron sharpens iron: Exploring the experiences of female college student leaders. *Advancing Women in Leadership Journal, 31*, 86–101.

Haber-Curran, P., & Sulpizio, L. (2017). Student leadership development for girls and young women. In D. Tillapaugh & P. Haber-Curran (Eds.), *Critical perspectives on gender and student leadership* (New Directions for Student Leadership, No. 154, pp. 33–46). San Francisco, CA: Jossey-Bass.

Haber-Curran, P., & Tillapaugh, D. (2018). Beyond the binary: Advancing socially just leadership through the lens of gender. In K. L. Guthrie & V. S. Chunoo (Eds.), *Changing the narrative: Socially just leadership education* (pp. 77–92). Charlotte, NC: Information Age Press.

Hall, R. J., & Lord, R. G. (1995). Multi-level information-processing explanations of followers' leadership perceptions. *Leadership Quarterly, 6*, 265–287.

Hall, R. M., & Sandler, B. R. (1982). *The classroom climate: A chilly one for women?* Washington DC: Association of American Colleges Project on the Status and Education of Women.

Halpert, J. A., Wilson, M. L., & Hickman, J. L. (1993). Pregnancy as a source of bias in performance appraisals. *Journal of Organizational Behavior, 14*, 649–663.

Hamill, P. (2013). *Embodied leadership: The somatic approach to developing your leadership.* London, UK: Kogan Page Limited.

Hanh, T. N. (1992). *Peace is every step: The path of mindfulness in everyday life.* New York, NY: Bantam Books.

Harro, B. (2013a). The cycle of liberation. In M. Adams, W. J. Blumenfeld, R. Castaneda, H. W. Hackman, M. L. Peters, & X. Zuñiga (Eds.), *Readings for diversity of social justice,* (3rd ed., pp. 618–625). New York, NY: Routledge.

Harro, B. (2013b). The cycle of socialization. In M. Adams, W. J. Blumenfeld, R. Castaneda, H. W. Hackman, M. L. Peters, X. Zuñiga (Eds.), *Readings for diversity of social justice,* (3rd ed., pp. 45–52). New York, NY: Routledge.

Harts, M. (2019). *The memo: What women of color need to know to secure a seat at the table.* New York, NY: Seal Press.

Harwarth, I., Maline, M., & DeBra, E. (2005). *Women's colleges in the United States: History, issues, and challenges.* Washington DC: U.S. Department of Education National Institute on Post-secondary Education, Libraries, and Lifelong Learning.

Heifetz, R. A. (1994). *Leadership without easy answers.* Cambridge, MA: Harvard University Press.

Hersey, P., & Blanchard, K. H. (1969). Life cycle theory of leadership. *Training & Development Journal, 23*(5), 26–34.

Hewlett, S. A. (2002). Executive women and the myth of having it all. *Harvard Business Review.* Retrieved from https://hbr.org/2002/04/executive-women-and-the-myth-of-having-it-all

Hewlett, S. A. (2007). Off-ramps and on-ramps: Women's nonlinear career paths. In B. Kellerman & D. D. Rhode (Eds.), *Women and leadership: The state of play and strategies for change,* pp. 407–430. San Francisco, CA: Jossey-Bass.

Hewlett, S. A., & Luce, C. B. (2005). Off-ramps and on-ramps: Keeping talented women on the road to success. *Harvard Business Review, 83*(3), 43-46.

Higher Education Research Institute. (1996). *A social change model of leadership development: Guidebook version III.* College Park, MD: National Clearinghouse for Leadership Programs.

Hinze, C. F. (2015). *Glass ceilings and dirt floors: Women, work, and the global economy.* New York, NY: Paulist Press.

Hollis, R. (2018). *Girl, wash your face: Stop believing the lies about who you are so you can become who you were meant to be.* New York, NY: Thomas Nelson.

Hollis, R. (2019). *Girl, stop apologizing: A shame-free plan for embracing and achieving your goals.* New York, NY: Harper Collins.

hooks, b. (2000a). *Feminism is for everybody.* Cambridge, MA: South End Press.

hooks, b. (2000b). *Feminist theory: From margin to center.* Cambridge, MA: South End Press.

hooks, b. (2011). *Ain't I a woman? Black women and feminism* (2nd ed.). New York, NY: Routledge.

hooks, b. (2013, October 28). Dig deep: Beyond *Lean In. The Feminist Wire.* Retrieved from https://thefeministwire.com/2013/10/17973/

Howes, S. D. (2016). *You're kind of just conditioned: Women and female college students' defiance of dominant social messages in the development of leader self-efficacy.* (Doctoral dissertation). Loyola University, Chicago, IL. Retreived from https://ecommons.luc.edu/luc_diss/2135

Hoyt, C. L., Burnette, J. L., & Innella, A. N. (2012). I can do that: The impact of implicit theories on leadership role model effectiveness. *Personality and Social Psychology Bulletin, 38*(2), 257–268. doi:10.1177/0146167211427922

Hoyt, C. L., & Murphy, S. E. (2016). *Managing to clear the air: Stereotype threat, women, and leadership.* Paper #238. Richmond, VA: Jepson School of Leadership Studies.

Hughes, B. E., & Hurtado, S. (2018). Thinking about sexual orientation: College experiences that predict identity salience. *Journal of College Student Development, 59*(3), 309–326.

Human Rights Campaign. (2019). *Glossary of terms.* Retrieved from https://www.hrc.org/resources/glossary-of-terms

Hymowitz, C., & Schellhardt, T. D. (1986). The glass-ceiling: Why women can't seem to break the invisible barrier that blocks them from top jobs. *Wall Street Journal, 57*, D1, D4–D5.

Inceoglu, I., Thomas, G., Chu, C., Plans, D., & Gerbasi, A. (2018). Leadership behavior and employee well-being: An integrated review and a future research agenda. *Leadership Quarterly 29*(1), 179–202.

Institute for Women's Policy Research. (2016, May). Mothers in college have declining access to on-campus child care. IWPR Quick Figures report #Q059. Retrieved from https://iwpr.org/wp-content/uploads/wpallimport/files/iwpr-export/publications/Q049.pdf

Iskra, D. M. (2008). *Breaking through the brass ceiling: Strategies of success for elite military Women.* Riga, Latvia: VDM Verlag.

Jacoby, B. (2015). *Service-learning essentials: Questions, answers, and lessons learned.* San Francisco, CA: Jossey-Bass.

Johnson, A. G. (2005). *Privilege, power, and difference* (2nd ed.). New York, NY: McGraw-Hill.

Jones, B. (2014). *Breaking through the stained-glass ceiling: Shattering myths and empowering women for leadership in the church.* Tulsa, OK: Harrison House Publishers.

Jones, S. (2016). Authenticity in leadership: Intersectionality of identities. In K. L. Guthrie, T. Bertrand Jones, & L. Osteen (Eds.), *Developing culturally relevant leadership learning* (New Directions for Student Leadership, No. 152, pp. 23–34). San Francisco, CA: Jossey-Bass.

Jordan, J. (1980). *Passion: New poems 1977-1980.* New York, NY: Beacon Press.

Kahneman, D. (2011). *Thinking, fast and slow.* New York, NY: Farrar, Straus and Giroux.

Katuna, B. (2019). *De-gendering leadership in higher education.* West Yorkshire, UK: Emerald.

Kaufman, S. B. (2011, January 28). Does the Implicit Association Test (IAT) really measure racial prejudice? Probably not. *Psychology Today.* Retrieved from https://www.psychologytoday.com/us/blog/beautiful-minds/201101/does-the-implicit-association-test-iat-really-measure-racial-prejudice

Kellaway, M. (2014, September 3). First of "seven sisters" schools to admit trans women. *Advocate.* Retrieved from https://www.advocate.com/politics/transgender/2014/09/03/watch-first-seven-sisters-schools-admit-trans-women

Kezar, A. J., & Wheaton, M. M. (2017). The value of connective leadership: Benefitting from women's approach to leadership while contending with traditional views. *About Campus, 21*(6), 19–26.

Kimmel, M. (2008). *Guyland: The perilous world where boys become men.* New York, NY: Harper Collins.

Kingston, M. H. (1976). *The woman warrior: Memoirs of a girlhood among ghosts.* New York, NY: Knopf.

Kinzie, J., Thomas, A. D., Palmer, M. M., Umbach, P. D., & Kuh, G. D. (2007). Women students at coeducational and women's colleges: How do their experiences compare? *Journal of College Student Development, 48*(2), 145–165.

Kollmayer, M., Schultes, M., Schober, B., Hodosi, T., & Spiel, C. (2018). Parents' judgments about the desirability of toys for their children: Associations with gender role attitudes, gender-typing of toys, and demographics. *Sex Roles, 79*(5), 329–341. Retrieved from https://doi.org/10.1007/s11199-017-0882-4

Komives, S. R., & Dugan, J. P. (2010). Contemporary leadership theories. In R. A. Couto (Ed.), *Political and civic leadership: A reference handbook,* pp. 109–125. Thousand Oaks, CA: SAGE.

Komives, S. R., Longerbeam, S. D., Mainella, F. C., Osteen, L., & Owen, J. E. (2009). Leadership identity development: Challenges in applying a developmental model. *Journal of Leadership Education, 8*(1), 11–47.

Komives, S. R., Longerbeam, S. D., Owen, J. E., Mainella, F. C., & Osteen, L. (2006). Leadership identity development model: Applications from a grounded theory. *Journal of College Student Development, 47*(4), 401–418.

Komives, S. R., Lucas, N., & McMahon, T. R. (2013*). Exploring leadership: For college students who want to make a difference* (3rd ed.). San Francisco, CA: Jossey-Bass.

Komives, S. R., Owen, J. E., Longerbeam, S. D., Mainella, F. C., & Osteen, L. (2005). Developing a leadership identity: A grounded theory. *Journal of College Student Development, 46,* 593–611.

Kuruvilla, C. (2014). These are the religious denominations that ordain women. *Huffington Post.* Retrieved from https://www.huffpost.com/entry/religion-ordain-women_n_5826422

Labyrinth Society. (2019). *About labyrinths.* Retrieved from https://www.labyrinthsociety.org/about-labyrinths

Lam, B. (2015, October 13). Jennifer Lawrence calls out the wage gap. *The Atlantic.* Retrieved from https://www.theatlantic.com/business/archive/2015/10/jennifer-lawrence-wage-gap/410311/

Lawless, J. L., & Fox, R. L. (2013). *Girls just wanna not run: The gender gap in young Americans' political ambition.* Washington DC: Women & Politics Institute.

LeGuin, U. (1987). *The left hand of darkness.* New York, NY: Ace Books.

Leaper, C. (2014). Parents' socialization of gender in children. In R. E. Tremblay, M. Boivin, & R. Peters (Eds.), *Encyclopedia on early childhood development.* Retreived from http://www.child-encyclopedia.com/gender-early-socialization/according-experts/parents-socialization-gender-children

Lear, M. W. (1968, March 10). The second feminist wave. *New York Times.*

Levensen, J. C., Shensa, A., Sidani, J. E., Coldits, J. B., & Primack, B. A. (2017). Social media use before bed and sleep disturbance among young adults in the United States: A nationally representative study. *Sleep, 40*(9).

Light, P. (2013, April 19). Why 43% of women with children leave their jobs, and how to get them back. *The Atlantic.* Retrieved from https://www.theatlantic.com/sexes/archive/2013/04/why-43-of-women-with-children-leave-their-jobs-and-how-to-get-them-back/275134/

Linder, C. (2015). Navigating guilt, shame, and fear of appearing racist: A conceptual model of antiracist white feminist identity development. *Journal of College Student Development, 56*(6), 535–550.

Linder, C., & Myers, J. S. (2018). Institutional betrayal as a motivator for campus sexual assault activism. *NASPA Journal About Women in Higher Education, 11*(1), 1–16.

Livers, A. B., & Caver, K. A. (2003). *Leading in Black and white: Working across the racial divide in corporate America.* San Francisco, CA: Jossey-Bass.

Lopez, G. (2017, March 7). For years, this popular test measured anyone's racial bias. But it might not work after all. *Vox.* Retrieved from https://www.vox.com/identities/2017/3/7/14637626/implicit-association-test-racism

Lorber, J. (1994). Night to his day: The social construction of gender. In J. Lorber (Ed.), *Paradoxes of gender* (pp. 13–36). New Haven, CT: Yale University Press.

Lord, R. G., DeVader, C. L., & Alliger, G. M. (1986). A meta-analysis of the relation between personality traits and leadership perceptions: An application of the validity generalization procedures. *Journal of Applied Psychology, 71*, 402–410.

Lorde, A. (1983). There is no hierarchy of oppressions. *Bulletin: Homophobia and Education, 14*(3/4), 9.

Lorde, A. (1984). *Sister, outsider: Essays and speeches.* New York, NY: The Crossing Press.

Lorde, A. (2015). The master's tool will never dismantle the master's house. In C. Moraga, & G. Anzaldúa, G. (Eds.), *This bridge called my back* (4th edition), pp. 94–97. Albany, NY: State University of New York Press.

Love, B. J. (2013). Developing a liberatory consciousness. In M. Adams, W. J. Blumenfeld, R. Castaneda, H. W. Hackman, M. L. Peters, & X. Zuñiga (Eds.), *Readings for diversity and social justice* (3rd ed., pp. 600–605). New York, NY: Routledge.

Marine, S. B., Helfrich, G., & Randhawa, L. (2017) Gender-inclusive practices in campus women's and gender centers: Benefits, challenges, and future prospects. *NASPA Journal About Women in Higher Education, 10*(1), 45–63.

Martin, C. L., & Ruble, D. N. (2010). Patterns of gender development. *Annual Review of Psychology, 61*(1), 353–381.

Martínez Alemán, A. M., & Renn, K. A. (Eds.). (2002). *Women in higher education: An encyclopedia.* Santa Barbara, CA: ABC CLIO.

Micheletti, L. M. (2002). Coeducation. In A. M. Martinez Aleman, & K. A. Renn (Eds.), *Women in higher education: An encyclopedia* (pp. 21–25). Santa Barbara, CA: ABC CLIO.

Miller, C. C. (2014, April 23). Pay gap is because of gender, not jobs. *New York Times*. Retrieved from https://www.nytimes.com/2014/04/24/upshot/the-pay-gap-is-because-of-gender-not-jobs.html

Miller, C. C. (2016, March 18). As women take over a male-dominated field, the pay drops. *New York Times*. Retrieved from https://www.nytimes.com/2016/03/20/upshot/as-women-take-over-a-male-dominated-field-the-pay-drops.html

Miller, C. C., Quealy, K., & Sanger-Katz, M. (2018, April 24). The top jobs where women are outnumbered by men named John. *New York Times*. Retrieved from https://www.nytimes.com/interactive/2018/04/24/upshot/women-and-men-named-john.html

Miller, D., & Wai, J. (2015, February 17). The bachelor's to Ph.D. STEM pipeline no longer leaks more women than men: A 30-year analysis. *Frontiers of Psychology*.

Moraga, C., & Anzaldúa, G. (2015). *This bridge called my back* (4th ed.). Albany: State University of New York Press.

Moya, P. (2001). Chicana feminism and postmodern theory. In C. McCann & S. Kim (Eds.), *Feminist theory reader: Local and global perspectives* (pp. 463–481). New York, NY: Routledge.

Muhr, S. L., & Sullivan, K. R. (2013). "None so queer as folk": Gendered expectations and transgressive bodies in leadership. *Leadership, 9*(3), 416–435.

Nash, R. J., Bradley, D. L., & Chickering, A. W. (2008). *How to talk about hot topics on campus: From polarization to moral conversation.* San Francisco, CA: Jossey-Bass.

National Association of Women Business Owners. (2018). *Women business owner statistics*. Retrieved from https://www.nawbo.org/resources/women-business-owner-statistics

National Coalition for Women and Girls in Education. (2017). *Title IX at 45: Advancing opportunity through equity in education.* Washington DC: NCWGE.

National Eating Disorders Association. (2019). *Body image.* Retrieved from https://www.nationaleatingdisorders.org/body-image-0

National Institute of Mental Health. (2019). *Statistics.* Retrieved from https://www.nimh.nih.gov/health/statistics/mental-illness.shtml

National Multicultural Greek Council (NMGC) (2019). *About.* Retrieved from https://nationalmgc.org/about/

National Panhellenic Conference. (2019). *About.* Retrieved from https://www.npcwomen.org/about/

National Pan-Hellenic Council. (2019). *About.* Retrieved from https://www.nphchq.org/quantum/our-history/

National Sexual Violence Resource Center. (2019). *Statistics.* Retrieved from https://www.nsvrc.org/statistics

Neumark-Sztainer, D. (2005). Can we simultaneously work toward the prevention of obesity and eating disorders in children and adolescents? *International Journal of Eating Disorders, 38*(3), 220–227.

Newman, J. (March 16, 2018). "Lean In": Five years later. *New York Times*. Retrieved from https://www.nytimes.com/2018/03/16/business/lean-in-five-years-later.html

Nicolazzo, Z. (2016). *Trans* in college: Transgender students' strategies for navigating campus life and the institutional politics of inclusion.* Sterling, VA: Stylus.

North, D. L., & Matsoukas, M. (Writer & Director). (2016, October 23). Racist as fuck. (Season 1, episode 3) [TV series episode]. In I. Rae & L. Wilmore (Creators), *Insecure.* 3 Arts Entertainment.

Northouse, P. G. (2018). *Leadership: Theory and practice* (8th ed.). Los Angeles, CA: SAGE.

Olcott, D., & Hardy, D. (2005). *Dancing on the glass ceiling: Women, leadership, and technology.* Madison, WI: Atwood Publishing.

Oliver, B. (2018, October 12). Why leaning in has not worked for women of color. *Fast Company.* Retrieved from https://www.fastcompany.com/90243134/why-leaning-in-has-not-worked-for-women-of-color

Ortiz, A. M., & Rhoads, R. A. (2000). Deconstructing whiteness as part of a multicultural educational framework: From theory to practice. *Journal of College Student Development, 41*(1), 81–93.

Owen, J. E. (2012). Using student development theories as a conceptual framework in leadership education. In K. L. Guthrie & L. Osteen (Eds.), *Developing student leadership capacity* (New Directions for Student Services, No. 140, pp. 17–36). San Francisco, CA: Jossey-Bass.

Owen, J. E. (2016). Fostering critical reflection: Moving from a service to a social justice paradigm. In W. Wagner & J. M. Pigza (Eds.), *Innovative learning for leadership development* (New Directions for Student Leadership, No. 145, pp. 49–55). San Francisco: CA. Jossey-Bass.

Owen, J. E., Hassell-Goodman, S., & Yamanaka, A. (2017). Culturally relevant leadership learning: Identity, capacity, and efficacy. *Journal of Leadership Studies, 11*(3), 48–54.

Owen. J. E., & Wagner, W. (2010). Situating service-learning in the context of civic engagement. In B. Jacoby & P. Mutascio (Eds.), *Looking in, reaching out: A reflective guide for community service-learning professionals* (pp. 231–253). Providence, RI: Campus Compact.

Palmieri, J. (2018). *Dear madame president: An open letter to the women who will run the world.* New York, NY: Grand Central.

Pascarella, E. T., Hagedorn, L. S., Whitt, E. J., Yeager, P. M., Edison, M. I., Terenzini, P. T., & Noura, A. (1997). Women's perceptions of a "chilly climate" and their cognitive outcomes during the first year of college. *Journal of College Student Development, 38*, 109–124.

Pascarella, E., & Terenzini, P. (2005). *How college affects students (Vol. 2): A third decade of research.* San Francisco, CA: Jossey-Bass.

Pavlovich, L. (2017, July 30). *The gender equality debate: A boost for women in sport.* Retrieved from https://athleteassessments.com/gender-equality-debate/

Pew Center on Religion and Public Life. (2016). *The gender gap in religion around the world.* Retrieved from https://www.pewforum.org/2016/03/22/the-gender-gap-in-religion-around-the-world/

Pew Research Center. (2016). *Racial, gender wage gaps persist in U.S. despite some progress*. Retrieved from https://www.pewresearch.org/fact-tank/2016/07/01/racial-gender-wage-gaps-persist-in-u-s-despite-some-progress/

Pew Research Center. (2017). *Six facts about the U.S. military and its changing demographics*. Retrieved from https://www.pewresearch.org/topics/military-and-veterans/project/social-trends/

Pew Research Center. (2018). *The data on women leaders*. Retrieved from http://www.pewsocialtrends.org/fact-sheet/the-data-on-women-leaders/

Picillo, A., & Devine, L. (2017). *Breaking the grass ceiling: Women, weed, and business*. Scotts Valley, CA: Createspace Independent Publishing.

Pierce, A. (July 7, 2015). *Leaning in won't liberate us*. National Organization for Women. Retrieved from https://now.org/blog/leaning-in-wont-save-us/

Pigza, J., Owen, J. E., & Associates. (in press). *Women and leadership development in college: A facilitation resource*. Sterling, VA: Stylus.

Pipher, M. B. (1994). *Reviving Ophelia: Saving the selves of adolescent girls*. New York, NY: Putnam.

Pittinsky, T. L., Bacon, L. M., & Welle, B. (2007). The great women theory of leadership? Perils of positive stereotypes and precarious pedestals. In B. Kellerman & D. D. Rhode (Eds.), *Women and leadership: The state of play and strategies for change* (pp. 93–125). San Francisco, CA: Jossey-Bass.

Preskill, S., & Brookfield, S. D. (2009). *Learning as a way of leading: Lessons from the struggle for social justice*. San Francisco, CA: Jossey-Bass.

Proudford, K. L. (2007). Isn't she delightful? Creating relationships that get women to the top (and keep them there). In B. Kellerman & D. L. Rhode (Eds.), *Women and leadership: The state of play and strategies for change* (pp. 431-452). San Francisco, CA: Jossey-Bass.

Reason, R., Broido, E., Davis, T., & Evans, N. (2005). *Developing social justice allies* (New Directions for Student Services, No. 110). San Francisco, CA: Jossey-Bass.

Renn, K. A. (2007). LGBT student leaders and queer activists: Identities of lesbian, gay, bisexual, transgender, and queer identified college student leaders and activists. *Journal of College Student Development, 48*, 311–330.

Renn, K. A., & Patton, L. D. (2011). Campus ecology and environments. In J. H. Schuh & S. R. Harper (Eds.), *Student services: A handbook for the profession* (5th ed.). San Francisco, CA: Jossey-Bass.

Renn, K. A., & Reason, R. D. (2012). *College students in the United States: Characteristics, experiences, and outcomes*. San Francisco, CA: Jossey-Bass.

Rhode, D. L. (2014). *What women want: An agenda for the women's movement*. New York, NY: Oxford University Press.

Rhode, D. L. (2017). *Women and leadership*. New York, NY: Oxford University Press.

Riggio, R. E. (1988). *The charisma quotient: What it is, how to get it, how to use it*. New York, NY: Dodd Mead.

Rocco, M. L. (2017). *Moving beyond common paradigms of leadership: Understanding the development of advanced leadership identity* (Doctoral dissertation). University of Maryland, College Park, MD. Retrieved from https://doi.org/10.13016/M2T727G5V

Rokeach, M. (1973). *The nature of human values*. New York, NY: Free Press.

Roosevelt, R. (1960). *You learn by living: Eleven keys to a more fulfilling life*. New York, NY: Harper & Row.

Ryan, M. K., & Haslam, S. A. (2005). The glass cliff: Evidence that women are over-represented in precarious leadership positions. *British Journal of Management, 16,* 81–90.

Sanchez-Hucles, J. V., & Davis, D. D. (2010). Women and women of color in leadership: Complexity, identity, and intersectionality. *American Psychologist, 65*(3), 171–181.

Sanchez-Hucles, J. V., & Sanchez, P. (2007). From margin to center: The voices of diverse feminist leaders. In J. L. Chin, B. Lott, J. K. Rice, & J. Sanchez-Hucles (Eds.), *Women and leadership: Transforming visions and diverse voices* (pp. 211–227). Malden, MA: Blackwell.

Sanchez, P., Hucles, P., Sanchez-Hucles, J., & Mehta, S. C. (2007). Increasing diverse women leadership in corporate America: Climbing concrete walls and shattering glass ceilings. In J. L. Chin, B. Lott, J. K. Rice, & J. Sanchez-Hucles (Eds.), *Women and leadership: Transforming visions and diverse voices* (pp. 228–244). Malden, MA: Blackwell.

Sandberg, S. (2013). *Lean in: Women, work, and the will to lead*. New York, NY: Knopf.

Sax, L. J., Bryant, A. N., & Harper, C. E. (2008). The differential effects of student-faculty interaction on college outcomes for men and women. *Journal of College Student Development, 46,* 642–657.

Schein, E. H. (2015). *Organizational culture and leadership* (5th ed.). San Francisco, CA: Jossey-Bass.

Seemiller, C., & Grace, M. (2016). *Generation Z goes to college*. San Francisco, CA: Jossey-Bass.

Shambaugh, R. (2007). *It's not a glass ceiling, It's a sticky floor: Free yourself from the hidden behaviors sabotaging your career success*. New York, NY: McGraw-Hill.

Shankman, M. L., Allen, S. J., & Haber-Curran, P. (2015). *Emotionally intelligent leadership: A guide for students* (2nd ed.). San Francisco, CA: Jossey-Bass.

Shea, H. D., & Renn, K. A. (2017). Gender and leadership: A call to action. In D. Tillapaugh & P. Haber-Curran (Eds.), *Critical perspectives on gender and student leadership* (New Directions for Student Leadership, No. 154, pp. 83–94). San Francisco, CA: Jossey-Bass.

Sidani, J. E., Shensa, A., Hoffman, B., Hammer, J., & Primack, B. A. (2016). The association between social media use and eating concerns among U.S. young adults. *Journal of the Academy of Nutrition and Dietetics, 116*(9), 1465–1472.

Simon, S., & Hoyt, C. L. (2012). Exploring the effect of media images on women's leadership self-perceptions and aspirations. *Group Processes & Intergroup Relations, 16*(2), 232–245.

Sinno, S. M., & Killen, M. (2009). Mom's at work and dad's at home: Children's evaluations of parental roles. *Applied Developmental Science, 13*(1), 16–29.

Sixteen Days Campaign (2019). *About*. Retrieved from https://16dayscampaign.org/

Slaughter, A. (2012). Why women still can't have it all. *The Atlantic.* Retrieved from https://www.theatlantic.com/magazine/archive/2012/07/why-women-still-cant-have-it-all/309020/

Smith, C. P., & Freyd, J. J. (2014). Institutional betrayal. *American Psychologist, 69*(6), 575–587.

Smith, M., & Strauss, V. (2019, January 28). Activists call on education department to take action for "menstrual equity." *Washington Post.* Retrieved from https://www.washingtonpost.com/local/education/activists-call-on-education-department-to-take-action-for-menstrual-equity/2019/01/28/

Smith, S. (n.d.). *Loving-kindness mantra.* Retrieved from http://www.contemplative mind.org/practices/tree/loving-kindness

Smith, W. A. (2010). Toward an understanding of Black misandric microaggressions and racial battle fatigue in historically white institutions. In V. C. Polite (Ed.), *The state of the African American male in Michigan: A courageous conversation* (pp. 265–277). East Lansing: Michigan State University Press.

Sollee, K. (October 30, 2015). Six things to know about fourth wave feminism. *Bustle.* Retrieved from https://www.bustle.com/articles/119524-6-things-to-know-about-4th-wave-feminism.

Spears, L. C. (2010). Character and servant leadership: Ten characteristics of effective, caring leaders. *Journal of Virtues & Leadership, 1*(1), 25–30.

Stanton, E. C., Anthony, S. B., Gage, M. J., & Harper, I. (1922). *History of woman suffrage: Six volumes.* Rochester, Susan B. Anthony and Charles Mann Press.

Stein, J. (2018, September 15). Census shows gender pay gap is narrowing. *Washington Post.*

Steinem, G. (1987). *Outrageous acts and everyday rebellions.* New York, NY: Henry Holt.

Stice, E., & Shaw, H. E. (2002). Role of body dissatisfaction in the onset and maintenance of eating pathology: A synthesis of research findings. *Journal of Psychosomatic Research, 53*(5), 985–993.

Stogdill, R. M. (1974). *Handbook of leadership: A survey of theory and research.* New York, NY: Free Press.

Tillapaugh, D., & Haber-Curran, P. (Eds.). (2017). *Critical perspectives on gender and student leadership* (New Directions for Student Leadership, No. 154). San Francisco, CA: Jossey-Bass.

Tillapaugh, D., Mitchell, D., Jr., & Soria, K. M. (2017). Considering gender and student leadership through the lens of intersectionality. In D. Tillapaugh & P. Haber-Curran (Eds.), *Critical perspectives on gender and student leadership* (New Directions for Student Leadership, No. 154, pp. 23–32). San Francisco, CA: Jossey-Bass.

Tolentino, J. (2016, April 12). How "empowerment" became something for women to buy. *New York Times.* Retrieved from https://www.nytimes.com/2016/04/17/magazine/how-empowerment-became-something-for-women-to-buy.html

Turk, D. B. (2004). *Bound by a mighty vow: Sisterhood and women's fraternities, 1870–1920.* New York, NY: NYU Press.

Turner, M. (2001). Don't forget about the women. *Black Issues in Higher Education, 18*(6), 34–35.

UNESCO Institute of Statistics. (2017). *Women in science.* Retrieved from http://uis.unesco.org/en/topic/women-science

United States Bureau of Labor Statistics. (2018). *Healthcare occupations.* Retrieved from https://www.bls.gov/ooh/healthcare

United States Census Bureau. (2019). *Equal pay day.* Retrieved from https://www.census.gov/newsroom/stories/2019/equal-pay.html

United States Equal Employment Opportunity Commission. (2019). *Facts about equal pay and compensation discrimination.* Retrieved from https://www.eeoc.gov/eeoc/publications/fs-epa.cfm

United States Glass Ceiling Commission. (1995). A solid investment: Making full use of the nation's human capital (Final Report of the Commission). Washington DC: U.S. Government Printing Office.

University of Michigan University Health Services. (2019). *Body image.* Retrieved from https://www.uhs.umich.edu/bodyimage

Valoy, P. (June 8, 2015). Transnational feminism: Why feminist activism needs to think globally. *Everyday Feminism.* Retrieved from https://everydayfeminism.com/2015/01/why-we-need-transnational-feminism/

Vasan, N., & Przybylo, J. (2013). *Do good well: Your guide to leadership, action, and social innovation.* San Francisco, CA: Jossey-Bass.

Wade, L., & Ferree, M. M. (2015). *Gender: Ideas, interaction, institutions.* New York, NY: W. W. Norton.

Waldron, J. J., Semerjian, T. Z., & Kauer, K. (2009). Doing 'drag': Applying queer-feminist theory to the body image and eating disorders across sexual orientation and gender identity. In J. J. Reel & K. A. Beals (Eds.), *The Hidden Faces of Eating Disorders,* 63–81. Reston, VA: American Alliance for Health, Physical Education, Recreation, and Dance

Walker, A. (1983). *In search of our mothers' gardens: Womanist prose.* New York, NY: Harcourt Brace Jovanovich.

Watson, E. (2014). *Gender equality is your issue too.* Speech to the United Nations. Transcript retrieved from https://www.unwomen.org/en/news/stories/2014/9/emma-watson-gender-equality-is-your-issue-too

Williams, J. C. (2004, October). The maternal wall. *Harvard Business Review.* Retrieved from https://hbr.org/2004/10/the-maternal-wall

Wing Sue, D. (2010). Microaggressions in everyday life. *Psychology Today* [online]. Retrieved from https://www.psychologytoday.com/us/blog/microaggressions-in-everyday-life/201010/racial-microaggressions-in-everyday-life

Wiseman, R. (2009) *Queen bees & wannabes: Helping your daughter survive cliques, gossip, boyfriends, and other realities of adolescence.* New York, NY: Three Rivers Press.

Women Are Getting Even. (2019). *Causes of the wage gap.* Retrieved from http://www.wageproject.org/

Woman's Rights Convention. (1848). *The first convention ever called to discuss the civil and political rights of women.* Seneca Falls, NY. Retrieved from the Library of Congress, https://www.loc.gov/item/27007548/.

Women's Sports Foundation. (2019). *Advocate equality.* Retrieved from https://www.womenssportsfoundation.org/

Workplace Bullying Institute. (2010). *Workplace bullying survey.* Retrieved from https://www.workplacebullying.org/wbiresearch/2010-wbi-national-survey/

Yamanaka, A. (2018). *Phenomenological exploration on the experience of microaggression by women faculty of color and its relations to self-efficacy.* (Unpublished doctoral dissertation). George Mason University, Fairfax, VA.

Yates, E. L. (2001). Noteworthy news: Women's colleges receive high marks for learning effectiveness. *Black Issues in Higher Education, 17*(24), 22–23.

Zaccarro, S. J., Kemp, C., & Bader, P. (2004). Leader traits and attributes. In J. Antonakis, A. T. Cianciolo, & R. J. Sternberg (Eds.), *The nature of leadership* (pp. 101–124). Thousand Oaks, CA: SAGE.

Zamudio, M. M., Russell, C., Rios, F. A., & Bridgeman, J. L. (2010). *Critical race theory matters: Education and ideology.* New York, NY: Routledge.

Zimmerman, H. (2017). *Navigating the labyrinth toward college student government presidency: A phenomenological study of women who run for student government president.* (Doctoral dissertation). University of California–Los Angeles. Retrieved from https://escholarship.org/uc/item/8h10w4z6

ABOUT THE AUTHOR

Julie E. Owen, PhD, is an associate professor of leadership studies in the School of Integrative Studies at George Mason University (GMU), where she coordinates the leadership studies major and minor, and is affiliate faculty with the higher education program, and with women and gender studies. Owen has authored over 30 publications, including serving as coeditor of "Innovative Learning for Leadership Development" (*New Directions for Student Leadership*, Series No.1, 2015), coeditor of *Women and Leadership Development in College: A Facilitation Guide* (Stylus, 2020), and both editions of the *Handbook for Student Leadership Development* (Jossey-Bass, 2011). She has collaborated on several research initiatives, including the Multi-Institutional Study of Leadership—Institutional Survey (MSL—IS) and the Leadership Identity Development (LID) project. Owen has received grants from the Council for the Advancement of Standards in Higher Education (CAS) and Bringing Theory to Practice (BTtP). Owen has received AAC&U's K. Patricia Cross Future Leaders Award and ACPA's Annuit Coeptis and Diamond Honoree awards. At GMU, Owen was honored with the Teaching Excellence Award, the Undergraduate Research Mentoring Excellence Award, and was named Engaged Faculty Member of the Year for 2018. She was recognized with NASPA's SLPKC Komives Research Award and the University of Maryland's Distinguished Alumni Magoon Award. She is a frequent presenter, consultant, and keynote speaker on topics related to leadership, social change, and civic engagement.

Sulpizio, L., 79
support system, 184

Talent Reimagined report, 146–48
target identities, 46–47, 199
technical problems, 39, 189
technology, 69–70
Teig, Trisha, 167
Tillapaugh, Daniel, 154, 156, 158, 174
Title IX
  benefits and implications of, 67, 87, 113
  enforcement of, 150
tokenism, 165–66, 199
Tolentino, Jia, 159
toys/games, 63
traditional leader prototypes, 153–55
traits
  gender differences in leadership, 157
  theory, 19
trans*. See transgender
  definition of, 23, 200
  MSL on, 155
transformational leadership, 154–55
transgender
  definition of, 23, 200
  MtF and FtM, 155
transnational feminism, 18, 200
triple jeopardy, 165, 200

underlying assumptions of
  organizational culture, 86
United Nations, 14, 180

values
  clarification of, 37–39
  definition of, 200
  espoused, 86

Vasan, N., 177
Violence Against Women Act, 88
Virginia Student Power Network (VSPN), 187–88
volunteer opportunities, 146
VSPN. *See* Virginia Student Power Network
vulnerability
  to burnout, 162
  preparation and, 37

Walker, Alice, 17, 200
Watson, Emma, 14, 180
Welle, B., 160–61
What Women Want (Rhode), 13
Wheaton, M. M., 155, 158, 159–60
When Women Ruled the World (Cooney), 153
Wiest, Amber, 167
Williams, J. C., 131
Wing Sue, Derald, 74, 75–76
Wiseman, Rosalind, 66–67, 69, 73
Womanist movement, 17, 200
women
  campus issues impacting leadership and, 85–96
  campus organizations for leadership and, 96–101
  career barriers to advancement of, 138–44
  current situation for leadership and, 12–13
  in higher education, history of, 83–85
  metaphors for leadership, 130–36
  national organizations supporting, 102–3
  power and, 158–59
  powerful historic, 20

Also available from Stylus

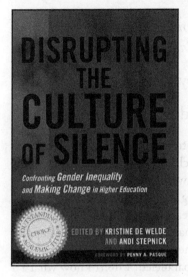

Disrupting the Culture of Silence

Confronting Gender Inequality and Making Change in Higher Education

Edited by Kristine De Welde and Andi Stepnick

Foreword by Penny A. Pasque

CHOICE 2015 Outstanding Academic Title

"Although frequently considered the ultimate bastion of liberalism, academia in the United States remains plagued with inequalities. Shining a spotlight on this dirty little secret, revealing how specific inequities operate, and offering solutions to them are the subjects of this superb volume edited by Kristine De Welde and Andi Stepnick. Although their focus is on gender inequality within the United States, attention is also given to the situation of minorities who suffer the double-whammy of being in more than one discriminated-against group, such as women of color or transgendered academics.

"This volume does an exceptional job of tracing the history of change within the academy and is required reading for courses and scholars in the field."—*Sex Roles*

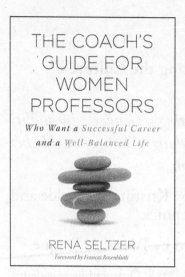

The Coach's Guide for Women Professors

Who Want a Successful Career and a Well-Balanced Life

Edited by Rena Seltzer

Foreword by Frances Rosenbluth

"I needed to transform how I approached my research. Rena was instrumental in ensuring I was incredibly productive. From goal-setting to structuring my time effectively to creating metaphors that facilitated my ability to push through challenges, she has helped to make me a happier and more efficient academic. Her positive energy is infectious and her ability to help her clients see the big picture is unparalleled. I don't know what I'd do without her!"—*Modupe Akinola*, *Assistant Professor, Columbia University*

"Rena Seltzer's workshops are perennial favorites with Yale faculty. Workshop alumni get more writing done, have more control over their schedules, and feel increased confidence in their leadership skills. Rena has also served as a coach for a number of Yale faculty leaders. Here as well, her work has been transformative. I am delighted to recommend *The Coach's Guide for Women Professors* to anyone aspiring to learn from this wise and inspiring academic coach."—*Tamar Szabó Gendler*, *Dean of the Faculty of Arts and Science, Vincent J. Scully Professor of Philosophy, and Professor of Psychology and Cognitive Science, Yale University*

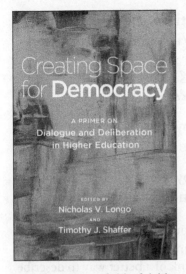

Creating Space for Democracy

A Primer on Dialogue and Deliberation in Higher Education

Edited by Nicholas V. Longo and Timothy J. Shaffer

Published in association with Campus Compact and AAC&U

"If democracy is in trouble, higher education is in trouble, so it is encouraging to see the cast of scholars who are mounting a response. This book is a vital contribution to the emerging field of deliberative pedagogy . . . . It is particularly encouraging to see new themes like the role of professionals in our democracy. Well done!"—*David Mathews*, *Kettering Foundation*

"Reaffirming higher education's civic mission, *Creating Space for Democracy* issues a compelling enjoinder for colleges and universities to play a leadership role in fostering participatory democracy. Positing college and university campuses as vital sites for democratic engagement, the authors in this volume offer tools for speaking across differences, while providing innovative models for revitalizing democracy through dialogue and deliberation, both within and beyond the gates of the academy."—*Lynn Pasquerella*, *President, AAC&U*

Intersections of Identity and Sexual Violence on Campus

Centering Minoritized Students' Experiences

Edited by Jessica C. Harris and Chris Linder

Edited by Jessica C. Harris and Chris Linder

"It may sound like hyperbole when I say, 'It changed my life,' but I honestly cannot think of a better way to describe its impact on my beliefs on organizing to eradicate sexual violence—on campuses and off. This book outlines what I've needed as a survivor during my times as a student and activist; this book should be mandatory reading for every individual who works with the issue of campus gender–based violence. Journalists, activists, and administrators alike stand to gain the knowledge needed to spur the transformative work of a power-conscious, history-informed, and intersectional understanding of the dynamics of sexual violence."—*Wagatwe Wanjuki*, *feminist writer and activist*

22883 Quicksilver Drive
Sterling, VA 20166-2019

Subscribe to our e-mail alerts: www.Styluspub.com